Modern REST API Development in Go

Design performant, secure, and observable web APIs
using Go's powerful standard library

Jesús Espino

‹packt›

Modern REST API Development in Go

Copyright © 2025 Packt Publishing

Portfolio Director: Ashwin Nair

Relationship Lead: Aaron Lazar

Project Manager: Ruvika Rao

Content Engineer: Nisha Cleetus

Technical Editor: Sweety Pagaria

Copy Editor: Safis Editing

Indexer: Hemangini Bari

Proofreader: Nisha Cleetus

Production Designer: Pranit Padwal

Growth Lead: Anamika Singh

First published: August 2025

Production reference: 1280725

Published by Packt Publishing Ltd.

Grosvenor House

11 St Paul's Square

Birmingham

B3 1RB, UK.

ISBN 978-1-83620-537-1

www.packtpub.com

To Paula, thank you for your love, patience, and constant support. To my kids, Lola and Máximo, you remind me how to see the world with wonder. In memory of my mother, Florencia, whose sacrifices made everything possible.

— Jesus Espino

Contributors

About the author

Jesús Espino is a principal software engineer at Gitpod and a veteran Go developer whose career spans more than a decade building and scaling open source platforms. Before joining Gitpod in 2025, he spent seven years at Mattermost, where he helped develop the company's high-traffic REST API. A relentless seeker of knowledge, Espino is well known for unpacking Go's internals in advanced talks at conferences such as GoLab and GopherCon UK. He has also significantly contributed to open source projects such as Taiga, Penpot, and Focalboard, among others.

About the reviewer

Clément Jean is the founder of ShareAble OÜ, a start-up providing online courses (Udemy, Linux Foundation, and other) and books (Packt) on technologies such as Protobuf and gRPC. With his passion for both education and technology, he strives to empower other people with the educational content he publishes.

Table of Contents

Chapter 14: Using the Echo Framework   243

Chapter 15: Unlock Your Book's Exclusive Benefits   257

Other Books You May Enjoy   263

Index   267

Preface

In today's extremely interconnected environment, REST APIs are the lingua franca for different software to communicate with each other. The industry has tried different communication systems in the past, such as SOAP, CORBA, and custom-made solutions, but REST has been the de facto standard. Its simplicity and ability to leverage the underlying technologies, such as the HTTP protocol, have positioned REST as the go-to option for most developers.

REST is a solid option, but REST can be executed with many languages, such as Python, Ruby, PHP, Rust, and so on. But we are going to talk about how to do it with Go, but why Go? Go is a modern, robust, fast, and easy-to-learn language, making it ideal for REST APIs. Its native compilation makes it an amazing candidate for the speed requirement of modern APIs; its strong typing makes it perfect for ensuring safety and robustness in your services, and its simplicity ensures that incorporating new developers, even if they need to learn the language, is not going to become a nightmare.

This book covers REST and Go, but I'm a firm believer in understanding the foundations of things, so we will also discuss topics such as the HTTP protocol used under the hood, cache approaches, observability, security, and much more. It provides you with the skills to develop REST APIs in Go and teaches you why we follow that approach and what the technological concepts are behind it.

I want to focus on the concepts and keep things as simple and close to the Go standard library as possible, covering specialized libraries only when no built-in package provides that for us. However, we will also provide examples for those who prefer different approaches to doing things, such as using query builders, ORMs, frameworks, or testing assertion libraries, giving you the final say on where you want to put the fine-grain control, and where you want to delegate to libraries that make your life easier.

Who this book is for

This book is for developers who want to gain a practical understanding of how to build REST APIs in general and, more specifically, using the Go programming language. While knowledge about Go is not strictly needed to get value from this book, some minimal understanding is required to get the most out of it.

What this book covers

Chapter 1, Introduction to APIs, goes through the fundamental concepts of REST APIs and explores other alternatives such as SOAP and GraphQL.

Chapter 2, Exploring REST APIs, covers the tools needed to explore and analyze existing APIs, such as cURL and Postman. It enables you to explore and test your own APIs in the following chapters.

Chapter 3, Building a REST Client, exposes the tools provided by Go's standard library for accessing APIs, and how you can build your own client library for consuming an existing API.

Chapter 4, Designing Your REST API, introduces the main concepts of REST APIs such as routes, resources, and actions, and the semantics associated with them in the REST API ecosystem.

Chapter 5, Authentication and Authorization, explores the needs and methods used for enforcing proper authentication in authorization in your API, exposing concepts such as JWT or the authentication HTTP header.

Chapter 6, Data Persistency, provides the knowledge needed to create the persistency layer of your application, including SQL database usage, the repository pattern, and building queries using the Squirrel query builder.

Chapter 7, API Security, goes through the different security features provided by the HTTP protocol and leveraged by the REST APIs. The chapter covers things such as data validation, sanitization, and password handling.

Chapter 8, API Performance, focuses on making your API fast, including topics such as cache control from the HTTP protocol, the Go profiler, and building and understanding benchmarks in Go code.

Chapter 9, Deploying Your API, examines the different options for deploying REST APIs, from deploying your API in bare metal to a more sophisticated approach such as Kubernetes or function as a service.

Chapter 10, Testing, exposes the different tools that Go provides for testing, and the different kinds of tests that you can build, from unit to integration tests, exploring all of them. We also explore the testify assertion library as an alternative to the Go standard library testing tools.

Chapter 11, Documenting with OpenAPI, shows the value of properly documenting your REST API with the standard tooling out there provided by the OpenAPI initiative. It includes generating documentation and exposing that to tools such as Postman.

Chapter 12, Metrics, Logs, and Traces, introduces the concepts of observability for your REST API application. This chapter explores the data that we collect (metrics, logs, and traces). It also explores the tools that help you understand the collected data, such as Jaeger and Grafana.

Chapter 13, Using GORM, offers an alternative approach for the storage layer, building it with GORM instead of the standard library, or the Squirrel library.

Chapter 14, Using the Echo Framework, explores other ways of generating your API that are not based on the standard library; instead, it uses a third-party framework.

To get the most out of this book

You will need Go 1.23 or greater installed in your computer to follow the examples. Also, we are going to extensively use tools such as cURL to verify the correct behavior, and in some chapters, we will explore approaches that require tools such as Docker, Grafana, or Node.js, among others.

Software/hardware covered in the book	Operating system requirements
Go 1.23 or greater	Windows, macOS, or Linux
cURL	
Postman	

If you are using the digital version of this book, we advise you to type the code yourself or access the code from the book's GitHub repository (a link is available in the next section). Doing so will help you avoid any potential errors related to the copying and pasting of code.

Download the example code files

The code bundle for the book is hosted on GitHub at https://github.com/PacktPublishing/Modern-REST-API-Development-in-Go. We also have other code bundles from our rich catalog of books and videos available at https://github.com/PacktPublishing. Check them out!

Download the color images

We also provide a PDF file that has color images of the screenshots/diagrams used in this book. You can download it here: https://packt.link/gbp/9781836205371

Conventions used

There are a number of text conventions used throughout this book.

CodeInText: Indicates code words in text, database table names, folder names, filenames, file extensions, pathnames, dummy URLs, user input, and Twitter handles. For example: "With this simple Create call, we are inserting our User model into the database. Not only that, but because we add the gorm.Model embedding, GORM, after creating the record, also automatically sets the ID, CreatedAt, and UpdatedAt fields.

A block of code is set as follows:

```
user := User{
  Username: "johndoe",
  Password: "password123",
  Role: "user",
}
result := db.Create(&user)

if result.Error != nil {
  log.Fatal(result.Error)
}
```

When we wish to draw your attention to a particular part of a code block, the relevant lines or items are set in bold:

```
func (r *Repository) DeleteList(id uint) error {
  result := r.db.Where("id = ?", id).Delete(&ShoppingList{})
  if result.Error != nil {
    return result.Error
  }
  return nil
}
```

Bold: Indicates a new term, an important word, or words that you see on the screen. For instance, words in menus or dialog boxes appear in the text like this. For example: " If everything went well, you should see the text **Hello World**, as shown in *Figure 1.1*."

Warnings or important notes appear like this.

Tips and tricks appear like this.

Get in touch

Feedback from our readers is always welcome.

General feedback: If you have questions about any aspect of this book or have any general feedback, please email us at customercare@packt.com and mention the book's title in the subject of your message.

Errata: Although we have taken every care to ensure the accuracy of our content, mistakes do happen. If you have found a mistake in this book, we would be grateful if you reported this to us. Please visit http://www.packt.com/submit-errata, click **Submit Errata**, and fill in the form.

Piracy: If you come across any illegal copies of our works in any form on the internet, we would be grateful if you would provide us with the location address or website name. Please contact us at copyright@packt.com with a link to the material.

If you are interested in becoming an author: If there is a topic that you have expertise in and you are interested in either writing or contributing to a book, please visit http://authors.packt.com/.

Share your thoughts

Once you've read *Modern REST API Development in Go*, we'd love to hear your thoughts! Scan the QR code below to go straight to the Amazon review page for this book and share your feedback.

https://packt.link/r/1836205376

Your review is important to us and the tech community and will help us make sure we're delivering excellent quality content.

1

Introduction to APIs

In today's highly connected, highly competitive world, where the efficacy of processes can mean the difference between success and failure, one of the most important players, from a technology standpoint, is **application programming interfaces** (**APIs**). They help us connect our systems, automate processes in those systems, and adapt those systems to our needs instead of our needs to those systems. All that is done thanks to APIs.

This book will explore how to build APIs in Go from scratch. We'll start with the basics of an API and how to explore it. Then, we'll go through the incremental process of creating an API, from adding the basic endpoints to incorporating things such as security and telemetry. As an optional exercise, we'll use a web framework instead of the standard library and an ORM instead of SQL queries.

In this chapter, we'll cover the following topics:

- The different kinds of APIs
- The basic concepts around REST APIs
- How to build a very basic API in Go

But let's start from the beginning. What exactly is an API? Let's talk about this.

Getting the most out of this book — get to know your free benefits

Unlock exclusive **free** benefits that come with your purchase, thoughtfully crafted to supercharge your learning journey and help you learn without limits.

Here's a quick overview of what you get with this book:

Next-gen reader

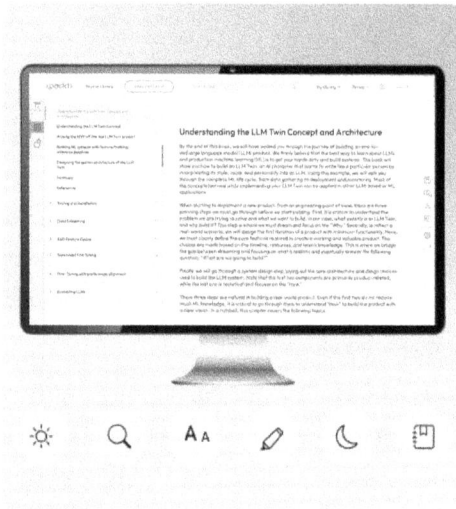

Figure 1.1: Illustration of the next-gen Packt Reader's features

Our web-based reader, designed to help you learn effectively, comes with the following features:

Multi-device progress sync: Learn from any device with seamless progress sync.

Highlighting and notetaking: Turn your reading into lasting knowledge.

Bookmarking: Revisit your most important learnings anytime.

Dark mode: Focus with minimal eye strain by switching to dark or sepia mode.

Interactive AI assistant (beta)

Our interactive AI assistant has been trained on the content of this book, to maximize your learning experience. It comes with the following features:

✦ Summarize it: Summarize key sections or an entire chapter.

✦ AI code explainers: In the next-gen Packt Reader, click the Explain button above each code block for AI-powered code explanations.

Note: The AI assistant is part of next-gen Packt Reader and is still in beta.

Figure 1.2: Illustration of Packt's
AI assistant

DRM-free PDF or ePub version

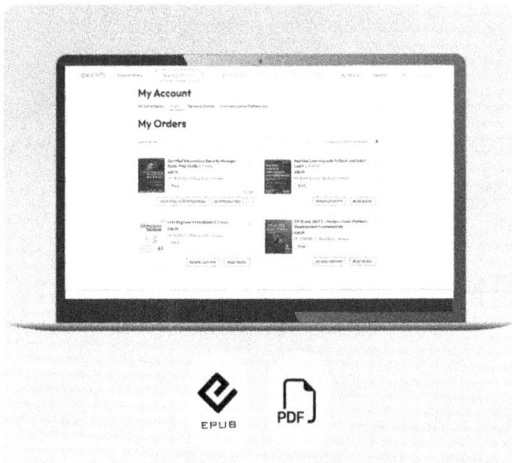

Learn without limits with the following perks included with your purchase:

📄 Learn from anywhere with a DRM-free PDF copy of this book.

📱 Use your favorite e-reader to learn using a DRM-free ePub version of this book.

Figure 1.3: Free PDF and ePub

Technical requirements

All the code examples for this chapter are included in this book's GitHub repository: `https://github.com/PacktPublishing/Modern-REST-API-Development-in-Go`. You only need the Go compiler installed on your system to compile and execute the code.

What's an API?

One of the first questions we should answer here is, what's an **API**? As mentioned in the introduction, it's an **application programming interface**, but what does that even mean?

In general terms, it's an interface for programmers to interact with an application. However, there are different definitions of an API, depending on the context. One of them could be the set of methods/functions that are exposed by a library. That's known as a library API. Of course, as a software engineer, you're dealing with these kinds of APIs all day long – your Go packages, your exported functions, and the standard library are all APIs, but they focus on in-process communication, organizing your code, and separating concerns. But, in modern systems, when we talk about APIs, we're usually talking about remote APIs.

So… what's a **remote API**? A remote API is a set of functionalities that are exposed to other processes, generally through a communication channel (such as a socket), allowing independent programs to interact with each other.

But that's still abstract, so let's be more specific about what we'll discuss in this book. We'll talk specifically about REST APIs, one of the most common ways of inter-process communication used today. In REST, the communication channel that's used is an HTTP connection that uses the HTTP protocol, so the API behaves like a web server and uses the same technology to communicate with other processes.

Before we explore REST and why we chose it over other options (maybe the best option for you is a different one), let's explore the most popular options that are available.

GraphQL

GraphQL is one of the modern approaches to providing APIs. It was born from the necessity to provide more flexible APIs to consumers without enforcing a rigid structure (REST APIs are normally less flexible for consumers). It has a lot of exciting advantages, such as the ability to request only specific fields or embed substructures in the same response on demand by asking the client for it. That's all doable in REST, but it isn't standardized like it is in GraphQL. **GraphQL** is a great option when many clients access your data in very different ways and patterns, and you must provide that flexibility. Also, GraphQL provides lots of value when you don't know how the consumer will query your data.

gRPC

gRPC Remote Procedure Calls (gRPC) is also one of the newest approaches for creating APIs. It's widely used in Go and has a lot of advantages. One of the main advantages is that it's agnostic from the language, and most of the code for serialization/deserialization and remote calls is automatically generated by the tools available. The degree of communication performance in gRPC is outstanding for multiple reasons, but mainly due to its binary protocol and usage of HTTP 2 as the transport layer. gRPC is ideal for the internal communication of services/microservices but isn't widely used in things such as web applications or public APIs. This is because HTTP 2 is a requirement and developers are normally more familiar with other technologies, such as REST.

SOAP

Simple Object Access Protocol (SOAP) is a very old technology that uses similar principles to gRPC. It uses HTTP as a transport layer, and the protocol is 100% XML. The main problem with SOAP is that compatibility between libraries is suboptimal. SOAP works well when you use the same library and language in all the services that you're communicating with, but not so well when you have a heterogeneous environment. Also, web clients rarely use SOAP as a communication protocol.

Custom API

You can build a custom API mechanism, selecting how you serialize and deserialize the data, transport it, and define the actions you allow. You could define a whole protocol and use TCP to communicate directly, but that's normally not needed, and there are a lot of problems that have already been solved in the previously explained technologies and, of course, in REST.

I'm adding this option for completeness, but unless you know why you're deciding to go with this option, you should probably be using one of the existing well-known solutions.

In summary, there are multiple mechanisms for generating APIs and communicating with applications, but in this book, we'll be using REST. So, what's REST, and why should you use it?

What's REST?

Representational State Transfer (REST) is one of the most common ways of building remote APIs in modern software, especially on public APIs that need to be consumed by third-party services/clients. The main reasons why REST is so widely used are the simplicity of the concepts it embraces and its flexibility to adapt whenever those concepts don't 100% apply to your use case.

I'm going to take a pragmatic rather than a formal approach to describing REST. If you want a more formal definition of REST, you can go to Wikipedia's REST page and follow some of the references there. So, let's jump into the concepts.

REST concepts

In REST, there are **resources** and **entities**. An entity is an instance of a resource. For example, "users" is a resource that represents the users in the system, but "John Doe" is an instance of that resource, so "John Doe" is an entity. Every resource and entity has a unique way of being identified in the context of REST applications – that is, via a **Uniform Resource Identifier (URI)**. This is the URL that you use to access the resource or entity. For example, resource users could have a URI of `https://example.com/api/v1/users`, whereas the "John Doe" entity could have a URI of `https://example.com/api/v1/users/42`.

Now that we know what resources and entities are and how we can identify them by their URIs, we need a way to represent their data. How is the "John Doe" entity data represented?

REST doesn't impose any form of data representation, but the communicating applications need to at least be able to understand the same representation. The reality is that the de facto standard that's used for representing entities in REST is **JavaScript Object Notation (JSON)**. In some scenarios, you may wish to select a different representation for whatever reason (for example, for performance or compatibility purposes). Other common options are MessagePack, **Binary JSON (BSON)**, and XML.

Now that you understand the basic concepts of entities, resources, URIs, and representation, you have a solid foundation for building applications around REST. However, it's also important to understand how we operate in those concepts and how we communicate them.

So, let's talk about how REST leverages HTTP to communicate the operations that we want to apply to resources and entities.

REST and HTTP

Most REST APIs are based on the HTTP protocol and leverage multiple features.

In HTTP, the URL is the URI of a resource or an entity. You can put it in your browser or call it through your code, but at the end of the day, it's the same concept: it's a URL that represents a unique resource or entity in REST.

Once you've identified the resource or the entity and its URL, you must decide what you're going to do. What action are you going to take? Are you going to delete the entity? Are you going to create a new one? Are you going to get an existing one?

The way we express the action that we want to execute in REST is done through **HTTP verbs**. The HTTP protocol defines a set of **verbs** or actions that you can execute on a URL; these are known as **methods** in HTTP.

There are multiple methods in HTTP, including GET, POST, and DELETE, and each has an action associated with it in the context of REST, depending on whether it's a resource or an entity. Let's take a look:

- REST resource (for example, /users):
    - GET: List the entities of the resource
    - POST: Create a new entity for this resource
    - DELETE: This is normally not accepted, but it can mean removing all the entities of the resource
    - PUT: Normally not accepted
    - PATCH: This is normally not accepted, but it can mean partially updating all the entities of the resource
- REST entity (for example, /users/123):
    - GET: Get the entity's information
    - POST: Normally not accepted
    - DELETE: Delete the entity
    - PUT: Update the entire entity
    - PATCH: Partially update the entity

Once we have a way to identify resources and entities and execute actions on them, we need a way to pass information in some instances. For example, if I want to create a new entity, I need information about that entity. If I'm creating a user, I need their username, email, name, surname, and any other information that I want to store.

For that, we can use the HTTP body of the request. This body needs to be serialized in a certain format – as I mentioned previously, the de facto standard for serialization is JSON – and we also need to communicate to the server that we're using that serialization mechanism. To do so, we can use the `Content-Type: application/json` header. So, the combination of the `Content-Type` header and the request body is enough for the client to convey the necessary information to the server.

The server now knows what action the client wants to execute – and with what data – due to the method in the request being serialized and included in the body of the request. However, we need a way to respond to that. This can also be handled using the HTTP protocol.

HTTP provides two things that are handy in this case: the response body (similar to the request body) and the status code. In REST, the response body will contain the information you're requesting, as well as the entity or the list of entities. The status code gives you information about what happened with the operation itself.

It's very important to pay attention to the status code because it gives you information about what happened with your request, and maybe you need to take action and handle something differently. The following are some of the most common HTTP status codes:

- `200 OK`: Everything went well
- `201 Created`: A new entity has been created
- `202 Accepted`: The request has been accepted but hasn't necessarily been processed
- `204 No Content`: Everything went well, but no data is available
- `301 Moved Permanently`: Permanent redirect
- `302 Moved`: Temporary redirect
- `304 Not Modified`: The data hasn't changed (used for caches)
- `400 Bad Request`: The client sent the wrong data
- `401 Unauthorized`: Authentication needed
- `403 Forbidden`: Authorization needed
- `404 Not found`: Resource or entity doesn't exist
- `405 Method Not Allowed`: The action that you're trying to execute isn't allowed
- `500 Internal Server Error`: Something went wrong on the server side

There are other status codes, but they aren't as widely used as the ones mentioned here.

Once you know the status code and the data that you want to return, which can be done in the request body, you must serialize that to JSON and communicate to the client that you're using JSON format by using the `Content-Type` header.

So, now that we know we need a URI, an HTTP method, an HTTP request body, an HTTP status code, an HTTP response body, and a couple of `Content-Type` headers, let's see some examples of this using `curl`.

Let's imagine we have an API with `users` resources in the `http://localhost:8888/api/v1/users` URI, and we want to create a new entity for that. We know the resource URI, and because we want to create a new entity, we know that we have to use the `POST` verb on the resource URI and pass new user information in the request's body in JSON format. So, we can do something like this:

```
$ curl -X POST -d'{"username": "john.doe", "name": "John", "surename":
"Doe"}' -H "Content-Type: application/json" http://localhost:8888/api/v1/
users
```

> 💡 **Quick tip:** Enhance your coding experience with the **AI Code Explainer** and **Quick Copy** features. Open this book in the next-gen Packt Reader. Click the **Copy** button
>
> (1) to quickly copy code into your coding environment, or click the **Explain** button
>
> (2) to get the AI assistant to explain a block of code to you.

```
                                                          Copy        Explain
function calculate(a, b) {                                 (1)          (2)
    return {sum: a + b};
};
```

> 📖 **The next-gen Packt Reader** is included for free with the purchase of this book. Scan the QR code OR go to `packtpub.com/unlock`, then use the search bar to find this book by name. Double-check the edition shown to make sure you get the right one.

If something isn't OK in the request, we could get something such as a 400 Bad Request error from our API, but if everything goes well, we expect to receive a 201 Create status code and an output similar to the following:

```
{
    "id": 42,
    "username": "jonh.doe",
    "name": "John",
    "surname": "Doe",
}
```

Here, we can see how the HTTP protocol conveys all the information that we need in both directions to decide what to do, how to do it, and what the final result of the operations will be. But that's only part of the power that comes with the fact that REST is usually built on top of HTTP. Let's take a look at some of its other advantages.

Other HTTP features used in REST

HTTP is a very rich protocol that provides many different HTTP features that we, as API developers, can leverage to improve our APIs.

Probably the most widely used one is the use of query parameters to convey extra information, such as pagination or filtering. For example, if I don't want to get all the users in the system, I could use something such as /api/v1/users?page=0&perPage=100, providing parameters to the users resource to get only page number 0 and only 100 entities per page. The parameters that are used and their effects are defined by the REST API developer, so there's no standard way of doing this. However, common patterns are used frequently in REST services.

Another important HTTP feature that's widely used is **cache headers**. HTTP provides a set of HTTP headers related to the cache that instruct the server or the client on how we want the cache on the other side to behave. This can imply substantial performance improvements. For example, I can use the Cache-Control: max-age=60 HTTP header to instruct the client to cache this request's result and use it for 60 seconds. That would help me avoid requesting the same data again during the next 60 seconds if there are more petitions.

The HTTP protocol provides security, authorization, and authentication mechanisms. CORS and the Authorization header are good examples. HTTP also provides security-related headers, something we're going to explore more deeply in *Chapter 7*.

Custom headers are something that can be seen in the REST API. It's another way to send or receive information between the programs that are communicating. Custom headers are prefixed with X- to differentiate them from the official headers. For example, I could deliver pagination information by adding headers such as X-Page: 0 and X-Entities-Per-Page: 100, and perhaps the server could reply with the entities and another header, such as X-Has-Next-Page: true. This kind of approach isn't especially common or widely used, but it's good to know that there's that possibility.

The last important aspect that has made REST so successful is the fact that it uses a "human-readable" data representation. A huge percentage of APIs use JSON as their serialization mechanism, allowing the API consumers to inspect and debug the data they get from the API service quickly. This "easy-to-read" data provides developers with a boost in understanding the API and/or the errors that occur due to bad usage or service implementation errors.

So, REST defines resources and entities and is built on top of HTTP. But what does all this have to do with Go, and why should you use Go and not any other language? Let's see.

Why use Go for API development?

First, there are very good reasons to use Go for API development, and they're the same for other languages. I'm heavily biased because I love the Go programming language for multiple reasons. Still, I'm going to explain why I think Go is a great language for API development and why I think it's ahead of other languages.

One of the main reasons is the language itself. If you know Go, you already know how simple, elegant, and fast it can be. Having a language that keeps your problem straightforward is ideal for REST API development. Go tends to provide low-complexity solutions and avoid boilerplate code. APIs are often created as small functions that give access to your logic. A language that gets straight to the point and allows you to write that code succinctly and directly is a blessing in this context.

Another good reason why you should use Go for REST is its extensive standard library, which provides you with most of the building blocks you'll need to build an API without any external dependencies. JSON encoding/decoding, HTTP servers, URL routing, query parameters parsing, and header handling are all built into the standard library. When you start writing your API in Go, you already have all that you need to build the API. You may need some other libraries, depending on the project, but even if that's required, the Go ecosystem surrounding APIs is, in general, very mature.

Apart from the standard library, the language itself provides particular advantages when you're working with programs that operate concurrently, such as an API where you have multiple clients consuming that API at the same time. In those scenarios, its built-in concurrency primitives and lightweight processes (goroutines) make your applications ultra-performant out of the box, almost without you needing to think about it. The built-in HTTP server handles the requests in independent goroutines, so your API will be running concurrently, even if you don't use goroutines anywhere in your code.

There are other popular language options out there for API development, from Python to Rust to others such as C# and Java. But, from my experience, Go falls in the sweet spot between performance, a high degree of control, development speed, and robustness. Of course, I'm biased because Go is my language of choice, but I've worked with other languages, and I haven't found something in the same sweet spot that Go has for building APIs.

In conclusion, you can build APIs with any language, but not all of them provide the same value as Go. While we explore this in this book, I will show you how good Go is at writing APIs and how far you can go using the standard library almost exclusively.

Building a simple API in Go

As mentioned in the *Technical requirements* section, you'll need the Go compiler to build our examples. If you haven't done so yet, you can learn how to install it at `http://go.dev`.

Let's start building a very simple API from scratch in Go. We aren't going to dive too deep into the details here, but I'm going to explain what's going on in general terms. We'll explore the specifics in the following chapters. For now, we only want to get a very simple API up and running.

Creating the project

The first step is to create our project. For that, we're going to need to create a directory and initialize our project package there:

```
$ mkdir myapi
$ cd myapi
$ go mod init myapi
```

In the first and second lines, we're creating the new directory and entering it.

In the third line, when we run `go mod init myapi`, we're defining the root import path of our project. I'm using `myapi` here, but it's more common to use something such as `github.com/username/reponame` as the import path as it refers to the path of the repository in GitHub, or any other service that you use to host your code.

Once you've initialized the Go project, we can start writing the first version of our program. For now, we're going to build a "Hello World" program as an HTTP server in a file called main.go.

Writing a "Hello World" program

In this section, we're going to write one of the simplest APIs that we can build: a Hello World API that allows us to make requests and always returns Hello World as a string. Let's see the code:

```go
package main

import (
    "fmt"
    "net/http"
)

func main() {
    http.HandleFunc("/", func(w http.ResponseWriter, r *http.Request) {
        fmt.Fprint(w, "Hello World")
    })
    http.ListenAndServe(":8888", nil)
}
```

If you're familiar with Go, then most of the code here will be very straightforward. You only need to pay a bit more attention to http.HandleFunc, which registers a new available URL in our HTTP server. This tells our server how to handle requests on that URL using the handler defined inline there.

To handle these requests, we can just write the response handler alongside the result that we want to transmit. Don't worry too much about the details here – we'll dive deeper into this in the following chapters.

Once the handler has been defined and bound to a URL, we need to start listening on a port and run the web server. We can do this using the http.ListenAndServe function.

With that, we already have an HTTP server that gets requests and gives responses. Now, let's execute the server from the command line.

Running your server

Your API server runs just like every other program in Go, so you have two options. The first option is to run the program directly by executing the following command:

```
$ go run .
```

Alternatively, you can build your program and run the final executable:

```
$ go build .
$ ./main
```

In both cases, you'll end up with a process running that exposes port 8888 and accepts HTTP requests. But you don't need to believe me; let's check it out.

Accessing the API

The most straightforward approach that you can follow to check whether your server is running and behaving as expected is to open your web browser and go to http://localhost:8888. If everything went well, you should see the text **Hello World**, as shown in *Figure 1.1*.

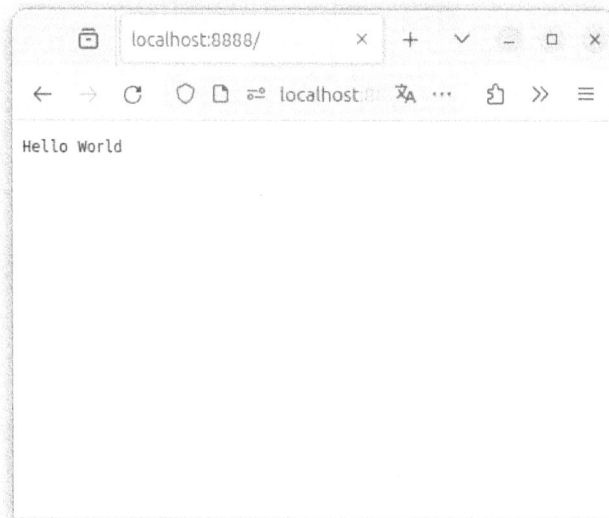

Figure 1.4 – Hello World in a browser

Another option is to use curl, a command-line-based HTTP client, to get this same information:

```
$ curl http://localhost:8888
Hello World
```

However, there are other ways to access our API apart from using HTTP clients such as a web browser or curl. You can also build your API client. For that, you'll still need to use HTTP under the hood, but you'll access the API using code, not other applications.

Creating the client project

We need to create a project for the client, similar to what we did for the server. To do so, we can execute similar commands:

```
$ mkdir myclient
$ cd myclient
$ go mod init myclient
```

With that, our project is ready and we can start working on the code.

Writing the API client

An API client is nothing other than the code that accesses the API. In our case, we'll access the API directly using an HTTP request and print the response to the terminal:

```go
package main

import (
    "fmt"
    "io"
    "net/http"
)

func main() {
    result, err := http.Get("http://localhost:8888/")
    if err != nil {
        panic(err)
    }
    defer result.Body.Close()
    data, err := io.ReadAll(result.Body)
    if err != nil {
        panic(err)
    }
    fmt.Println("Response:", string(data))
}
```

Here, we use the `http.Get` function to make a `GET` request to our API server. Our server will generate `Hello World` and send that as a response to our request.

So, we read the body that's sent by the server and use that data to print the necessary information to the console. Easy, right?

Running the client

Before running the client, be sure that your server is up and running. If not, the client will fail because it won't be able to connect to the server. Again, you can run the client however you prefer. I prefer using the go run option because it's just one command:

```
$ go run .
Response: Hello World
```

With that, we receive the response from the server and print it to the terminal.

Hooray! You've created your first API server and client in Go and communicated two independent programs through that new API. But this is just the beginning.

Summary

In this chapter, we conveyed a lot of general information about APIs in general – specifically REST APIs. We talked about other alternatives, such as gRPC, GraphQL, and SOAP before diving deeper into the principles and concepts that are used in REST and how they're used in the HTTP protocol.

Regarding REST, we took a closer look at how REST leverages HTTP verbs, status codes, headers, and request/response bodies to communicate the data, format, and actions required to provide us with a solid foundation to build our APIs.

Finally, we learned how to build a very simple API server and client and how to communicate information between them using the Go standard library using the HTTP package.

In the next chapter, we'll explore the different options and tools that we have to better understand existing REST APIs.

Unlock this book's exclusive benefits now

Scan this QR code or go to packtpub.com/unlock, then search this book by name.

Note: Keep your purchase invoice ready before you start.

2

Exploring REST APIs

A REST API can be simple or complicated, have thousands of different resources with millions of entities, or expose only one resource with a few entities. Every developer can decide how to use query parameters, HTTP headers, and HTTP verbs. Nothing is written in stone here because REST provides the guiding principles, but the developer always makes the final decision.

For this reason, it's essential to have the right tools and resources to understand an API properly before consuming it, as well as the right tools to explore and investigate how to use that API in real life.

This chapter will explore three tools I consider the *bread and butter* of any API user:

- **OpenAPI**: The OpenAPI documentation defines our REST API, declaring the resources, entities, and operations we can perform on each resource, as well as the authentication mechanism; everything is exposed in OpenAPI.
- **Postman**: Postman is one of the most popular applications for interacting with APIs from the developer's perspective, allowing us to explore them in greater detail. It also supports the OpenAPI standard and many public APIs documented out there that you can use directly.
- **curl**: The `curl` application is one of my favorites. It lets you craft any request you need from the terminal, enabling you to quickly test and loop on API endpoints and tweak parameters rapidly.

Technical requirements

We won't be writing any code in this chapter; instead, we'll explore an API using the methods mentioned previously. To do so, we'll need to have Postman and `curl` installed. We'll also need to create a free account in Postman so that we can use the application to its fullest potential.

OpenAPI

OpenAPI is a standard from the OpenAPI Initiative that describes HTTP APIs and is the de facto standard for REST APIs.

It imparts a detailed description of all the URLs, methods, parameters, resources, entities, and serialization mechanisms available while also providing examples of how to use the API in code.

In this section, we'll explore the basic shape of OpenAPI and the main things you need to look at to understand an API. However, we won't get into the details of the OpenAPI format. Instead, I'll help you understand an API through its OpenAPI documentation.

We'll explore how to document APIs using OpenAPI in *Chapter 11*.

For now, let's talk more about the OpenAPI file and its format.

The OpenAPI file

The OpenAPI file is a **YAML Ain't Markup Language** (**YAML**) file containing general API information and a list of paths. Each path represents a URL in your API; you can have a set of accepted methods for that URL. For each method, you define the expected request format, the body, the parameters, the headers, and the possible responses: the possible status codes, bodies, headers, and so on.

With these simple concepts, you can express almost everything you need to declare how your API accepts and responds to requests. And even if that isn't enough for your case because you have some particular way of doing certain things, such as authentication, OpenAPI still has some ways to define that kind of exception.

But this is a bit abstract. Let's see an example.

OpenAPI example

The following is an OpenAPI file representing a straightforward API:

```
openapi: 3.0.0
info:
  title: My API
  description: My brand new API written in Go
  version: 0.0.1
servers:
  - url: http://example.com/api/v1
```

```
      description: My API public server
    - url: http://test.example.com/api/v1
      description: My API test server
paths:
  /users:
    get:
      summary: Returns the list of users.
      description: List all the user ids
      responses:
        '200':
          description: A JSON array of user ids
          content:
            application/json:
              schema:
                type: array
                items:
                  type: string
```

As I mentioned previously, here, we define some API metadata, such as the name, description, and version of the API and the list of servers. After, we enter the most essential part for exploring the API: its **paths**.

Each path provides a URL – in this case, the /users URL. Here, we define the GET method and give it a description, summary, and possible responses. In this case, we only respond to these requests with a 200 status code that provides an array of strings containing the user ID list in JSON format.

All this information is easy to find and access in YAML format. However, this isn't ideal because people aren't that comfortable reading YAML. Fortunately, there are tools that can transform our OpenAPI format into something more straightforward to use and navigate, such as **Redoc**.

Let's see a real-world example of an API endpoint's documentation and using OpenAPI and Redoc to expose that documentation to consumers.

OpenAPI documentation example

You want your API to be documented in an easy-to-consume way. That's what Redoc does for us – it takes our OpenAPI and builds a web-based document that exposes all the details of our API in a very easy-to-consume way.

Figure 2.1 shows an example of the Mattermost API documentation, which you can use to get a Mattermost channel by name (`https://api.mattermost.com/#tag/channels/operation/ GetChannelByName`):

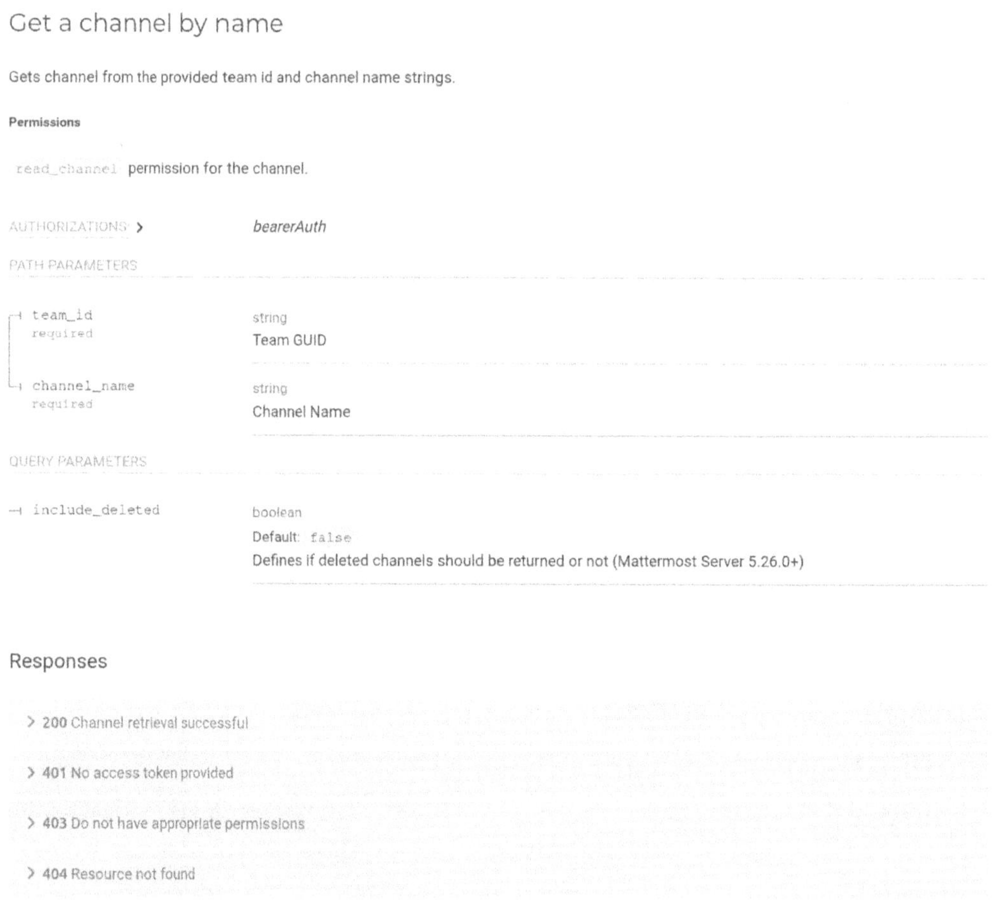

Get a channel by name

Gets channel from the provided team id and channel name strings.

Permissions

`read_channel` permission for the channel.

AUTHORIZATIONS >	*bearerAuth*
PATH PARAMETERS	
┌┤ team_id required	string Team GUID
└┤ channel_name required	string Channel Name
QUERY PARAMETERS	
┤ include_deleted	boolean Default: false Defines if deleted channels should be returned or not (Mattermost Server 5.26.0+)

Responses

> 200 Channel retrieval successful

> 401 No access token provided

> 403 Do not have appropriate permissions

> 404 Resource not found

Figure 2.1 – OpenAPI endpoint documentation

As you can see, you have all the information that you need to call this API endpoint: the parameters that you can use in the URL, the parameters that you can pass through the query string, the authorization required, the permissions needed, and all the possible responses. This information is a game changer for the API consumer because they have all the required details on using the API at a glance.

But that's not all; you can also see examples of accessing it from the code. Mattermost is a **Go project**, so we expose our OpenAPI examples in Go by default. An example of this is shown in *Figure 2.2*:

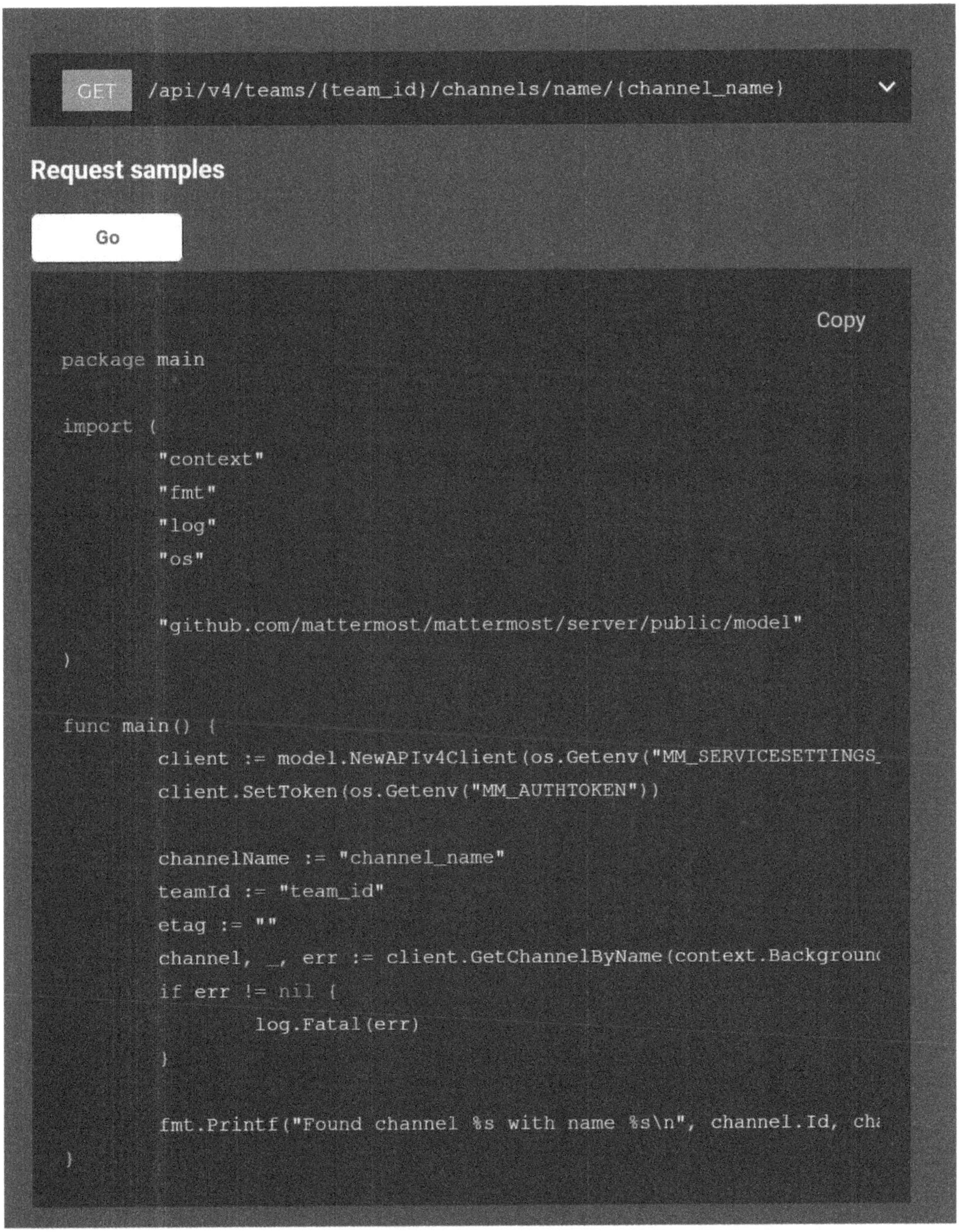

```
GET   /api/v4/teams/{team_id}/channels/name/{channel_name}          ∨

Request samples

  Go

                                                                  Copy

package main

import (
        "context"
        "fmt"
        "log"
        "os"

        "github.com/mattermost/mattermost/server/public/model"
)

func main() {
        client := model.NewAPIv4Client(os.Getenv("MM_SERVICESETTINGS_
        client.SetToken(os.Getenv("MM_AUTHTOKEN"))

        channelName := "channel_name"
        teamId := "team_id"
        etag := ""
        channel, _, err := client.GetChannelByName(context.Backgroun(
        if err != nil {
                log.Fatal(err)
        }

        fmt.Printf("Found channel %s with name %s\n", channel.Id, cha
}
```

Figure 2.2 – OpenAPI code example

The most outstanding part is the tailor-made example for the API, so you aren't dealing with an autogenerated API call example. Instead, you're exploring a real-world example provided by the creator of the API.

I recommend exploring the Mattermost API or any other OpenAPI-based generated documentation. You'll quickly get used to it and better understand the APIs rapidly.

OpenAPI is an excellent resource for understanding an API, but if you want to master it, you must interact with it. OpenAPI doesn't allow you to do that out of the box; instead, you have tools such as Postman to do so.

Postman

Postman is an HTTP client specially designed to consume APIs. It's the de facto standard in the industry to explore and try APIs with a graphical interface. It's compatible with OpenAPI and allows us to explore APIs but also interact with them directly there.

In this section, we're going to explore the basic usage of Postman and give you a sneak peek at its potential. We'll start by importing an API definition, studying it, and interacting with it by sending a request.

So, let's start by installing the tool and importing an API.

Importing an API

You can download and install Postman locally from `https://www.postman.com/downloads/` or directly from their web page at `https://web.postman.co`. It works perfectly fine in both cases, but you should consider using the installable application for local development.

One of the fantastic things about Postman is that it comes with many already existing APIs that are easy to incorporate and start exploring. As an example, we'll go through the Mattermost API and show you how to import, analyze, and start testing it manually.

Once you have Postman installed and registered an account, you only need to search for the API you want – in this case, Mattermost – in Postman's search field and click on the result, as shown in *Figure 2.3*:

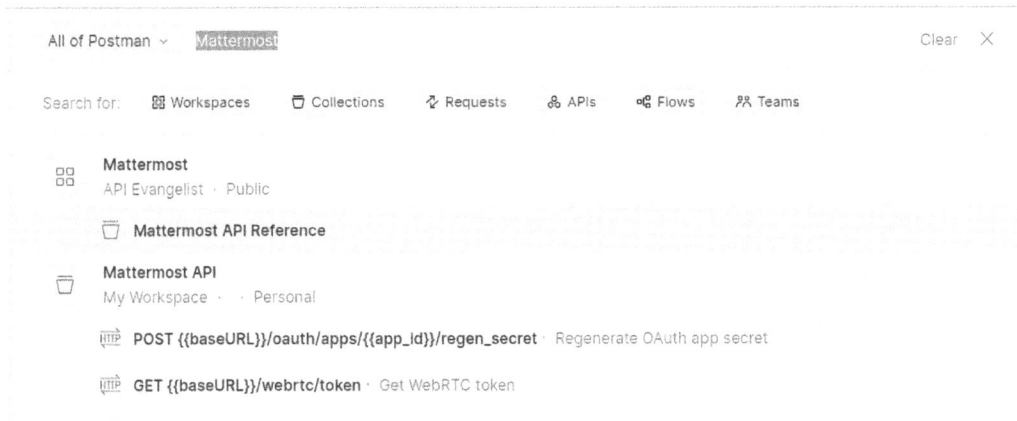

All of Postman ⌄   Mattermost   Clear   ✕

Search for: 🔲 Workspaces   🗂 Collections   ⌁ Requests   ⅋ APIs   ⅇ Flows   ⧉ Teams

⬚⬚ **Mattermost**
⬚⬚ API Evangelist · Public

    🗂 Mattermost API Reference

🗂 **Mattermost API**
    My Workspace · · Personal

    📋 POST {{baseURL}}/oauth/apps/{{app_id}}/regen_secret · Regenerate OAuth app secret

    📋 GET {{baseURL}}/webrtc/token · Get WebRTC token

Figure 2.3 – Postman API search

Here, we can see a list of search results and the APIs that were found, and we can select the one we want to explore. In this case, we'll select **Mattermost API Reference**.

After that, we can start exploring the Mattermost API and look at the different methods and endpoints we can use. Let's take a look.

Exploring API endpoints

APIs come in different sizes. Some are bigger, and some are smaller, but grasping an API's shape and behavior takes time. Postman provides a very convenient way of visualizing this to ease the process of exploration and understanding, giving you the big picture while allowing you to dig into the details.

Let's start with the big picture. Postman exposes a tree view of the API, which shows the different endpoints, routes, and methods you can execute, as shown in *Figure 2.4*:

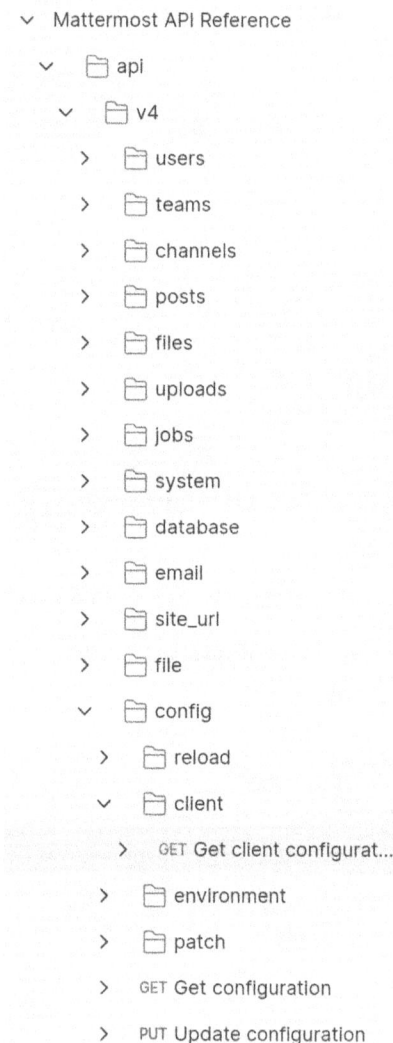

```
∨   Mattermost API Reference
    ∨   📂 api
        ∨   📂 v4
            >   📁 users
            >   📁 teams
            >   📁 channels
            >   📁 posts
            >   📁 files
            >   📁 uploads
            >   📁 jobs
            >   📁 system
            >   📁 database
            >   📁 email
            >   📁 site_url
            >   📁 file
            ∨   📁 config
                >   📁 reload
                ∨   📁 client
                    >   GET Get client configurat...
                >   📁 environment
                >   📁 patch
                >   GET Get configuration
                >   PUT Update configuration
```

Figure 2.4 – Postman API tree view

Here, we can see everything that we can do at a glance in the API's different endpoints. In this case, it's a very extensive API with many endpoints and methods you can execute.

Once you have this whole view of the API, you can dig into the details. For that, you must go to a specific method in an endpoint and click on it.

Figure 2.5 shows Postman showing you what you can do, the supported parameters, and the expected headers:

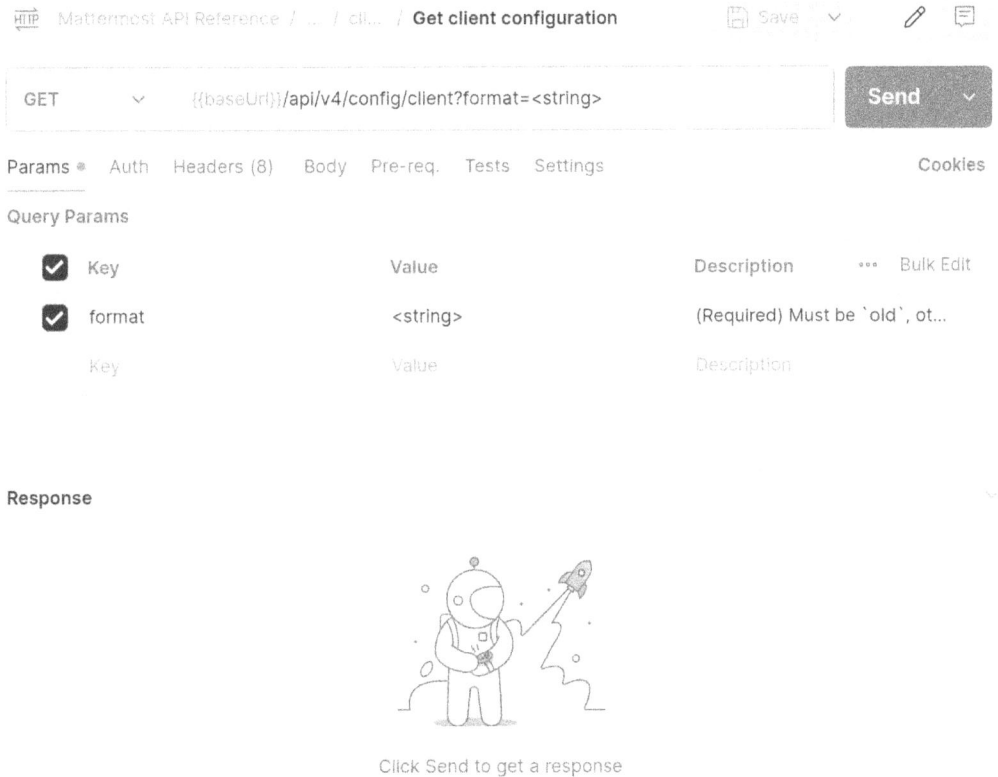

Figure 2.5 – Postman endpoint details

In this detailed view, you get information about that endpoint. In this case, we can see an endpoint for getting the client configuration, and we can see that it receives the format parameter. There's also a description of the field. We can set the value of that parameter by clicking the <string> text and introducing our value. For example, here, we can write old as our value.

But seeing this information isn't the only thing you can do. You can also interact with the API.

Sending requests using Postman

To send a request using Postman, you usually have to set some variables to let Postman know things such as where to find the API or the session token. The variables always depend on the definition of the API, but this is a widespread practice.

So, let's define our new environment with the necessary variables. In this case, we'll be using {{baseUrl}}, which is shown in the URL of the endpoint in *Figure 2.5*.

To do so, we must click the **Environments** option that's available in the menu on the left. You'll see the **New Environment** configuration panel, as shown in *Figure 2.6*:

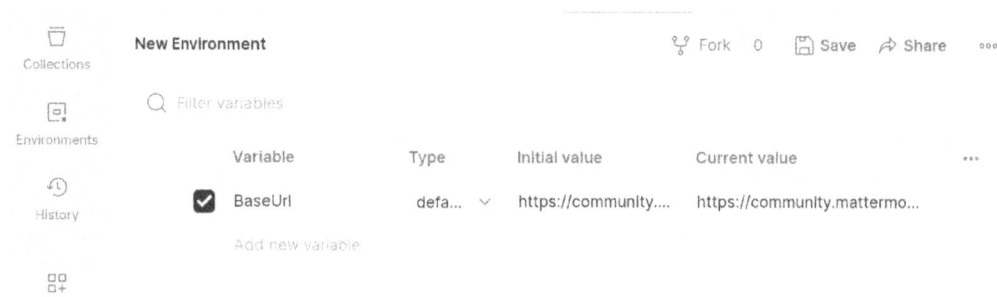

Figure 2.6 – Postman environment variables

Add a new environment with the name you want and set the baseUrl variable to the correct value there. We're going to use https://community.mattermost.com.

With that, we're ready to send a request to the server using Postman. To do so, we must return to the endpoint interface, select the newly created environment, and hit **Send**. You can see the result in *Figure 2.7*:

Figure 2.7 – Postman request response

🔍 **Quick tip:** Need to see a high-resolution version of this image? Open this book in the next-gen Packt Reader or view it in the PDF/ePub copy.

📖 **The next-gen Packt Reader** and a **free PDF/ePub copy** of this book are included with your purchase. Scan the QR code OR visit packtpub.com/unlock, then use the search bar to find this book by name. Double-check the edition shown to make sure you get the right one.

As you can see, we sent the request to the server, and we're getting a response in JSON format. Of course, you can make this more complex by changing the headers, the body, and other parameters. Note that you receive more information alongside the data, such as the headers, the status code, and the time the request took to complete.

This is just a tiny percentage of what you can do with Postman. This tool makes developing and testing APIs easier using your mouse. Still, I know that not everybody is a mouse person. So, let's explore a command-line option called curl that you can use to interact with APIs or even automatize API usage or testing with simple scripts.

curl

curl is the Swiss Army knife of REST API testing. It can build any request you need with the headers and parameters you want, all in a compact and easy-to-use CLI. If you don't have it installed on your system, you can use your system package manager or follow the instructions at https:// curl.se/.

If you're like me and prefer to interact with the command line, you'll love curl (and you probably already know it). Not only that, but curl is used everywhere and is supported by a lot of applications, so it isn't rare to have curl command-line examples in API documentation that provide support for extracting curl calls from places such as the Web Developers Tools of Firefox and Chrome in the **Network** tab, allowing you to reproduce network calls in your command line by copy and pasting.

In this section, we'll explore using the curl command to send requests and get information such as headers in the response.

Getting information

The first thing we can do with curl is send a simple HTTP GET request. This is the simplest form of curl request that you can do, and it consists of calling curl with the URL you want to get.

As an example, we can write the following in the command line:

```
$ curl https://www.google.com
<!doctype html><html itemscope="" itemtype="http://schema.org/WebPage"
lang="es"><head><meta...
```

This will send an HTTP GET request to https://www.google.com and return the resulting HTML.

But we're talking about REST APIs, so let's make a REST API call. As an example, let's use the Mattermost API:

```
$ curl "https://community.mattermost.com/api/v4/config/client?format=old"
{"AboutLink": "https://about.mattermost.com/default-about/",
"AndroidAppDownloadLink": "https://about.mattermost.com/mattermost-
android-app/", "AndroidLatestVersion":"   ", "AndroidMinVersion":"   ",
"AppDownloadLink": "https://about.mattermost.com/downloads/"...
```

This is getting better now. We're hitting an API endpoint and getting a JSON response. But sometimes, you might be more interested in the headers because you're evaluating something on the API or want to obtain specific information that comes only in the headers, not in the body. For those cases, you can use the –i parameter to get the headers, like so:

```
$ curl -i "https://community.mattermost.com/api/v4/config/
client?format=old"
HTTP/2 200
date: Wed, 26 Jun 2024 15:17:03 GMT
content-type: application/JSON
expires: 0
permissions-policy:
referrer-policy: no-referrer
vary: Origin
vary: Accept-Encoding
x-content-type-options: nosniff
x-request-id: 7ien4txkuibkbqfdjnywh7e1io
...
```

As you can see, you can get a lot of useful information very quickly with the curl command line, but you can do way more than that – you can also send information to create new resources or interact with the API. Let's see how.

Sending information

We usually use the POST or PUT method to send information to an API, but we can also use the –d parameter to pass the data of the request. In this case, we're going to use the POST method to log in to the Mattermost server using the API. We're going to need the headers, so let's use the –i parameter here:

```
$ curl -i https://community.mattermost.com/api/v4/users/login -d '{"login_
id": "jespino", "password": "secret"}'
```

```
HTTP/1.1 200 OK
Content-Type: application/json
Permissions-Policy:
Referrer-Policy: no-referrer
Token: bd7gjeunojdb5rtrpzek65myre
Vary: Origin
Vary: Accept-Encoding
X-Content-Type-Options: nosniff
...
```

In this case, if we've already created a session, we'll receive a Token header in the response that we can use to make calls to the API.

Now, let's see an example of updating my status via a PUT request. This time, I must specify the HTTP method to use. For that, I'll use the –X parameter. Before, curl was smart enough to know that you wanted to use GET or POST based on the data you were passing, but in this case, you need to expose that explicitly. Let's see how:

```
$ curl -X PUT https://community.mattermost.com/api/v4/users/me/status
-H 'Authorization: Bearer bd7gjeunojdb5rtrpzek65myre' -d'{"user_id":
"ys3pzdbewpn1dedpnj9or1888a", "status": "away"}'
{"user_id": "ys3pzdbewpn1dedpnj9or1888a", "status": "away", "manual":true,
"last_activity_at":1719417893301, "dnd_end_time":0}
```

In this call, I'm passing -H to provide the Authorization header and the Token header I received in the login request. I also passed userID and received that information in the login response.

Diving deeper into the details

As you've seen, you can do everything needed to explore and test your API using curl. You can make requests using different methods, add headers, and provide the body with the information you want to submit. All this is cool, but curl provides more information when needed.

If you want to learn more about the requests that have been made, you can use the -v parameter; it provides detailed information about the request and the response. In the response, you get different prefixes – > means data sent, < means date received, and * means additional information. Let's take a look at an example by using -v:

```
$ curl -v -X PUT https://community.mattermost.com/api/v4/users/me/status
-H 'Authorization: Bearer bd7gjeunojdb5rtrpzek65myre' -d'{"user_id":
"ys3pzdbewpn1dedpnj9or1888a", "status": "away"}'
```

```
* processing: https://community.mattermost.com/api/v4/config/
client?format=old
*   Trying 104.18.1.109:443...
* Connected to community.mattermost.com (104.18.1.109) port 443
* ALPN: offers h2,http/1.1
* TLSv1.3 (OUT), TLS handshake, Client hello (1):
*  CAfile: /etc/ssl/certs/ca-certificates.crt
*  CApath: /etc/ssl/certs
* TLSv1.3 (IN), TLS handshake, Server hello (2):
* TLSv1.3 (IN), TLS handshake, Encrypted Extensions (8):
* TLSv1.3 (IN), TLS handshake, Certificate (11):
...
```

As we can see, it provides a lot of information about how the connection was initialized, the HTTP version used, the TLS connection, and more:

```
> PUT /api/v4/users/me/status HTTP/1.1
> Host: community.mattermost.com
> User-Agent: curl/8.2.1
...
```

It also provides details of the request:

```
< HTTP/1.1 200 OK
< Content-Type: application/json
...
```

Finally, it provides details of the response that was received from the server.

This level of detail in the information provided is handy when you're figuring out why something isn't behaving as expected.

If you want to keep digging into curl, you'll discover that it's a potent tool that's used for many different use cases, not only for REST and HTTP.

Summary

In this chapter, we explored different ways to understand APIs better. First, we looked at using OpenAPI to get information on what we can do and how to use an API. We can explore APIs in read-only and "map" fashion using the YAML format or the OpenAPI-generated documentation pages. We saw how powerful and valuable this can be by looking at some examples and details about various parameters and methods.

Then, we considered another option – not only for exploring but also for interacting with APIs quickly and powerfully: Postman. We learned how to explore and interact with well-known public APIs or build our own and test them through the Postman interface.

Finally, we explored `curl`, a great CLI tool that provides us with everything we need to interact with our APIs from the command line and helps us with testing and debugging.

But this has nothing to do with Go, which is what this book is about. So, let's jump into the next chapter and learn how to build our client library for a REST API using the Go standard library.

Unlock this book's exclusive benefits now

Scan this QR code or go to `packtpub.com/unlock`, then search this book by name.

Note: Keep your purchase invoice ready before you start.

3

Building a REST Client

So far, we have seen what a REST API is and how to explore it, but the whole point of an API is to interact with it. For that, you need to build a client to make API requests and process the responses.

In this chapter, we will explore building a REST client in Go using only the standard library. Go is an excellent language for this task because it comes with the batteries included, and the standard library has everything you need to build a REST client.

As part of the exploration, we are going to cover the following:

- The Go HTTP client
- Request and Response objects
- Building your API client

Technical requirements

For this chapter, we need the Go compiler installed in your system.

The Go HTTP client

The http package in Go is a powerful library that allows you to make HTTP requests to HTTP servers and, in consequence, to your REST APIs. It is part of the standard library, so you don't need to install anything.

As an example of its simplicity, let's see the code needed for making a simple HTTP GET request:

```
resp, err := http.Get("https://example.com")
if err != nil {
    log.Fatal(err)
```

```
}
defer resp.Body.Close()
body, err := ioutil.ReadAll(resp.Body)
```

💡 **Quick tip:** Enhance your coding experience with the **AI Code Explainer** and **Quick Copy** features. Open this book in the next-gen Packt Reader. Click the **Copy** button (**1**) to quickly copy code into your coding environment, or click the **Explain** button (**2**) to get the AI assistant to explain a block of code to you.

Copy　　　Explain

```
function calculate(a, b) {
    return {sum: a + b};
};
```
                                                       ①   ②

📱 **The next-gen Packt Reader** is included for free with the purchase of this book. Scan the QR code OR go to packtpub.com/unlock, then use the search bar to find this book by name. Double-check the edition shown to make sure you get the right one.

This code allows us to make a GET request to https://example.com and read the response body. Also, as is usual in Go, it encourages us to handle any errors that may happen during the process.

The previous example is from a simplified API provided by the http package, but if you need more control over the request, you can go deeper and use a more granular API exposed by the http package. We will talk about this later in the chapter.

Under the hood, it uses DefaultClient, which is a client structure that is responsible for making the requests. You can normally use the default client and it is okay, but whenever you need more control, you can create your own client and customize it. Let's see how.

Customizing the client

First, you must understand that Go will create a default HTTP client for you. Whenever you run `http.Get`, you are calling the `Get` method of `DefaultClient`.

If you want more control, you can create a client and customize the transport mechanism or the timeouts of the requests. Here is an example of how to make a custom client:

```
var client := http.Client{
    Timeout: time.Second * 10,
}
resp, err := client.Get("https://example.com")
...
```

Now, you have a client with a timeout of 10 seconds, so if the server does not respond in 10 seconds, the request will be canceled automatically and return an error.

Apart from the timeouts, we mention **the transport mechanism**. What is that?

The transport mechanism is how the client will communicate with the server, handling things such as the maximum number of connections, the maximum idle times, or the proxy mechanism if there is one. It handles the low-level details of the communication.

So, if you want to have fine control over the transport mechanism and configuration, the client's `Transport` field is the way to go.

Once a client is set up and configured with the details we want, we can make requests using functions such as `client.Get` or `client.Post`, but we can also customize a request object before sending it.

Customizing the request

The `http` package provides a `Request` object that allows you to customize the request to your needs. We will explore the `request` object in more detail in the next section, but I want to explain how it interacts with the client.

Whenever you want to send a request, you can create a `request` object and set the specific parameters you need, such as headers, cookies, or the request's body. Once the `request` object is ready, you can send it to the server using the `client.Do` method. Here is an example of that:

```
req, err := http.NewRequest("GET", "https://example.com", nil)
if err != nil {
    log.Fatal(err)
```

```
}
req.Header.Set("User-Agent", "my-client")
resp, err := client.Do(req)
...
```

This code creates a new Request object, sets the User-Agent header, and sends the request using the client that we made before. Sometimes, client.Get is good enough, but when writing an API client, you usually need to customize the request to add headers or use special methods such as PUT or DELETE.

Now, we have a general vision of how the http package works when you are writing a client. Let's look into the details of what request and response objects are.

Request and Response objects

The request and response objects are the core of the http package. They can represent all the data you can generate in a request and all the data you can receive in a response. Not only that but the http package provides you with functionality for building HTTP clients and servers, and http.Request and http.Response provide that functionality to both sides. So, let's explore them.

The request object

We typically create the request object with the http.NewRequest function. This function provides the basic Request object creation with the minimum data it needs, the method, the URL, and the body. Here is an example of how to create a request object:

```
request, err := http.NewRequest("GET", "https://example.com", nil)
```

It is simple, right? However, the request object has a lot of methods that allow you to configure every piece of it, such as setting the headers or changing the cookies. I don't want to get into the details of everything here, so I will focus on the most important one whenever you are building a REST API: the **headers**.

To modify the headers, you can use the Header field of the request object. For example, let's see how you can set the Content-Type header:

```
request, err := http.NewRequest("POST", "https://example.com", b
    ytes.NewBuffer([]byte(`{"example": "Example"}`))
if err != nil {
    log.Fatal(err)
}
request.Header.Set("Content-Type", "application/json")
```

This code will set the Content-Type header to application/json, so the server knows what kind of data I'm sending in my request, in this case, a JSON object.

It doesn't look that powerful, but HTTP provides many functionalities through the headers, such as setting cookies, authorization, security-related tasks, cache control, and so on. Let's see another example of a header that is widely used in REST APIs, the Authorization header:

```
myToken := "my-very-secret-token-provided-by-the-server"
request.Header.Set("Authorization", "Bearer: " + myToken)
```

This code sets your Authorization header to a Bearer token, a common way to authenticate in REST APIs. The server will check the token and allow you to access the resources if the token is valid.

There are other headers that we are going to explore in the following chapters, such as the security-related ones in *Chapter 7* and the cache control in *Chapter 8*.

The request objects have one and only one purpose, obtaining a response, and we haven't explored the response object yet, so let's do it.

The response object

The response object is the one that is going to hold the data that the server has sent to you. You will get the status code, headers, and response body on the response object. Handling the status code is simple. Depending on the status code, you will behave differently, but the headers and the body are more complex.

Headers in the response can contain information you should consider, such as Content-Type, Cache-Control, or Etag. Ignoring them can lead to crashes or poor performance. We will cover a wide range of headers over the course of the book, so don't stress about it now.

Another important thing you need to understand about responses when using them as a client is to close the body of the response when you are done with it. Not closing the response body is a common pitfall of the Go developers; they forget to close the body, and the connection is not closed, leading to memory leaks or connection leaks. So, the recommended approach is always to call a defer of the body's close function whenever you make an HTTP request. Let me show you an example:

```
resp, err := http.Get("https://example.com")
if err != nil {
    log.Fatal(err)
}
defer resp.Body.Close()
```

As you can see here, right after making the request and ensuring there was no error, I enforced the closure of the response body by using defer. That allows me to be sure that the body will be closed when the function ends, no matter what happens in the middle. There are some cases where you may want to handle the closure in another way, but in such cases, you have to be sure that you end up closing it.

Now that we understand the basics of the Request and Response objects and how they interact with the client, let's build a simple API client that can interact with a simple REST API server.

Building your API client

We will build a simple client with an elementary API server here. In this case, the API server will be an API that returns a random number between 1 and 100, allows the seed to be set, and has a login process.

For that, we are going to need three endpoints. The first one is /random, which will receive a GET request and return JSON containing the random value like this: {"value": 42}. The second one will be /seed, which will receive a POST request with a JSON body containing the seed like this: {"seed": 123}. And the last one will be /login, which will receive a POST request with a JSON body containing the user and the password like this: {"user": "user", "password": "password"}, and it will return a token.

The following code is for the API server. You don't need to understand it now, but you can take a look at it if you want. It is not a good code example, so don't take it as a reference. We are going to explain how to build a proper API server in more detail in the following chapters:

```go
package main

import (
    "encoding/json"
    "log"
    "math/rand"
    "net/http"
    "strconv"
)

var token string
var randomGen *rand.Rand
```

```go
func random(w http.ResponseWriter, r *http.Request) {
    if r.Header.Get("Authorization") != "Bearer "+token {
        w.WriteHeader(http.StatusUnauthorized)
        return
    }
    w.Header().Set("Content-Type", "application/json")
    json.NewEncoder(w).Encode(map[string]int{
        "value": randomGen.Intn(100)})
}

func setSeed(w http.ResponseWriter, r *http.Request) {
    if r.Header.Get("Authorization") != "Bearer "+token {
        w.WriteHeader(http.StatusUnauthorized)
        return
    }
    var data map[string]int
    json.NewDecoder(r.Body).Decode(&data)
    randomGen = rand.New(rand.NewSource(int64(data["seed"])))
}

func login(w http.ResponseWriter, r *http.Request) {
    var data map[string]string
    json.NewDecoder(r.Body).Decode(&data)
    if data["user"] == "user" && data["password"] == "password" {
        token = strconv.Itoa(rand.Intn(100000000000))
        w.Header().Set("Content-Type", "application/json")
        json.NewEncoder(w).Encode(map[string]string{"token": token})
    } else {
        w.WriteHeader(http.StatusUnauthorized)
    }
}

func main() {
    token = strconv.Itoa(rand.Intn(100000000000))
    randomGen = rand.New(rand.NewSource(0))
    http.HandleFunc("/random", random)
    http.HandleFunc("/seed", setSeed)
```

```
    http.HandleFunc("/login", login)
    log.Fatal(http.ListenAndServe(":8888", nil))
}
```

As you can see, we have defined our three endpoints, and there are some authorization checks and a login process. With this in place, we can start working on building our client.

So, let's jump in with the client code and start creating our client structure. For that, we will develop the client in an independent package called `client`:

```
package client

import (
    "bytes"
    "encoding/json"
    "errors"
    "io"
    "net/http"
)

type Client struct {
    baseURL string
    token   string
}

func NewClient(baseURL string) *Client {
    return &Client{
        baseURL: baseURL,
    }
}
```

This basic structure allows us to define our client, pointing to a specific URL and saving the token whenever we have it. That is an excellent first step, so let's continue with the login process:

```
type LoginRequest struct {
    User     string `json:"user"`
    Password string `json:"password"`
}

type LoginResponse struct {
```

```go
        Token string `json:"token"`
}

func (c *Client) Login(user, password string) error {
    data := LoginRequest{
        User:     user,
        Password: password,
    }
    body, err := json.Marshal(data)
    if err != nil {
        return err
    }
    req, err := http.NewRequest("POST", c.baseURL+"/login",
            bytes.NewBuffer(body))
    if err != nil {
        return err
    }
    req.Header.Set("Content-Type", "application/json")
    resp, err := http.DefaultClient.Do(req)
    if err != nil {
        return err
    }
    defer resp.Body.Close()

    if resp.StatusCode != http.StatusOK {
        return errors.New("invalid login")
    }

    responseBody, err := io.ReadAll(resp.Body)
    if err != nil {
        return err
    }
    loginResponse := LoginResponse{}
    json.Unmarshal(responseBody, &loginResponse)

    c.token = loginResponse.Token
    return nil
}
```

This code allows us to log in to the server and save the token in the client. For that, we're construct-
ing the POST request and sending it with the default HTTP client defined by the http package. We
are also reading the body from the response in JSON format and unmarshalling that information
into a Go struct that contains the token. Now, we can use this token to make other requests. Let's
see how to make the random request:

```go
type RandomResponse struct {
    Value int 'json:"value"'
}

func (c *Client) Random() (int, error) {
    req, err := http.NewRequest("GET", c.baseURL+"/random", nil)
    if err != nil {
        return 0, err
    }
    req.Header.Set("Authorization", "Bearer "+c.token)
    resp, err := http.DefaultClient.Do(req)
    if err != nil {
        return 0, err
    }
    defer resp.Body.Close()


    if resp.StatusCode != http.StatusOK {
        return 0, errors.New("server invalid response")
    }

    responseBody, err := io.ReadAll(resp.Body)
    if err != nil {
        return 0, err
    }
    randomResponse := RandomResponse{}
    json.Unmarshal(responseBody, &randomResponse)

    return randomResponse.Value, nil
}
```

In this case, we can see how we are setting the Authorization header to be able to call the random endpoint. And finally, let's see how to set the seed:

```go
type SeedRequest struct {
    Seed int 'json:"seed"'
}

func (c *Client) SetSeed(seed int) error {
    data := SeedRequest{
        Seed: seed,
    }
    body, err := json.Marshal(data)
    if err != nil {
        return err
    }
    req, err := http.NewRequest("POST", c.baseURL+"/seed",
                                bytes.NewBuffer(body))
    if err != nil {
        return err
    }
    req.Header.Set("Authorization", "Bearer "+c.token)
    req.Header.Set("Content-Type", "application/json")
    resp, err := http.DefaultClient.Do(req)
    if err != nil {
        return err
    }
    defer resp.Body.Close()
    if resp.StatusCode != http.StatusOK {
        return errors.New("server invalid response")
    }

    return nil
}
```

Again, we are setting the Authorization header. This time, we are also setting the Content-Type header to let the server know that we are sending the data in JSON format and we are sending the seed to the server.

This code is for a straightforward client. For more complex clients, you may want to share more code in things such as setting the headers or handling the different status codes better, but this is a good starting point.

Now, let's see how cool our new API client is using this inside a Go application:

```go
package main

import (
    "fmt"
    "log"
    "github.com/your-user/your-repo/client"
)

func main() {
    c := client.NewClient("http://localhost:8888")
    if err := c.Login("user", "password"); err != nil {
        log.Fatal(err)
    }

    value, err := c.Random()
    if err != nil {
        log.Fatal(err)
    }
    fmt.Println("Random value:", value)

    if err = c.SetSeed(42); err != nil {
        log.Fatal(err)
    }

    value, err = c.Random()
    if err != nil {
        log.Fatal(err)
    }
    fmt.Println("Random value with seed 42:", value)
}
```

As you can see, as soon as you have your client implemented in Go, using it feels pretty natural.

Summary

This chapter showed how to build a REST client using the standard library in Go. We started with some theory about the http package and how we build the Request and Response objects. Finally, we built our REST API client with authentication support and requests for reading and storing data.

The learnings so far get us to the point where we can interact with REST APIs programmatically using Go. The next step is to start building our API.

In the next chapter, we will explore how to design and develop a REST API server in Go using the standard library exclusively.

Unlock this book's exclusive benefits now

Scan this QR code or go to packtpub. com/unlock, then search this book by name.

Note: Keep your purchase invoice ready before you start.

4

Designing Your REST API

So far, we have explored many concepts and tools that help us on the client side, but it's now time to explore the server side. This chapter will explore how to design and implement a REST API using Go and the standard library. You will learn enough to have your very first REST API written in Go, understanding which HTTP methods to use and which status code to return. Also, you will be able to define the URLs used for your resources.

We will go through the following topics:

- Exploring HTTP methods and status codes
- Understanding routing
- Building middleware
- Using API versioning
- Building a CRUD API

Technical requirements

For this chapter, you will need to have Go version 1.22 or later and cURL installed on your machine.

HTTP methods and status codes

We already talked about HTTP methods and status codes in the first chapter, but let's go through them now in greater detail. Let's start with the HTTP methods.

HTTP methods

HTTP methods are the verbs that we use to tell the server what we want to do with the resource. The most common methods used in REST APIs are GET, POST, PUT, PATCH, and DELETE. They are commonly used to build **CRUD** (which stands for **create, retrieve, update, and delete**) APIs. Here is a brief explanation of each one of those methods.

GET

In REST, the GET method is synonymous with the RETRIEVE verb, allowing you to get data from the server. It should be idempotent, meaning that if you make the same request multiple times, the result should be the same. In REST APIs, we use the GET method in two situations.

The first situation is when you need to get a single resource. Let's say you send a GET request to a specific resource instance, as in this example:

```
$ curl https://api.example.com/users/1
{
  "id": 1,
  "username": "john.doe",
  "name": "John",
  "surname": "Doe",
}
```

This way, we get the user with the ID of 1 from the server.

The other situation is to get a list of resources. Let's say you send a GET request to a resource, as in this example:

```
$ curl https://api.example.com/users
[
  {
    "id": 1,
    "username": "jonh.doe",
    "name": "John",
    "surname": "Doe",
  },
  {
    "id": 2,
    "username": "jane.doe",
    "name": "Jane",
```

```
      "surname": "Doe",
    }
  ]
```

In this case, we are getting the list of users from the server. Another common practice is to use query parameters to apply options to the list of resources, as in this example:

```
$ curl https://api.example.com/users?filter=John&orderby=name&limit=10
[
  {
    "id": 2,
    "username": "jane.doe",
    "name": "Jane",
    "surname": "Doe",
  },
  {
    "id": 1,
    "username": "jonh.doe",
    "name": "John",
    "surname": "Doe",
  }
]
```

If you implement that on the server side, you can filter by some text, order the results in a certain way, and limit the number of results. Query parameters are most frequently used with the GET method. They can also be used with other HTTP methods, but it is less common.

POST

In REST, the POST method is synonymous with the CREATE verb and allows you to create a new resource instance on the server. Here is an example:

```
$ curl -X POST https://api.example.com/users --ddata '{"username": "jesus.
espino", "name": "Jesus", "surname": "Espino"}'
```

This way, we create a new user on the server with the data provided. The server should return the created resource with the ID assigned to it:

```
{
  "id": 3,
  "username": "jesus.espino",
```

```
    "name": "Jesús",
    "surname": "Espino",
}
```

Another common usage of the POST method, which is not strictly RESTful, is to send a request to a resource to perform an action. For example, if you want to notify a user, you could do something like this:

```
$ curl -X POST https://api.example.com/users/3/notify --data '{"message":
"Hello, Jesús"}'
```

Of course, that requires you to implement it on the server side. It's a common practice to implement this kind of action because it's easy to understand and implement. If not, you would end up with a new resource that represents notifications and is, by nature, ephemeral, so you "create" a notification instance that triggers something in the server that notifies the user; it differs from the common pattern where we store and retrieve persisted instances. It feels more natural to say notify Y message the user X than create a notification with user X as the recipient and message Y as the content.

Another excellent example of this is the login/logout actions. You could create a session resource, but again, it looks odd. So, I prefer using the concept of actions in the REST API, but it's up to you.

Some developers also use the POST method to update a resource, but it's not the best practice. The PUT and PATCH methods are the way to go for that. So, let's discuss PUT and PATCH.

PUT

The PUT method in REST is synonymous with the UPDATE verb, allowing you to update a resource instance on the server. Here is an example:

```
$ curl -X PUT https://api.example.com/users/3 --data '{"username": "jesus.
espino", "name": "Jesús", "surname": "Espino García"}'
```

This way, we update the user with ID 3 on the server. The server should return the updated instance:

```
{
    "id": 3,
    "username": "jesus.espino",
    "name": "Jesús",
    "surname": "Espino García",
}
```

Take into account that the PUT method is used to fully replace an object. For partial updates, you should use the PATCH method.

PATCH

The PATCH method in REST is synonymous with the PARTIAL UPDATE verb, allowing you to update a resource instance partially. Here is an example:

```
$ curl -X PATCH https://api.example.com/users/3 -d '{"surname": "Other"}'
```

This way, we update the surname field of the user with ID 3 on the server. The server should return the updated instance:

```
{
  "id": 3,
  "username": "jesus.espino",
  "name": "Jesús",
  "surname": "Other",
}
```

As you can see, we are only updating the surname field. The other fields remain the same. Now, we know how to retrieve, create, and update, but what about deleting? Let's talk about the DELETE method.

DELETE

The DELETE method in REST is synonymous with the DELETE verb, allowing you to delete a resource instance on the server. Here is an example:

```
$ curl -X DELETE https://api.example.com/users/3
```

This request will delete the user with ID 3 from the server. It usually returns an empty body, unless an error occurred. DELETE is normally only used on specific instances, but can also be used on whole resources to delete all the instances (if you have it implemented). However, it is not a common practice.

We have talked about HTTP methods and the response bodies, but we haven't said anything about the status codes, so let's jump into it now.

HTTP status codes

The server uses HTTP status codes to communicate to the client the outcome of their requests. In *Chapter 1*, we already explored some of them, but let's go through the most common ones in REST APIs with some examples to understand them better.

2XX

When the server successfully handled a request, it returns a 2XX status code: a status code from 200 to 299. Some examples of this are the following:

- The 200 OK status code means everything went well and is the typical response whenever you retrieve or update resources.
- The 201 Created status code means the resource was created successfully. When creating a new resource, this is the typical reply if everything has gone well, generally as a result of a POST request.
- The 204 No Content status code is used when the request has been successfully processed, but the content result is empty. This status code is the one you use in DELETE requests.

3XX

From 300 to 399, the status codes mean the client should take additional action to complete the request. Some examples of this are as follows:

- The 301 Moved Permanently status code means that the resource has been moved to another URL, or in other words, a permanent redirect; the client has to handle it and go to the new URL to get the resource.
- The 302 Found status code means that the resource has been temporarily moved to another location, and the client should use the new location to access the resource.
- The 304 Not Modified status code means that the resource has not been modified; for that, the client has to provide some information about the cached version, such as the **entity tag** (ETag) or the date of the version that it has. With this status code, the client can use the cache.

4XX

From 400 to 499, the status codes mean an error on the client side. Some examples of this are as follows:

- The 400 Bad Request status code means the request was malformed and the server could not understand it. A malformed request can be missing a required field, using an invalid type, using the wrong content type, and so on.
- The 401 Unauthorized status code means that the client is not authorized to access the resource and should authenticate first.

- The 403 Forbidden status code means the user doesn't have permission to access that resource.

- The 404 Not Found status code means the server didn't find the resource.

5XX

From 500 to 599, the status codes mean an error on the server side. Some examples of this are as follows:

- The 500 Internal Server Error status code means the server failed unexpectedly, and the client should try again later

- The 501 Not Implemented status code means the server does not support the functionality required to fulfill the request

- The 503 Service Unavailable status code means the server is not available (usually returned by a proxy that was not able to reach the underlying service), and the client should try again later

Of course, there are more status codes, but the ones explained here are the ones that are more commonly used in REST APIs. We will learn about other status codes through the book whenever we use them for specific cases. Also, if you want to see a detailed list of them, you can find it at https://developer.mozilla.org/en-US/docs/Web/HTTP/Status.

Now that we know about HTTP methods and status codes, let's talk about routing.

Understanding routing

An essential part of the design of a REST API is the routing. This involves defining how you will structure the URLs and HTTP methods that your API responds to. For example, you can have the /api/v1/users resource, the /api/v1/films resource, and so on. But you can decide to follow a more nested approach. For example, you can have /api/v1/users/1/films. It's up to you to decide how you want to structure your API, but consistency is important. I like the *flat* approach, but in my opinion, there's nothing wrong with the *nested* approach.

For routing in Go, we will use the standard library's http package in this book; however, there are other libraries you can use, such as gorilla/mux, gin, chi, and others.

Let's say that I want to define my users' resource in the /api/v1/users path using the standard library router (this routing is only available since Go 1.22). I would do something like this:

```
http.HandleFunc("GET /api/v1/users", listUsers)
http.HandleFunc("POST /api/v1/users", createUsers)
```

```
http.HandleFunc("GET /api/v1/users/{id}", getUser)
http.HandleFunc("PUT /api/v1/users/{id}", updateUser)
http.HandleFunc("PATCH /api/v1/users/{id}", partialUpdateUser)
http.HandleFunc("DELETE /api/v1/users/{id}", deleteUser)
```

This way, I'm defining the routes for the users' resources and pointing each of them to the right handler. Here, listUsers, createUsers, getUser, updateUser, partialUpdateUser, and deleteUser are functions that I have implemented in my code. In the route, we can find {id} as part of the path, which represents a URL parameter.

For example, let's say we have a User struct defined like this:

```
type User struct {
  ID int `json:"id"`
  Username string `json:"username"`
  Name string `json:"name"`
  Surname string `json:"surname"`
}
```

An implementation of the listUsers handler could be something like this:

```
func listUsers(w http.ResponseWriter, r *http.Request) {
  users := []User{
    {ID: 1, Username: "john.doe", Name: "John", Surname: "Doe"},
    {ID: 2, Username: "jane.doe", Name: "Jane", Surname: "Doe"},
  }

  w.Header().Set("Content-Type", "application/json")
  w.WriteHeader(http.StatusOK)
  err = json.NewEncoder(w).Encode(users)(users)
  if err != nil {
    http.Error(w, err.Error(), http.StatusInternalServerError)
    return
  }
}
```

This is a function that receives a request and populates the response with the correct data.

With this in mind, you can envision what we are achieving here. Whenever you request any of the routes using the appropriate method, the request will be handled by the function we defined, and the response we build is returned to the client. That way, you have the whole cycle covered.

So, in general terms, the routing and handlers are your REST API's main building blocks. But there are some convenient utilities that you can use to make your life easier, such as middleware.

Middleware

A **middleware** is a function executed before and/or after the handler, allowing you to do everyday tasks such as logging, authentication, authorization, and so on. The approach we will follow to build middleware in Go is to wrap our handler function with another function. This approach is known in other languages as the **decorator pattern**. I think it is going to be easier to understand with an example.

Let's say that I want to log every request that is made to my API before it is done, and after it is done, I could do something like this:

```go
func logRequest(next http.HandlerFunc) http.HandlerFunc {
  return func(w http.ResponseWriter, r *http.Request) {
    log.Printf("Before %s %s %s", r.Method, r.URL.Path, r.RemoteAddr)
    next(w, r)
    log.Printf("After %s %s %s", r.Method, r.URL.Path, r.RemoteAddr)
  }
}
```

As you can see here, a middleware is a function that receives a handler function and returns a new handler function, which is the one that we are going to execute. In this case, we log the request before and after the handler is executed.

To use this middleware, we just need to wrap our handler with it, like this:

```go
http.HandleFunc("GET /api/v1/users", logRequest(listUsers))
```

This way, whenever we register the handler, we are not registering the listUser function. We are registering the decorated function returned by the logRequest function. This pattern is powerful because you can chain multiple middlewares and reuse them across different handlers, as in this example:

```go
http.HandleFunc("GET /api/v1/users", logRequest(loginRequired(listUsers)))
```

Or we can even combine them in a common middleware:

```
func compose(next http.HandlerFunc) http.HandlerFunc {
  return logRequest(loginRequired(next))
}


http.HandleFunc("GET /api/v1/users", compose(listUsers))
```

This powerful pattern allows us to apply our common logic to all the handlers in our API. In the next section, we will talk about API versioning.

API versioning

When designing a REST API, you genuinely believe you are doing it right and will not need significant changes. Maybe some new features and extra fields, but nothing backward incompatible. However, the reality is that you never know where the project will take you. Sometimes, a slight change in the data model leads to a breaking change. Sometimes, you have to restructure how you access the data for performance reasons. Anyway, it is good to be prepared for changes in the future, and even if you did it 100% right since the beginning, there is almost no cost to being ready for the need for a new version of your API.

The standard practice on this is to build your API using a version in the URL, as we have seen in the /api/v1/users examples. If you need to create a new version of your API, you can keep your /api/v1/users route with the current existing behavior and create a new /api/v2/users with the new behavior, allowing you to have both versions running at the same time, and giving the consumers time to upgrade. The idea is to eventually deprecate the v1 version and only keep the v2 version in the future.

The changes in the versions of the API are not an everyday event, and they shouldn't be. You are probably doing something wrong if your version is changing frequently.

But all this theory around routes, methods, middleware, and versioning is not what you are here for, right? You are here to learn how to build a REST API in Go. So, let's put all these concepts together in the next section.

Building a CRUD API

Before we build our API, we need to define it and decide which resources we will expose and how we will expose them. For that, we are going to follow CRUD. This is a very well-known pattern that means "create, retrieve, update, and delete," which are the operations that are implemented on each resource.

As an example, we will create an API for a shopping list. The simplicity of that API will allow us to build all we need to learn about how to make a complex API without writing a lot of code. So, let's think a bit about what will be required.

As we said, we must decide our methods, status codes, and routes. For that, we need to know which resources we are going to expose. For simplicity, we will not implement authentication just yet, so we will not include users for now (we will do so in the next chapter). The two resources we need for now are the *shopping list* and the *list item*. From a purist perspective of REST, you would have two resources that work independently and are managed independently. Still, you could decide that the API only has the shopping list, and the items are just part of that shopping list. It is a matter of how you want to design it, and it depends on your context. In my case, I will use one single resource, the shopping list, and the list of items will be a list inside the resource.

Let's see an example of the structure that we are going to define for our resource, the ShoppingList struct:

```
type ShoppingList struct {
    ID int
    Name string
    Items []string
}
```

As you can see here, we are defining a straightforward structure that contains an ID, a name, and a list of items on the list. This struct should be enough, but because we are going to be marshalling it with JSON, it's a good practice to add the JSON tags to instruct the JSON marshaler how to name the fields in the output JSON structure, so let's do it:

```
type ShoppingList struct {
    ID int `json:"id"`
    Name string `json:"name"`
    Items []string `json:"items"`
}
```

Those tags will instruct the JSON marshaler to use field names of id, name, and items in the final marshaled JSON.

Now that we have defined the shape of ShoppingList, let's start building the basic structure of our application.

Basic structure

To begin shaping our application, we have to initialize our structure to store the information and start serving HTTP requests. The following code would be a good starting point:

```go
package main

import (
  "net/http"
)

type ShoppingList struct {
  ID int `json:"id"`
  Name string `json:"name"`
  Items []string `json:"items"`
}

var allData []ShoppingList

func main() {
  http.ListenAndServe(":8888", nil)
}
```

This code will define a global variable called allData (a global variable is a very naive way to store the data; we will see the right way in *Chapter 6*), and it will start listening to requests.

The problem with this is that we are not handling any requests. Every request will generate a 404 response because we haven't defined any endpoint yet, so let's start defining an endpoint.

The creation endpoint

Before creating endpoints, we need to know exactly where we want to expose the resource. In this case, I will expose the resource in the /v1/lists URL. Also, we want to know what method we will use for this case. Because we are creating a new resource instance, we need to expose the POST method in the resource URL. So, the new route for that will look like POST /v1/lists, so we add that into the main function, leaving it as follows:

```go
func main() {
  http.HandleFunc("POST /v1/lists", handleCreateList)
  fmt.Println("listening on port :8888")
```

```
    http.ListenAndServe(":8888", nil)
}
```

You can see here that we are registering the POST /v1/lists handler, and we are connecting that to the handleCreateList function, but that function doesn't exist yet, so let's create it:

```
import (
    ...
    "encoding/json"
)

...

func handleCreateList(w http.ResponseWriter, r *http.Request) {
    var list ShoppingList
    err := json.NewDecoder(r.Body).Decode(&list)
    if err != nil {
        http.Error(w, err.Error(), http.StatusBadRequest)
        return
    }
    allData = append(allData, list)
    w.WriteHeader(http.StatusCreated)
    err = json.NewEncoder(w).Encode(list)
    if err != nil {
        http.Error(w, err.Error(), http.StatusInternalServerError)
        return
    }
}
```

In this case, we take the request from the user, extract the body, and unmarshal it into a ShoppingList structure. If there is any problem unmarshaling, we will return a 400 Bad Request status code (the data received is malformed somehow). If everything went well, we store the information in our allData variable and return the newly created instance. Easy, right? Now, we have a fully working API that allows you to store shopping lists, but that is entirely useless if you don't have a way to retrieve that data. Let's jump into that.

The list endpoint

In REST, we use the GET method on the resource URL to get a list of resource instances. In this case, it is GET /v1/lists, so we add the new route to the main function like this:

```
http.HandleFunc("GET /v1/lists", handleListLists)
```

And we implement our new handler like this:

```
func handleListLists(w http.ResponseWriter, r *http.Request) {
  data, err := json.Marshal(allData)
  if err != nil {
    http.Error(w, err.Error(), http.StatusInternalServerError)
    return
  }
  err = w.Write(data)
  if err != nil {
    http.Error(w, err.Error(), http.StatusInternalServerError)
    return
  }
}
```

This case is even simpler. We get our allData variable, marshal it, and return the JSON response in the body. Now, we can add and retrieve information to start checking whether it has the expected behaviour using, for example, curl. If you run your program using go run main.go (it will keep running there), then you can list the shopping lists using the following:

```
$ curl http://localhost:8888/v1/lists
[]
```

That will return you an empty JSON list (the [] string), which makes sense because you haven't added any data yet, so you can now add your first item using curl like this:

```
$ curl -X POST http://localhost:8888/v1/lists --data '{"id": 1, "name":
"my first shopping list", "items": ["eggs", "milk"]}'
{"id": 1, "name": "my first shopping list", "items": ["eggs", "milk"]}
```

It would return the newly created item and a 201 Created status code. If you get the list again, this time, you get the list of items that you have created:

```
$ curl http://localhost:8888/v1/lists
[{"id": 1, "name": "my first shopping list", "items": ["eggs", "milk"]}]
```

This is great! We have a way to create and list items in our resources, but eventually, you will need to delete items, right? So, let's add that feature.

The delete endpoint

Again, we need to consider what is needed from the URL and HTTP methods standpoint. In this case, the method is obvious: it is going to be the DELETE method, and the URL will point to the corresponding item, so the things end similar to DELETE /v1/lists/{id}. But what does it look like in the code? Here is the route:

```
http.HandleFunc("DELETE /v1/lists/{id}", handleDeleteList)
```

Here is the handler code:

```
func handleDeleteList(w http.ResponseWriter, r *http.Request) {
  id := r.PathValue("id")
  for i, list := range allData {
    if strconv.Itoa(list.ID) == id {
      allData = append(allData[:i], allData[i+1:]...)
      w.WriteHeader(http.StatusNoContent)
      return
    }
  }
  http.Error(w, "List not found", http.StatusNotFound)
}
```

We can see here that we register the handler, go through the allData slice, and remove the element with the corresponding ID, returning 204 No Content because there is no content to return. Another new thing is the usage of r.PathValue("id"), which gives you access to the URL parameters.

You can test it manually with curl. For that, insert some data using the curl commands that you already know, and use the following curl command for the deletion:

```
$ curl -X DELETE http://localhost:8888/v1/lists/1
```

Then, you can check whether the deletion worked by listing the instances of the shopping lists resource.

You can "update" a list by deleting it and creating it again, but that sounds wrong, doesn't it? So, let's see the right way for that.

The update endpoint

In this case, we will explain two different update approaches: full update and partial update. For the full update, we will use the PUT /v1/lists/{id} route and pass in the body the new version of the shopping list with all the data. Here is the code for the route:

```
http.HandleFunc("PUT /v1/lists/{id}", handleUpdateList)
```

And like in the other cases, here is the code of the handler:

```
func handleUpdateList(w http.ResponseWriter, r *http.Request) {
  id := r.PathValue("id")
  for i, list := range allData {
    if strconv.Itoa(list.ID) == id {
      var updatedList ShoppingList
      err := json.NewDecoder(r.Body).Decode(&updatedList)
      if err != nil {
        http.Error(w, err.Error(), http.StatusBadRequest)
        return
      }
      allData[i] = updatedList
      if err := json.NewEncoder(w).Encode(updatedList); err != nil {
        http.Error(w, err.Error(), http.StatusInternalServerError)
        return
      }
      return
    }
  }
  http.Error(w, "List not found", http.StatusNotFound)
}
```

In this case, we look for the element we need to update, replace it entirely with the new information, and return the updated version. Let's see an example of this using curl:

```
$ curl -X PUT http://localhost:8888/v1/lists/1 --data '{"id": 1, "name":
"updated shopping list", "items": ["eggs", "milk"]}'
{"id": 1, "name": "updated shopping list", "items": ["eggs", "milk"]}
```

But, as you can see in the example, it requires knowing the instance's information upfront, and sometimes, you just want to update one of the fields without caring about the rest of the data. For that, we have the partial update.

For a partial update, we use the PATCH method. The final route will look similar to PATCH /v1/lists/{id}, and the body will contain only part of the information. Let's see what it looks like in the code. Let's start with the new data structure needed to represent the changes:

```
type ShoppingListPatch struct {
  Name *string `json:"name"`
  Items []string `json:"items"`
}
```

In this case, we use a different data structure where all the parameters are pointers. Using pointers allows us to provide "optional" fields, so if the field is nil, you do not apply the changes. If the field is not nil, you apply the changes. Using pointers is only one way of doing it. There are other ways, such as using map[string]any or any other approach that you find sensible in your environment.

Of course, like any other endpoint, we need to register the route:

```
http.HandleFunc("PATCH /v1/lists/{id}", handlePatchList)
```

And finally, here is the handler function:

```
func handlePatchList(w http.ResponseWriter, r *http.Request) {
  id := r.PathValue("id")
  for i, list := range allData {
    if strconv.Itoa(list.ID) == id {
      var patch ShoppingListPatch
      err := json.NewDecoder(r.Body).Decode(&patch)
      if err != nil {
        http.Error(w, err.Error(), http.StatusInternalServerError)
        return
      }
      if patch.Name != nil {
        list.Name = *patch.Name
      }
      if patch.Items != nil {
        list.Items = patch.Items
```

```
      }
      allData[i] = list
      err = json.NewEncoder(w).Encode(list)
      if err != nil {
        http.Error(w, err.Error(), http.StatusInternalServerError)
        return
      }
      return
    }
  }
  http.Error(w, "List not found", http.StatusNotFound)
}
```

You can see in the code that we only update the not-nil fields whenever we find the field, and everything else stays unmodified. Let's try it with curl:

```
$ curl -X PATCH http://localhost:8888/v1/lists/1 --data '{"name": "updated
shopping list"}'
{"id": 1, "name": "updated shopping list", "items": ["eggs", "milk"]}
```

As you can see, now, I only need to know the instance ID and the fields that I want to change.

There is only one REST action that we are missing here, so for the sake of completeness, let's quickly see it.

The retrieve endpoint

The last method we are missing is retrieving a single resource instance. For that, we will use the GET /v1/lists/{id} route and expect to receive a 200 OK response with the instance data in the body. Here is the code for that, with the registration for the route:

```
http.HandleFunc("GET /v1/lists/{id}", handleGetList)
```

And here is the handler code:

```
func handleGetList(w http.ResponseWriter, r *http.Request) {
  id := r.PathValue("id")
  for _, list := range allData {
    if strconv.Itoa(list.ID) == id {
      data, err := json.Marshal(list)
      if err != nil {
```

```
        http.Error(w, err.Error(), http.StatusInternalServerError)
        return
      }
      err = w.Write(data)
      if err != nil {
        http.Error(w, err.Error(), http.StatusInternalServerError)
        return
      }
      return
    }
  }
  http.Error(w, "List not found", http.StatusNotFound)
}
```

In this case, we find the list in `allData` and return it to the user. There is nothing new here. We can test it using `curl`:

```
$ curl http://localhost:8888/v1/lists/1
{"id": 1, "name": "updated shopping list", "items": ["eggs", "milk"]}
```

We just run the `curl` request, without a method (`GET` is the default), and receive the resource instance data.

We implemented the most common REST actions that developers would usually need to work with a resource, and that gives you a lot of flexibility and power, but sometimes it is not enough. For those cases, you must create custom actions on lists and resources. Let's see an example of that.

The add-to-list action endpoint

We will create a new action to add items to the shopping list that will not require you to know anything about the existing content of the list upfront or even the structure of the list. You can use any method you want that fits the purpose of the actions. Still, the recommendation is that if it is a read-only action, it can be `GET`. In situations when a side effect (updating data, sending emails/notifications, or anything else) is expected, it is recommended to use the `POST` method (it is more secure because it prevents attacks such as CSRF, cache poisoning, or data leaks through the URL; we will see these security threats in more detail in *Chapter 7*).

For our action, we are going to use the POST /v1/lists/{id}/push route, and we are going to send JSON {"item": "name-of-the-item"}, so let's start creating the new type needed for the action data:

```go
type ListPushAction struct {
  Item string `json:"item"`
}
```

Once we have our struct defined, we can register the new route:

```go
http.HandleFunc("POST /v1/lists/{id}/push", handleListPush)
```

And finally, we define our action handler:

```go
func handleListPush(w http.ResponseWriter, r *http.Request) {
  id := r.PathValue("id")
  for i, list := range allData {
    if strconv.Itoa(list.ID) == id {
      var item ListPushAction
      err := json.NewDecoder(r.Body).Decode(&item)
      if err != nil {
        http.Error(w, err.Error(), http.StatusInternalServerError)
        return
      }
      list.Items = append(list.Items, item.Item)
      allData[i] = list
      err = json.NewEncoder(w).Encode(list)
      if err != nil {
        http.Error(w, err.Error(), http.StatusInternalServerError)
        return
      }
      return
    }
  }
  http.Error(w, "List not found", http.StatusNotFound)
}
```

As you can see here, the action hides a certain degree of complexity, but from the server side, it is the same. The server handles the request and processes the response. Now, it is easy to add elements using `curl`:

```
$ curl -X POST http://localhost:8888/v1/lists/1/push --data '{"item":
"new-item"}'
{"id": 1, "name": "updated shopping list", "items": ["eggs", "milk", "new-
item"]}
```

Summary

In this chapter, we explored the fundamentals of designing REST APIs, including the methods, routes, and status codes used.

We explored an example of how to do that in code using the standard library. We also went through the most common REST actions used to create, retrieve, list, update, and delete instances from a REST resource and how to create your custom actions for resources.

All this knowledge is helpful, but our API lacks two crucial features: authentication and authorization. Without them, you are exposing all your data to any user who has access to it without restrictions, which is unacceptable in almost all cases. In the next chapter, we are going to see how authentication and authorization can be incorporated into our shopping list app.

Unlock this book's exclusive benefits now

Scan this QR code or go to `packtpub.com/unlock`, then search this book by name.

Note: Keep your purchase invoice ready before you start.

5

Authentication and Authorization

We already have a new API exposing endpoints that accept requests and give responses. It can be sufficient for particular API cases, but you usually need some authentication and authorization. In this chapter, we are going to go through the following topics:

- Basic authentication
- Token-based authentication
- Authorization using the **role-based access control (RBAC)** approach
- Adding authentication to our API
- Adding authorization to our API

It is essential to have a clear understanding of what the difference is between authorization and authentication. Both features are related, but they have very different purposes. The authentication responsibility is to know the user and verify that the user is whoever they say they are. Authorization, on the other hand, uses authentication information (who the user is) to decide whether the user is allowed or not to execute specific actions. For example, you must authenticate your user by providing your username and password. Once the API has authenticated your user, you need authorization to execute specific actions, such as creating a new resource instance.

Let's see some authentication mechanisms that we can easily add to our APIs.

Basic authentication

The most basic authentication mechanism uses HTTP Basic Auth to authenticate requests. Developers rarely use it because it has some drawbacks, mainly because you send user credentials repeatedly and don't have the concept of sessions easily associated with it.

For this, the client sends the `Authorization` header to the server with something such as `Basic dXNlcjpwYXNzd29yZA==`. It is a concatenation of the user and the password separated by `:` and then converted into `base64`.

We won't go further into details or examples because this kind of authentication is rare in APIs and is not considered a good practice.

Token-based authentication

The use of token-based authentication is widespread today. The idea is that whenever you log in to the API, you get an opaque token, a string that shouldn't have any meaning for the client but has meaning for the server. For every subsequent request, you will send that token, and the server will check if that token is valid.

There are different models for token-based authentication. We are going to talk about two of them here: a server session token that associates a random token with the session information stored in the server, and the concept of **JSON Web Token (JWT)**. In both cases, from the user perspective, the token should be an opaque code, something meaningless that only has meaning for the server. But let's talk about each approach.

Server session token

The idea here is to generate a random string (a token) and store that string in the server, normally associated with a session, so that the client can send it inside every request, and the server will check it. For example, a straightforward implementation of this could be the following:

```
sessions := make(map[string]time.Time)

func generateToken() string {
  token := uuid.New().String()
  sessions[token] = time.Now().Add(1 * time.Hour)
  return token
}
```

This way, you will have a map of tokens and their expiration time. In this case, checking that the token is valid is as simple as checking if it is on the map and hasn't reached the expiration time. With this approach, you need to refresh that session from time to time when you use the token, and if you need to invalidate the token, you can remove it from the map – for example, when the user logs out.

This example is a naive implementation. I want to show here that the token itself is just a random string, and the server stores the information to assert the validity of the session. In an actual implementation, you must store it in a database table/collection with all session information, such as the user ID and any other data the server needs. However, the concept itself is the same.

JWT

The drawback of a random server token is that the server needs to store and maintain session information. The alternative to that is to use tokens that are self-contained and store session information inside. That is what JWT is about.

With JWT, you have session information stored inside the token, and then you sign it with a secret key that only the server can access. That means that nobody can tamper with the token to change the data. A common JWT contains information such as the user ID, expiration time, and any other information you need to store in the session.

Now, the validation process has changed drastically. We receive the token and check the signature, and then we can trust the information in the token. So, we only need to check that the user is who they claim to be and if the expiration time is still valid.

But let's talk a bit more about the details of a JWT to understand it better. A JWT is a string composed of three parts: a header, a payload, and a signature. The header is a JSON object containing the token type and the algorithm used to sign it. The payload is information you want to store in the token, such as the user ID, expiration time, and any other information you need. The signature results from the HMACSHA256 hash algorithm of the header and the payload using a secret key that only the server knows.

Then, all that information is encoded in base64 and concatenated with dots, so the final token looks like this:

```
xxxxxxxxxxxxxxxxxxxxxxxxxxxxxxxxxxxxxxx.xxxxxxxxxxxxxxxxxxxxxxxxxxxxxxxxxxxxxxx
xxxxxxxxxxxxxxxxxxxxxxxxxxxxxxxxxxxxxxx.xxxxxxxxxxxxxxxxxxxxxxxxxxxxxxxxxxxxxxx
xxxxxxx
```

But what does it look like in the code? Let's see it.

Creating a JWT

In this case, we can build a JWT using the `github.com/golang-jwt/jwt` package, a popular package for working with JWT in Go. Let's see how we can build a JWT:

```
import (
    "github.com/golang-jwt/jwt"
)

const secretKey = []byte("secret")

func generateJWTToken(userID string) (string, error) {
    claims := jwt.MapClaims{}
    claims["user_id"] = userID
    claims["exp"] = time.Now().Add(1 * time.Hour).Unix()
    token := jwt.NewWithClaims(jwt.SigningMethodHS256, claims)
    tokenString, err := token.SignedString(secretKey)
    if err != nil {
        return"", err
    }
    return tokenString, nil
}
```

As you can see, with the `golang-jwt` library, generating a new JWT that you would return in your login endpoint is easy. We create claims; that is, our data. We generate the token itself and sign it with a secret key.

Now, how can we validate the token? It is also straightforward; we just need to parse the token and check the signature, and then we can trust the information in the token. Let's see how we can do that:

```
func parseJWTToken(token string) (string, error) {
    claims := jwt.MapClaims{}
    _, err := jwt.ParseWithClaims(token, claims,
        func(token *jwt.Token) (interface{}, error) {
        return secretKey, nil
    })
    if err != nil {
        return"", err
    }
```

```
    userID, ok := claims["user_id"].(string)
    if !ok {
      return "", errors.New("invalid token")
    }
    return userID, nil
}
```

As you can see, we parse the token with the claims and check the signature with the secret key. If the signature is valid, we can trust the information in the token. In this case, we are returning the user ID, but you can return any information you need that was stored in the token.

Also, I want you to consider that JWTs are not private. They are not encrypted. They are only signed, so the information that you store in the token is accessible to anybody who has access to the token. You shouldn't store any sensitive information that only the server should know.

Now, we have a way to authenticate our users, and we can quickly identify and keep track of the user's session. But what about authorization? How can we decide if the user is allowed to execute specific actions? Let's see that in the next section.

Retrieving user information

In the previous examples, we used the user ID as information stored in the token. Still, in an actual application, you must retrieve the user information from the database. So, let's see how we can do that:

```go
func getUserFromRequest(r *http.Request) (User, error) {
  token := r.Header.Get("Authorization")
  if token == "" {
    return User{}, errors.New("no token")
  }
  userID, err := parseJWTToken(token)
  if err != nil {
    return User{}, err
  }
  user, err := getUserByID(userID)
  if err != nil {
    return User{}, err
  }
  return user, nil
}
```

This allows us to get user information from the request. Also, we can use this function to check if the user is authenticated as part of a middleware that we can use in our API. Let's see how we can do that:

```go
func authRequired(next http.HandlerFunc) http.HandlerFunc {
  return func(w http.ResponseWriter, r *http.Request) {
    user, err := getUserFromRequest(r)
    if err != nil {
      http.Error(w, "unauthorized", http.StatusUnauthorized)
      return
    }
    next(w, r)
  }
}

func main() {
  http.HandleFunc("GET /lists/{id}", authRequired(handleGetList))
  ...
}
```

This middleware ensures that specific API endpoints require the user to be authenticated. This way, you don't need to worry about that logic inside your API endpoints; you just "tag" them as required with the middleware, and you are done with that.

With this, we can authenticate users and ensure they are who they claim to be. But usually, that's not enough. You also want to allow users to do things depending on who they are. That is what is called authorization. Let's talk about authorization in more detail.

Authorization using the RBAC approach

There are different ways to authorize users in an API, but one of the most commonly used, due to its simplicity and scalability, is RBAC. The idea is to assign roles to users and then assign permissions to the roles. So, the user has a role, and the role has permissions, and the user can execute actions that the permissions allow. A simple permission system, for example, is to have two roles: regular users and administrators. Administrators can do all actions, and regular users can only execute a subset of API actions.

There are a lot of ways to define this. It can be simple, such as having a set of predefined roles, a role field in the user, and checking for the role in the API endpoints. But it can also be way more complex – for example, a system where you can create dynamic roles, have dynamically assigned permissions, and store all that information in a database. Also, you can decide that a user can belong to multiple roles simultaneously, define a hierarchy of roles, and many other things. But the underlying principle is simple: a role provides you access to actions.

For this, I will go with an elementary example because I think you can build the complexity needed for your system using a foundational understanding of the concept. So, let's see an example of this in code:

```
type Role string

const (
  RoleAdmin Role = "admin"
  RoleUser Role = "user"
)

type User struct {
  ID string `json: "id"`
  Role Role `json: "role"`
}

func handleUpdateUser(w http.ResponseWriter, r *http.Request) {
  user := getUserFromRequest(r)
  updatedUser = getUserFromBody(r)
  if updatedUser.ID != user.ID && user.Role != RoleAdmin {
    http.Error(w, "forbidden", http.StatusForbidden)
    return
  }
  // do the update
}
```

This code defines a simple RBAC approach where the user can only update their information, but the admin can update any user information. Another common approach to add authorization to endpoints and keep them separated is to use middleware.

Let's see how we can do that:

```
func adminRequired(next http.HandlerFunc) http.HandlerFunc {
  return func(w http.ResponseWriter, r *http.Request) {
    user := getUserFromRequest(r)
    if user.Role != RoleAdmin
      http.Error(w, "forbidden", http.StatusForbidden)
      return
    }
    next(w, r)
  }
}

func main() {
  http.HandleFunc("PUT /config",
        adminRequired(authRequired(handleUpdateConfig)))
  ...
}
```

Here, we are creating a middleware that checks that the user is an admin, and if they are not, it will return a 403 Forbidden error. This way, we can keep the authorization and business logic of the endpoint separate.

All this is great, but let's incorporate all this new knowledge into our previous API and add authentication and authorization.

Adding authentication to our API

Now that we understand the basic concepts of authentication and authorization, it is time to use them in our application. The first thing that we need to do is to create the new data structures that we are going to need.

We are going to need User and Session structures, so let's build those data structures:

```
type User struct {
  Role string
  Username string
  Password string
}
```

```
type Session struct {
  Expires time.Time
  Username string
}
```

You can see here that we are already defining a way to identify the user of the session and its expiration time. Also, you can see that the user has a Role field to determine the role in the system. That's all we need for now to handle sessions and users.

Also, we need login request data. In our case, we need a username string and a password string:

```
type LoginRequest struct {
  Username string `json: "username"`
  Password string `json: "password"`
}
```

We have to remember to add JSON tags to the fields to be able to parse the request data.

With all the data structures, we need a place to store that information. For now, we are going to store that directly in global variables. Remember that this is not the right way to do it. We are only doing it in this way for simplicity's sake. In the next chapter, we will talk about storing all this information in a database.

For storing the data, we create two new global variables:

```
sessions = map[string]*Session{}
allUsers = map[string]*User{
  "admin": {"admin", "admin", "password"},
  "user": {"user", "user", "password"},
}
```

We pre-populate the user map with two accounts, an admin and a regular user. We also store the password in plain text; that is not a good practice, but we will talk about that in *Chapter 7* when we cover security.

Now that we have our data defined, let's build our new login endpoint:

```
func main() {
  ...
  http.HandleFunc("POST /login", handleLogin)
  ...
}
```

We define our new login endpoint route and point it to the new `handleLogin` function that we are about to create:

```go
func handleLogin(w http.ResponseWriter, r *http.Request) {
  var data LoginRequest
  json.NewDecoder(r.Body).Decode(&data)
  user := allUsers[data.Username]
  if user != nil && user.Password == data.Password {
    token := strconv.Itoa(rand.Intn(100000000000))
    sessions[token] = &Session{
      Expires: time.Now().Add(7 * 24 * time.Hour),
      Username: user.Username,
    }
    w.Header().Set("Content-Type", "application/json")
    json.NewEncoder(w).Encode(map[string]string{"token": token})
  }
  w.WriteHeader(http.StatusUnauthorized)
}
```

In this handler, we read the `LoginRequest` variable sent by the user and check if the user exists and the password is correct. If everything is okay, we will generate a random token and store a new session with that token. Then, we return the token to the user. We will return a `401 Unauthorized` status code if your user is incorrect.

Now that we can authenticate the user, we can request authorization from our API endpoints. For that, we are going to use the following middleware:

```go
func authRequired(next http.HandlerFunc) http.HandlerFunc {
  return func(w http.ResponseWriter, r *http.Request) {
    token := r.Header.Get("Authorization")
    if !strings.HasPrefix(token, "Bearer ") {
      http.Error(w, "unauthorized", http.StatusUnauthorized)
      return
    }
    token = token[7:]
    if sessions[token] == nil {
      http.Error(w, "unauthorized", http.StatusUnauthorized)
      return
    }
  }
```

```
      if sessions[token].Expires.Before(time.Now()) {
        http.Error(w, "unauthorized", http.StatusUnauthorized)
        return
      }
      user := allUsers[sessions[token].Username]
      if user == nil {
        http.Error(w, "unauthorized", http.StatusUnauthorized)
        return
      }
      next(w, r)
    }
  }
```

This middleware checks the Authorization header to get the user token, then checks if the token is correctly formatted, if the token exists in the sessions and the session is valid, and, finally, if the user exists. If everything is okay, it lets the request pass to the next handler. If not, it will return a 401 Unauthorized status code.

We only have to add this middleware to the endpoint, which requires authentication. In our case, we are going to require authentication for all of them, with the exception of the login endpoint:

```
func main() {
  http.HandleFunc("GET /lists", authRequired(handleListLists))
  http.HandleFunc("POST /lists", authRequired(handleCreateList))
  http.HandleFunc("GET /lists/{id}", authRequired(handleGetList))
  http.HandleFunc("PUT /lists/{id}", authRequired(handleUpdateList))
  http.HandleFunc("DELETE /lists/{id}", authRequired(handleDeleteList))
  http.HandleFunc("PATCH /lists/{id}", authRequired(handlePatchList))
  ...
}
```

As you can see, the routes are clearly defined now for those endpoints you require to be authenticated.

So now, let's try it with curl:

```
$ curl -i http://localhost:8888/lists
HTTP/1.1 401 Unauthorized
Content-Type: text/plain; charset=utf-8
X-Content-Type-Options: nosniff
```

```
Date: Sat, 31 Aug 2024 12:06:32 GMT
Content-Length: 13

unauthorized
```

Cool! However, we are now unable to access our endpoints without being authenticated. So, let's authenticate:

```
$ curl -X POST -d '{"username": "user", "password": "password"}' -H
"Content-Type: application/json" http://localhost:8888/login
{"token": "87880698525"}
```

Now, we have our token, so we can try again to access the endpoint:

```
$ curl http://localhost:8888/lists -H "Authorization: Bearer 87880698525"
[]
```

Great! Now, we are authorized to access it. We get an empty list because we haven't created a list yet. But we got authenticated correctly.

But authentication is rarely enough. You need to be able to authorize users granularly based on some criteria, so let's add RBAC authorization to our API.

Adding authorization to our API

The good news is that almost everything we need is already done. We have users, we have sessions, we have roles, and we only need to check everything together, so let's build a middleware for that:

```
func adminRequired(next http.HandlerFunc) http.HandlerFunc {
  return authRequired(func(w http.ResponseWriter, r *http.Request) {
    token := r.Header.Get("Authorization")
    token = token[7:]
    user := allUsers[sessions[token].Username]
    if user.Role != "admin"
      http.Error(w, "forbidden", http.StatusForbidden)
      return
    }
    next(w, r)
  })
}
```

We are creating a middleware but are already using the existing one to ensure the session is already there. That is why I'm only checking the user role. If it is an admin, I keep going. If not, I return a `403 Forbidden` status code.

Now, we only need to apply the right middleware to my endpoints. In this case, we can apply this to all modifications' endpoints like this:

```
func main() {
    http.HandleFunc("GET /lists", authRequired(handleListLists))
    http.HandleFunc("POST /lists", adminRequired(handleCreateList))
    http.HandleFunc("GET /lists/{id}", authRequired(handleGetList))
    http.HandleFunc("PUT /lists/{id}", adminRequired(handleUpdateList))
    http.HandleFunc("DELETE /lists/{id}", adminRequired(handleDeleteList))
    http.HandleFunc("PATCH /lists/{id}", adminRequired(handlePatchList))
    ...
}
```

Now, we have endpoints that every user can call and endpoints that only admins can call.

Let's try this with `curl`:

```
$ curl -X POST -d '{"username": "user", "password": "password"}' -H
"Content-Type: application/json" http://localhost:8888/login
{"token": "90895591176"}
$ curl http://localhost:8888/lists -H "Authorization: Bearer 90895591176"
[]
```

Okay – I can log in as a regular user and retrieve all lists. But what happens if I try to create a new list? Let's see:

```
$ curl -i -X POST -d '{"id": 1, "name": "my first shopping list", "items":
["eggs", "milk"]}' -H "Authorization: Bearer 90895591176" http://
localhost:8888/lists
HTTP/1.1 403 Forbidden
Content-Type: text/plain; charset=utf-8
X-Content-Type-Options: nosniff
Date: Sat, 31 Aug 2024 12:17:24 GMT
Content-Length: 10

forbidden
```

Now, let's try to log in as an admin:

```
$ curl -X POST -d '{"username": "admin", "password": "password"}' -H
"Content-Type: application/json" http://localhost:8888/login
{"token": "3658125704"}
$ curl -X POST -d '{"id": 1, "name": "my first shopping list", "items":
["eggs", "milk"]}' -H "Authorization: Bearer 3658125704" http://
localhost:8888/lists
{"id": 1, "name": "my first shopping list", "items": ["eggs", "milk"]}
```

As we can see here, we are now correctly checking the proper role to access the endpoints.

Summary

In this chapter, we explored two fundamental concepts that almost every API needs: authorization and authentication. We investigated authentication options commonly used in APIs, such as session tokens and JWTs. Also, we talked about the simplicity behind RBAC and how, with this simple concept, you can go very far regarding authorization.

But all this information is only helpful if you use it, so we applied all this new knowledge to our API. Now, it can authenticate users and decide if they are authorized to execute specific actions based on their roles.

One of the things that is starting to feel wrong is how we store data using global variables. That is not the right way to do it. What any API developer out there would use to store that kind of data is a database. It doesn't matter if you prefer one database or another. The concepts are the same. In the next chapter, we will talk about data persistence in a database, and we will use SQLite as an example, but its principles apply to any other database.

6

Data Persistency

Our API is in good shape, but we have a huge problem: we are not persisting the data, which is a big deal in most APIs. The whole point of most APIs is to store and retrieve data, so we need to fix this. In this chapter, we are going to learn how to store data in real applications. We will see concepts such as accessing the database with the Go `sql` package, the repository pattern, and how to use a query builder. Also, we are going to implement the storage layer and persist the data in a database as we explore the following concepts:

- How to create and access a database
- What is the repository pattern?
- Exploring the sql package
- How to use a query builder
- Adding persistence to our API

Creating and accessing your database

In this section, we will explore SQL databases and how to use them in Go. I've selected SQL databases because they are the most widely used in APIs, but you can use any database you want. The concepts are the same. At the end of the day, what you want is to use the database that best fits your needs. For simplicity's sake, we are going to use **SQLite**.

Go is excellent when you use SQL databases because it includes, by default, a standard SQL interface that all the SQL database libraries share. This means that you can change the database you are using without changing the Go code that interacts with the database (but, probably, you need to adapt the SQL code to fit your database). So, you import and use the driver whenever you want to use a database.

For example, this is how you access a SQLite database in Go:

```go
package main

import (
  "database/sql"
  "fmt"
  _ "github.com/mattn/go-sqlite3"
)

func main() {
  db, err := sql.Open("sqlite3", "./foo.db")
  if err != nil {
  fmt.Println(err)
    return
  }
  defer db.Close()
}
```

💡 **Quick tip**: Enhance your coding experience with the **AI Code Explainer** and **Quick Copy** features. Open this book in the next-gen Packt Reader. Click the **Copy** button (1) to quickly copy code into your coding environment, or click the **Explain** button (2) to get the AI assistant to explain a block of code to you.

```
                                                    Copy      Explain
function calculate(a, b) {
  return {sum: a + b};
};                                                   1           2
```

📖 **The next-gen Packt Reader** is included for free with the purchase of this book. Scan the QR code OR go to packtpub.com/unlock, then use the search bar to find this book by name. Double-check the edition shown to make sure you get the right one.

One thing to consider is that in Go, when you want to use a database driver, you import it, but you usually don't use the imported package. You import it to ensure the driver is initialized and registered in the Go sql package. This is why you see the _ character in the import statement to let the compiler know that you are importing.

Another imported package is the database/sql package, which defines the SQL database interface. This is the one that you use to access your database. For example, we opened the database using sql.Open and passed the sqlite3 driver name (registered by the go-sqlite3 driver imported before) and the connection string. In this case, the connection string is a filename, ./foo.db, because we use SQLite. Whenever you are finished with it, you close the database connection using the db.Close() function. Easy, right?

But where do we put our code for database access? You can put it right between your existing code, but that is not a good idea, so let's look for a better option that doesn't spread your database calls all over your code base.

The repository pattern

I'm a big fan of single responsibility in code; a good example is the repository pattern. The idea behind the repository pattern is that a specific package handles every single database access. For example, if you want to get a list of users, you can directly query the database with something such as SELECT * FROM users. Still, with the repository pattern, you encapsulate that inside the repository package so you can call repository.GetUsers() and get the list of users. From the outside, you don't need to know anything about how the data is structured, stored, or retrieved. You just call the repository and get the data.

There are some exciting benefits of using a repository pattern. Some of them can apply to your project, some of them don't, but I think it is a good idea to know them:

- **Database-agnostic**: You can change your database without changing the code that interacts with the database. That means that you can have multiple database implementations.
- **Structure-agnostic**: You can change the database structure without changing the code that interacts with the database.
- **Testable**: You can mock the repository and test the code that uses the repository without touching the database.
- **Traceable**: You can trace the database access in a single place to see what is happening with the database.

This pattern is widely used in the industry; examples are everywhere. Later in this chapter, we will explore it more when we apply the repository pattern to our project. Before that, we need to get a bit deeper into the Go sql package, so let's jump into it.

The sql package

The database/sql package defines the SQL database interface. But it doesn't implement that interface. The drivers, such as go-sqlite3 or pq (the PostgreSQL driver), do it.

The database access always starts with connecting to the database itself using sql.Open. From there, we can decide what to do. Usually, we execute SQL queries. Some queries require data to be returned, such as SELECT queries, and others don't, such as INSERT or UPDATE queries. For the former, we can use Query or QueryRow methods that return Rows and Row objects, respectively. We can use Exec, which will return a `Result` object for cases where we don't need to get the results.

Let's look at the querying part in more detail.

Querying

As mentioned, the first thing that we need to do is open the database. As was shown in the previous example, we can do it like this:

```
db, err := sql.Open("sqlite3", "./database.db")
```

Once we have the database object, we can start running queries using Query or QueryRow, depending on the number of results we expect. Let's see an example expecting multiple rows:

```
rows, err := db.Query("SELECT id, username, password FROM users")
if err != nil {
  return err
}
defer rows.Close()
```

We can execute the query and receive a list of rows we must consume. Something important to remember is to notify that you have finished with the rows by closing it. If you don't, you could have a database connection leak. The usual way is, as you can see in the example, the usage of defer to close the rows after the error check.

We have to consume the rows one by one and assign the values to variables like this:

```
for rows.Next() {
  var id int
```

```go
    var username string
    var password string
    err = rows.Scan(&id, &username, &password)
    if err != nil {
      fmt.Println(err)
      return
    }
    fmt.Println(id, username, password)
  }
```

The rows value acts like a cursor and rows.Scan allows us to get the data from the current row we are processing. At every rows.Next call, move the cursor to the next row.

But sometimes, as mentioned, you only need one row. In that case, you can use QueryRow, which returns a single row. You can use it like this:

```go
row := db.QueryRow("SELECT id, username,
  password FROM users WHERE id = ?", 1)
var id int
var username string
var password string
if err := row.Scan(&id, &username, &password); err != nil {
  fmt.Println(err)
  return
}
fmt.Println(id, username, password)
```

As you can see, we only consume one row, so we don't need to loop. We can directly use row.Scan to obtain the data or the error if something goes wrong.

Sometimes, you don't even need the result data. For example, you don't need to access any row information if you delete data. You only need to get the data removed from the database. For that, you use the Exec method. Let's see an example of that:

```go
result, err := db.Exec("DELETE FROM users WHERE id = ?", 1)
```

Now, we only receive a Result object (or an error). If everything goes well, we can inspect the result for information such as the number of affected rows. For example, this specific query can be successfully executed but would delete one thing, nothing, or multiple things. With the Result object, you can distinguish between those cases.

Transactions

Another crucial thing to consider when using databases is transactions. Transactions are how to ensure that a set of queries gets executed in an atomic way and with a certain degree of isolation from other queries. For example, if you want to do a wire transfer, you want to ensure that the money is removed from one account and added to the other; that is, two things need to be executed atomically, and both are done or none is done.

The database/sql package comes with the necessary methods for executing transactions. Let's see an example:

```
tx := db.Begin()
_, err := tx.Exec("UPDATE accounts SET balance = balance - 100 WHERE id =
1")
if err != nil {}
  tx.Rollback()
  return
}
_, err := tx.Exec("UPDATE accounts SET balance = balance + 100
                WHERE id = 2")
if err != nil {}
  tx.Rollback()
  return
}
err := tx.Commit()
```

In this example, we generate a transaction and execute two queries. We want to be sure that we are updating the balance in both accounts or neither of them. If anything goes wrong, we roll back the transaction. If everything goes well, we will commit the transaction.

The transaction interface is very similar to the database interface, so you can run Query, QueryRow, Exec, and other methods used directly in the database object.

The sql package is potent and allows you to build database access very quickly, but some things can be improved. Let's see how to use a query builder to make our lives easier.

Using a query builder

Sometimes, writing SQL can be complicated, especially when you are building your query based on some conditions. For example, if you only want to apply particular filtering if the user sets an option, you must create the query using concatenation or string interpolation. I prefer to use a query builder. It makes my code more explicit and more manageable.

Let's see an example of this in action:

```
func (r *Repository) GetUsers(includeDeleted bool) ([]User, error) {
  query := sq.Select("*").From("users")
  if !includeDeleted {
    query = query.Where(sq.Eq{"deletedAt": 0})
  }
  ...
}
```

As you can see in the code, a specific part of the query is only included when needed. Also, the query is built using a fluent interface that makes it easy to read and understand.

Another option would be an ORM, but I prefer SQL builders because they give me more control over the executed SQL.

In this book, we will use SQuirreL as our SQL builder, but if you are more interested in ORMs, we will explore GORM in *Chapter 14*.

Let's jump into the details of how to use SQuirreL.

Querying

SQuirreL provides an excellent abstraction over the sql package and allows us to do all kinds of queries easily. The SQuirreL API is fluent. You build your queries by chaining function calls. For example, if you want to run the query SELECT * FROM users WHERE Surname LIKE 'A%' ORDER BY Surname LIMIT 10 OFFSET 0, you can do it with the following code:

```
query := sq.Select("*").From("users").Where(sq.Like{
  "Surname": "A%"}).OrderBy("Surname").Limit(10).Offset(0)
```

You can even write the code in a completely different way, and it would work perfectly fine, as follows:

```
query := sq.Select("*").Offset(0).Where(sq.Like{
  "Surname": "A%"}).Limit(10).OrderBy("Surname").From("users")
```

It doesn't matter because it generates the same SQL code at the end. This is great. We can build SQL queries by chaining things that we want to get from the database. But it is not SQL. It is a data structure that represents a query, so how do we convert it to SQL?

To convert a data structure to SQL, you can use the `ToSql` function, which returns the SQL query and the arguments to be passed to the query. Let's see it:

```
sql, args, err := query.ToSql()
```

In this case, the SQL result would be something like this:

```
SELECT * FROM users WHERE Surname LIKE ? ORDER BY Surname LIMIT 10 OFFSET
0
```

The arguments would be as follows:

```
[]string{"A%"}
```

With that information, you can simply use it in the `sql` package, as follows:

```
rows, err := db.Query(sql, args...)
```

This is not hard, but there is an even easier way to run this. You can use the `RunWith` method, which allows you to run the query with a database or a transaction. Let's see how to do that:

```
rows, err := query.RunWith(db).Query()
```

As you can see here, you can run the query and pass it to the database or transaction where you want to execute it. In both cases, we will have a set of SQL rows that we can handle like in the standard `sql` package.

Let's apply all this new knowledge to our API project.

Adding persistence to your API

To add persistence to our API, we will not write all the code needed in the book, but you can check the whole code in the book repository under the `chapter06` folder.

The first thing that we need to do is create the repository abstraction. We create a brand-new file named `repository.go` and put some code in it:

```
package main

import (
  "database/sql"

  sq "github.com/Masterminds/squirrel"
  _ "github.com/mattn/go-sqlite3"
```

```
)

type Repository struct {
  db *sql.DB
}

func NewRepository(database string) (*Repository, error) {
  db, err := sql.Open("sqlite3", database)
  if err != nil {
    return nil, err
  }
  return &Repository{db}, nil
}
```

With this, we define the basic structure of our repository and how to create a repository instance. As you can see, we are encapsulating the database connection inside our repository and opening the database using the SQLite driver.

The next step is to set up the tables that we need. For that, we are going to create an Init method, like the following:

```
func (r *Repository) Init() error {
  if _, err := r.db.Exec("CREATE TABLE IF NOT EXISTS users (role VARCHAR,
    username VARCHAR PRIMARY KEY, password VARCHAR)"); err != nil {
    return err
  }
  if _, err = r.db.Exec("CREATE TABLE IF NOT EXISTS sessions (
    token VARCHAR PRIMARY KEY, expires TIMESTAMP, username VARCHAR)");
    err != nil {
    return err
  }
  if _, err = r.db.Exec("CREATE TABLE IF NOT EXISTS shoping_lists (
    id VARCHAR PRIMARY KEY, name VARCHAR, items TEXT)"); err != nil {
    return err
  }
  return nil
}
```

This creates the required tables for storing the data if those tables don't exist. Once this is ready, let's implement repository methods that handle our data. For example, here's one to store a session:

```
func (r *Repository) AddSession(username string) (*Session, error) {
  token := strconv.Itoa(rand.Intn(100000000000))
  session := Session{Token: token, Expires: time.Now().Add(
    7 * 24 * time.Hour), Username: username}
  query := sq.Insert("sessions").Columns("token", "expires",
    "username").Values(session.Token, session.Expires, session.Username)
  _, err := query.RunWith(r.db).Exec()
  if err != nil {
    return nil, err
  }
  return &session, nil
}
```

Here, we are using SQuirreL to build and execute the query to store a new session. We are also creating a random session ID. But besides storing sessions, we need to retrieve them, right? Let's see how to do it:

```
func (r *Repository) GetSession(token string) (*Session, error) {
  query := sq.Select("token", "expires", "username").From(
    "sessions").Where(sq.Eq{"token": token}, sq.Gt{"expires": time.Now()})
  row := query.RunWith(r.db).QueryRow()
  session := Session{}
  if err := row.Scan(&session.Token, &session.Expires, &session.Username);
err != nil {
    return nil, err
  }
  return &session, nil
}
```

Again, we are using SQuirreL and building the query to get the session based on the session token, then we populate the Session object and return it to the caller.

The last example that I am going to show about the repository is the patch method for shopping lists, because it has an interesting usage of the SQuirreL library:

```
func (r *Repository) PatchShopingList(id string, patch *ShopingListPatch)
error {
```

```
  query := sq.Update("shoping_lists").Where(sq.Eq{"id": id})
  if patch.Name != nil {
    query = query.Set("name", *patch.Name)
  }
  if patch.Items != nil {
    query = query.Set("items", strings.Join(*patch.Items, ","))
  }
  _, err := query.RunWith(r.db).Exec()
  if err != nil {
    return err
  }
  return nil
}
```

You can see in this example how we build the query conditionally and only set the fields set in the patch object.

All of this is interesting, but how do we use it? Let's see the changes in our main.go file to use the new repository object.

The first thing that we need to do is initialize the repository. For that, we are going to update the main function like this:

```
var repository *Repository

func main() {
  var err error
  repository, err = NewRepository("./database.db")
  if err != nil {
    fmt.Println("Unable to open the database:", err.Error())
    os.Exit(1)
  }
  if err := repository.Init(); err != nil {
    fmt.Println("Unable to initialize the database:", err.Error())
    os.Exit(1)
  }
  ...
```

We define a global repository variable and initialize it at the beginning of the main function. You may want to use something such as an API struct that groups all your handlers and your state, such as the `repository` object, but for simplicity, we will keep this as a global variable.

Once we have the repository defined and initialized at the beginning of the program, we can use it everywhere we need, for example, in the session middleware:

```go
func authRequired(next http.HandlerFunc) http.HandlerFunc {
  return func(w http.ResponseWriter, r *http.Request) {
    token := r.Header.Get("Authorization")
    if !strings.HasPrefix(token, "Bearer ") {
      http.Error(w, "unauthorized", http.StatusUnauthorized)
      return
    }
    token = token[7:]
    _, err := repository.GetSession(token)
    if err != nil {
      http.Error(w, "unauthorized", http.StatusUnauthorized)
      return
    }
    next(w, r)
  }
}
```

Here, instead of getting the session from a global variable, we get the session from the repository, and the repository takes it from the database. This is a way better way of doing this.

For the rest of the application, we kept doing the same thing, finding where we were storing data in global variables, putting them in the repository, and implementing the needed methods to interact with those objects in the database.

You can try to implement it yourself or go directly to the book's repository and check the code in the `chapter06` folder.

Summary

In this chapter, we have explored how to properly persist our data using the database/sql package from Go and how to use SQuirreL as a query builder. We have explored the repository concept to abstract our data access from how the data is stored, in our case, a SQL database. In your case, it could be anything, from files in the filesystem to NoSQL databases. To finish, we explored how to include these concepts in our API project. With all this information, you can now store your data correctly. But storing it is only half the problem; we also need to keep it safe.

In the next chapter, we will explore some key security concepts for implementing APIs.

Unlock this book's exclusive benefits now

Scan this QR code or go to packtpub. com/unlock, then search this book by name.

Note: Keep your purchase invoice ready before you start.

7

API Security

Our API can now store data in a database; consequently, it's time to start talking about security. As soon as you store data, you must store it securely. That means you are storing the correct data, accessed only by the right people, and the data is always available. Security is not only critical, but also a very complex subject. The security field is constantly evolving, and attackers are finding new and different ways to attack systems as technologies evolve and change. Trying to cover all the security concepts in a chapter of a book is not realistic, so I'm going to cover the most important ones related to API development, including the following:

- How to validate and sanitize your inputs
- How to handle and store passwords
- How to leverage HTTP protocol security features
- How to encrypt your communication with TLS using `Let's Encrypt`

Also, as in previous chapters, we will integrate these concepts into our API, adding TLS and CORS. But let's start with something that sounds trivial but is a key part of API security: input validation and sanitization.

Input validation and sanitization

It sounds easy and trivial, but input validation is one of the most essential parts of the security of your API. Most of the time, the first thing an attacker will try to do is send you data you are not prepared to handle. Sometimes, it will be something that makes your system crash. Sometimes, it will be something that will allow the attacker to access or destroy your data, and other times, it is just an intermediate step from a more complex attack. So, the rule of thumb is: never trust the input.

Never trust the input. This is a great phrase, but what is the input? Some people think that the input is, for example, the query parameters and the body of the request, and that's input, for sure, but it is not the only input. The input is everything that the user can modify in any way. For example, any HTTP header is input, cookies are input, and a URL is input. Anything from the HTTP request in our API should be considered input, and we should never trust it.

To better understand why we validate input and what we are trying to avoid, let's start talking about the threats that you can find if you don't validate your data correctly.

Incorrect data validation threats

There are a lot of different threats that can happen from not validating your data correctly. Still, the most popular are injection attacks, mainly SQL injection and **cross-site scripting (XSS)** attacks.

Injection attacks

An **injection attack** is a type of attack that allows the attacker to execute something on your server; the most common example of that is the SQL injection attack. It happens when you don't validate your data properly before you pass it to the SQL query construction. If the attacker leverages that, they can execute arbitrary SQL commands in your database. Of course, you don't want that happening. Let's see an example of a SQL injection attack:

```
func myHandler(rw http.ResponseWriter, r *http.Request) {
    query := r.URL.Query().Get("query")
    db.Query("SELECT * FROM users WHERE name = '" + query + "'")
}
```

In this code, we have a SQL injection vulnerability. We allow the user to put arbitrary text from the query parameter in our SQL. You could think that adding the quotes around it fixes the problem, but that is a very naive solution. Imagine that the attacker passes something like '; DROP TABLE users; -- in the query parameter. You would end up executing the following SQL query:

```
SELECT * FROM users WHERE name = ''; DROP TABLE users; -- '
```

You can see how the quotes didn't work because the attacker used the quote to close the current existing started quote, then added their query, and finished using -- to comment out the rest of the query. Now, an attacker can run any SQL statement in your database. In this case, dropping the whole users table.

This is SQL injection, but there are other types of injection attacks, such as **Lightweight Directory Access Protocol (LDAP)** injection or shell injection. Anything you build as a string using user input can be the subject of an injection attack. As we said before, we never trust input, but in the case of injections, we can also say, "Never concatenate user input on queries or commands blindly."

For SQL, specifically, we have excellent tools that allow us to prevent SQL injections. The most important one is using parameters in the SQL query instead of building the query by concatenating strings. Let's see how we do it right with the previous example:

```
func myHandler(rw http.ResponseWriter, r *http.Request) {
  query := r.URL.Query().Get("query")
  db.Query("SELECT * FROM users WHERE name = ?", query)
}
```

This code is no longer vulnerable to SQL injection because we are passing it as a parameter, and because of that, the sql package is using a prepared statement to execute that, so the parameter is going to be correctly passed as a parameter, and not as part of the query. It doesn't matter what goes in the query variable; it will be scoped only for comparison with the name column.

Also, using tools such as ORMs or query builders can help you prevent SQL injections, but you need to be sure that the tool you are using handles them properly to avoid injections.

Now that we know the risks involved in injection attacks, let's talk about XSS attacks.

XSS attacks

XSS is an attack that allows the attacker to make your users execute arbitrary JavaScript code in your web app. If you are building an API that doesn't use HTML to expose the content, you are safe, but nowadays, the most common way to access APIs is through web clients.

An XSS attack consists of somebody saving JavaScript code inside your API data. If you don't correctly sanitize this data, you can end up sending that data to one of your users, and this user ends up executing arbitrary JavaScript code. It sounds bad, but it is probably worse than you think it is. The attacker can do many things with that access. First, they have access to the user session data, so they can directly impersonate the user and access any data the user has access to. Your system is at massive risk if this affects an administrator user. If it is a regular user, that user can spread the attack to other users.

Let's see an example of an XSS attack:

```go
func myHandler(rw http.ResponseWriter, r *http.Request) {
    query := r.URL.Query().Get("query")
    rw.Write([]byte("<h1>" + query + "</h1>"))
}
```

You can see here that, without any validation, we are just writing the user input into the HTML response, again concatenating user input into something without validating. So, what can I do to exploit it? If I go to my web browser and access the `http://localhost:8080/?query=<scri pt>alert(JSON.stringify(document.cookie))</script>` URL, my JavaScript code will be executed, showing me in an alert the content of my cookies. Instead of an alert, it could send that information to another server or do whatever the attacker wants.

To prevent XSS attacks, you must escape the HTML content you are receiving or sending. It is very common for template systems to do so automatically. Here is an example of how you can do it in Go:

```go
import "html/template"

...

func myHandler(rw http.ResponseWriter, r *http.Request) {
    query := r.URL.Query().Get("query")
    temp, err := template.New("myTemplate").Parse("<h1>{{.query}}</h1>")
    if err != nil {
        // handle error
    }
    temp.Execute(rw, map[string]string{"query": query})
}
```

We are using the `html/template` package to build a template that prints the query variable in HTML. But, in this case, the `template` library will escape the HTML content, so the script tag will be shown as text. The resulting HTML would be as follows:

```
<h1>&lt;script&gt;alert(JSON.stringify(document.cookie))&lt;/script&gt;
</h1>
```

We can see what we want in the generated HTML. The user input is shown properly as text, but is not being executed. If we don't want to use the template system in this case, we can simply use the `template.HTMLEscapeString` function on the data to get a similar result.

Here is an example:

```
func myHandler(rw http.ResponseWriter, r *http.Request) {
  query := r.URL.Query().Get("query")
  rw.Write([]byte("<h1>" + template.HTMLEscapeString(query) + "</h1>"))
}
```

There is a common pitfall that any Go developer should be aware of when using templates. The `html/template` package correctly handles HTML and escapes strings, but the `text/template` package doesn't escape strings. So, if you are using the `text/template` package, you must be sure that you are escaping strings properly by yourself. You should always use the `html/template` package when dealing with HTML content.

Now that we know about the most important threads that can affect your API, let's see how we should validate the data we receive in our API.

Data validation

Data validation is about ensuring that the data that gets into your system is correct, not only in type and format but also in semantics. For the types, we are using Go, which is strongly typed, so we are already safe from a lot of problems, but still, we need to be sure the data we are receiving is correct. For example, if I have an email field, I want it to be an email. If I have an age field, I don't want you to send me a negative number or 2000.

Sometimes, not having control or limits on specific parameters can lead to security issues. If your API is paginated, and you don't limit the number of items per page, an attacker could easily make a request that returns a considerable amount of data, leading to a **Denial of Service (DoS)** attack. Also, sometimes the internal code expects the data in the system to be already checked, so if you suddenly receive, for example, a negative number where it is not expected, your application can end up crashing.

But how do we validate our data in Go? The first thing that you can do is rely on your encoder/decoder to ensure types. For example, in JSON, we can do it like this:

```
import "encoding/json"

...

type User struct {
  Username string `json:"username"`
```

```
    Email     string `json:"email"`
    Age       int    `json:"age"`
}


...


func myHandler(rw http.ResponseWriter, r *http.Request) {
  var user User
  err := json.NewDecoder(r.Body).Decode(&user)
  if err != nil {
    // handle error
  }
  // user types are now as expected
}
```

In this example, we can see that the user data received from the request is parsed into the User struct, which allows us to ensure that what is in the User struct has the right types.

That's not enough because the age could be -100, the email could be "notanemail", and the username could be empty, for example. Those examples are correct regarding types but make no semantic sense for the application. So, we need a more detailed validation.

One option would be to build your validators, for example:

```
func validateUser(user User) error {
  if user.Username == "" {
    return errors.New("username is required")
  }
  if user.Email == "" {
    return errors.New("email is required")
  }
  if user.Age < 0 {
    return errors.New("age must be positive")
  }
  return nil
}
```

With this, we can be sure that our data has some of the fields correctly filled out, but still, the email could be something that is not an email, the username could be arbitrarily long, and the age could be a huge number. So, we would need to keep improving this `validateUser` function. Another option is using a library that does this for you, such as the `validator` package. Let's see how we can use it:

```
import "github.com/go-playground/validator/v10"



...



type User struct {
  Username string `json:"username" validate:"required,min=3,max=20"`
  Email    string `json:"email" validate:"required,email"`
  Age      int    `json:"age" validate:"required,gte=18,lte=130"`
}



func myHandler(rw http.ResponseWriter, r *http.Request) {
  var user User
  err := json.NewDecoder(r.Body).Decode(&user)
  if err != nil {
    // handle error
  }
  validate := validator.New()
  err = validate.Struct(user)
  if err != nil {
    // handle error
  }
  // user is now validated
}
```

As you can see here, the `validator` package uses the `struct` tags to define the validation rules for each field. In this case, we are only allowing people over 18, only valid emails, and users with usernames between 3 and 20 characters.

Now, in the rest of our API, we can be sure that the data is correct and that the mental burden of thinking about all the corner cases on the data is no longer there.

We already covered how we validate the data coming in, but what about the data we are sending? Sometimes, we need to clean up and sanitize the data before sending it, so let's discuss that.

Sanitization

Apart from validating the data that is coming in, we also want to sanitize the data that is going out. As we saw in the XSS attack example, this is critical to avoid attackers exploiting our system. However, there is also another kind of sanitization. For instance, if you send users' information to the client, such as the list of users belonging to your group, you want to expose only data that it is acceptable to reveal. For example, you don't want to send the users' passwords or password hashes in the response. This can be addressed in multiple ways – for example, by not generating it from the JSON encoder perspective. Here is an example:

```
type User struct {
  Username string `json:"username"`
  Email    string `json:"email"`
  Age      int    `json:"age"`
  Password string `json:"-"`
}
```

This way, we are not serializing the `Password` field, so it will not be sent to the client. There are also other ways to do it, but this is probably the most common one.

Other options include having different structs for the input and output or having a `sanitize` function that cleans up the data before sending it out. However, what is essential is that you are sure that only the right data is being exposed to the client.

Talking about passwords, how should we handle them? Let's explore how we should handle and store our passwords next.

Password handling

One vital thing is to keep your data private and secure. There are some especially sensitive types of data that you will store in your system; one of the most important ones is passwords, and you want to keep them secure. Storing passwords in plain text is considered a bad practice, and you should avoid it. The most widespread practice for password handling is to hash a password before storing it.

Hashing is a mechanism that, from a string, generates another string with a non-reversible operation. That means you can always generate the same hashed string with the original string, but you can't generate the original string with the hashed string. This is very interesting for passwords because, this way, you don't need to store the passwords of your users. You can simply store the hash, and if the hash gets leaked, it will not be easy to get the original password and use it anywhere else.

It sounds good, right? But there is a catch. The same string always generates the same hash, so people can build "rainbow tables," pre-computed tables of relations of hashes to the original string value that render the hashing mechanism useless. To avoid this, we use a technique called "salt." A salt is a random string concatenated with the password before hashing it. This way, the hash for the same password is always different, and with a long enough salt (for example, 16 bytes), it makes rainbow tables completely impractical.

Let's see an example of password hashing in Go using the bcrypt library (the de facto standard nowadays on password hashing):

```
import "golang.org/x/crypto/bcrypt"

...

func hashPassword(password string) (string, error) {
  bytes, err := bcrypt.GenerateFromPassword([]byte(password), 14)
  return string(bytes), err
}
```

In this example, we can see how we use the bcrypt library to hash the password. The second parameter is the work factor, which defines how "costly" it is to generate a hash. The higher the work factor, the more time it takes to create one hash, and the more resilient the password will be to brute force attacks. Also, the bcrypt library generates the salt for you, so you don't need to worry about it.

We need a way to check whether the password provided by the user matches the hash whenever the user is logging in, so let's see how to do it:

```
func validatePassword(password, hash string) bool {
  err := bcrypt.CompareHashAndPassword([]byte(hash), []byte(password))
  return err == nil
}
```

We use the CompaerHashAndPassword function from bcrypt to compare the provided password and the stored hash. It gives an error if the password wasn't used to generate the hash.

Now that our passwords are safely stored in our system, we can think about another abstraction layer, the HTTP protocol and its security features. Let's take a look at it.

HTTP security features

Hypertext Transfer Protocol (HTTP) provides a mechanism to interchange Hypertext, but also provides some security features that, as an API developer, you should be aware of. Let's start by talking about **Content Security Policy (CSP)**.

CSP

CSP is a mechanism that HTTP provides to have granular control over the restriction of loaded content. One of the most important features of CSP is XSS protection, which we already discussed in the *input validation* section. With CSP headers, you can restrict inline script execution, remote JavaScript execution, JavaScript eval code execution, and form submission, or even load iframes. CSP is a complex feature, so I would recommend investigating it in detail, but here is an example of how to use it from Go:

```go
func myHandler(rw http.ResponseWriter, r *http.Request) {
  rw.Header().Set("Content-Security-Policy", "default-src 'self'",
    "frame-ancestors 'none'")
  rw.Write([]byte("Hello World"))
}
```

In this example, we establish the loading content policy to only allow the browser to load content inside the same domain (`default-src 'self'`) and not allow it to load iframes in the page (`frame-ancestors 'none'`). This is a relatively secure way of configuring it, but it depends on your application's needs. Maybe you prefer to be more restrictive, for example, defining what scripts you can load. Let's see an example of that:

```go
func myHandler(rw http.ResponseWriter, r *http.Request) {
  rw.Header().Set("Content-Security-Policy",
    "script-src 'sha256-RlUYTu4FOqAM9/4rdDtHbr8Q/wg6B088iYXXoKvCPIg='")
  rw.Write([]byte("Hello World"))
}
```

In this example, we are setting the CSP header to only allow scripts with the right sha256 to be loaded. This way, you have complete control over what is loaded on your page.

Security is also a trade-off. Depending on your application needs, you have to decide whether you want to be more strict or more permissive. CSP has a lot of fine-grained settings to allow you to be sure that only what you want is loaded into your application, how you want it.

You can learn more about it in the **Mozilla Developer Network (MDN)** documentation here: https://developer.mozilla.org/en-US/docs/Web/HTTP/Headers/Content-Security-Policy.

Now that we know how to restrict what is loadable on our page, let's talk about how we allow our JavaScript to access resources from other domains through the **Cross-Origin Resource Sharing (CORS)** mechanism.

CORS

CORS is widely used but generally not as well known as it should be. CORS aims to define what is allowed to be done with other domains. For example, suppose you have a web application in https://mywebapp.com and you want to access an API in https://myapi.com. You need to explicitly add the CORS headers in the API to allow the web application to access it (the browser is responsible for checking the CORS headers).

So, CORS is not a restriction mechanism but a permission mechanism. The browser will disallow cross-domain access by default, and you need to explicitly allow it using CORS. That means the browser will block any JavaScript request to another domain by default unless the server explicitly allows it using the CORS headers. Also, it is crucial to understand that CORS is focused on the browser. It doesn't protect you from other ways of accessing your API. For example, if you use curl, CORS is not applied, and the request will be sent to the API.

But how does the browser know whether there is CORS or not? The browser will decide based on the type of requests whether a "pre-flight" (ask for the headers first or not) is needed, depending on the request. A definition of "simple request" in the CORS specification defines what is simple enough (or safe enough) to be sent without pre-flight, and the headers on the returned headers are checked directly.

For non-simple requests, for example, the creation of a new entity, the browser will send a pre-flight request to the server asking for the CORS headers. If the headers show that my request is allowed, the browser will proceed with the request; if not, the request will be blocked.

But I think all this will be clearer with an example, so let's see how we can add CORS to an API in Go.

```
import "github.com/rs/cors"

...

func main() {
  mux := http.NewServeMux()
```

```
    mux.HandleFunc("/api", myHandler)
    handler := cors.Default().Handler(mux)
    http.ListenAndServe(":8080", handler)
}
```

In this example, we use the github.com/rs/cors package to add our middleware to the handler, generating all the needed headers and pre-flight handlers for all our API endpoints. This adds an "OPTIONS" method handler to all the endpoints responding to the pre-flight requests.

The cors.Default() allows all, so you should configure it more strictly. A more sensible configuration would be as follows:

```
    handler := cors.New(cors.Options{
        AllowedOrigins: []string{"https://mywebapp.com"},
        AllowedMethods: []string{"GET", "POST", "PUT", "DELETE", "OPTIONS"},
        AllowedHeaders: []string{"Content-Type", "Authorization"},
    }).Handler(mux)
```

This would ensure that this API is only accessible from https://mywebapp.com. We clearly define what methods and headers are allowed. This way, we have fine-grained control over what can be called and from where. A widespread mistake is to allow all origins (AllowedOrigins: [] string{"*"}), which is very handy for developers because you don't need to know what you are doing, but it is a significant risk in production environments. In some cases, you want to allow all the domains, for example, for public APIs, but it is essential to know why you are doing it.

Now we know how to give specific permissions for specific domains using CORS, let's talk about a simple but vital header, Content-Type.

Content-Type

The Content-Type header defines the content that you are serving. It sounds more related to efficiency or ergonomics than security, but let me show you the following scenario. You have an endpoint that allows you to save a file or text exposed in another API. If you don't define the content type, the content type could be guessed by the browser. So, I can upload an HTML file and the browser will interpret that as HTML, and load it in the browser, with access to things such as cookies, sessions, and other data. If you ensure that the content type is set correctly to something such as application/octet-stream or text/plain, the browser won't interpret it as HTML.

So, I recommend always establishing the content type of your responses. In the case of an API, you can use the `application/json` content type, which is the most common one. Let's see an example of how to do it in Go:

```
func myHandler(rw http.ResponseWriter, r *http.Request) {
    rw.Header().Set("Content-Type", "application/json")
    rw.Write([]byte(`{"message": "Hello World"}`))
}
```

As you can see here, we are establishing `Content-Type` as the header for the request. Depending on the application, we can use a middleware to use a default content type.

These are only some HTTP features that help make your API more secure. There are some more that you can check in the OWASP Cheat Sheet about HTTP security response headers here: `https://cheatsheetseries.owasp.org/cheatsheets/HTTP_Headers_Cheat_Sheet.html`.

Now we know that the HTTP protocol provides security features that we can leverage to make our API users safer. Still, another layer of security related to HTTP is crucial – **Transport Layer Security (TLS)**. Let's talk about how to use it with `Let's Encrypt`.

HTTPS with Let's Encrypt

First of all, let's start by explaining what TLS is. TLS is a protocol to ensure that our client and server communication is encrypted and secure. It is the successor of **Secure Sockets Layer (SSL)** and uses certificate-based encryption to ensure that the server you are talking to is the one you think it is. When we have HTTP over TLS, we name it HTTPS, which is the most common way to access web pages nowadays.

We mentioned certificate-based encryption. What does it mean? It means that the server has a certificate signed by a certificate authority, which ensures that the server is the one it says it is. This is very important because if you don't have this, you could be talking to a server that is not the one you think it is, which can lead to many security issues. **Certificate authorities** (also known as **CAs**) are officially recognized as trustworthy entities, and most browsers trust them when evaluating certificate emissions.

Once your server has a valid certificate signed by a CA, you can use HTTPS. Any client that connects to the API through HTTPS will validate the TLS certificate, and if it is valid, start a "handshake" that establishes an encrypted communication between the client and the server. Any data that goes through that channel is secure and encrypted, so even if somebody is listening to the communication, they cannot read the data.

As I said, you can get your certificate from any CA that is globally accepted. But there is an exciting project called Let's Encrypt that provides free certificates for everybody. Let's Encrypt uses the **Automated Certificate Management Environment** (ACME) protocol to provide certificates, and it is very easy to use. Let's see how we can use it in Go:

```
import "golang.org/x/crypto/acme/autocert"


...


func main() {
  certManager := autocert.Manager{
    Prompt:     autocert.AcceptTOS,
    HostPolicy: autocert.HostWhitelist("example.com"),
    Cache:      autocert.DirCache("certs"),
  }
  server := &http.Server{
    Addr:      ":https",
    TLSConfig: certManager.TLSConfig(),
  }
  server.ListenAndServeTLS("", "")
}
```

This would ask for the certificate whenever you start the server. Other options exist, such as using the certbot tool from Let's Encrypt. If you are using the certbot tool (the recommended approach from Let's Encrypt), you can use the generated certificates directly like this:

```
func main() {
  http.ListenAndServeTLS(":https", "lets-encrypt-certs-path/mydomain.crt",
       "lets-encrypt-certs-path/mydomain.key", nil)
}
```

This way, you can have your API secured with HTTPS, and the certbot tool will properly refresh your certificates periodically. Also, you don't necessarily need to provide the HTTPS protocol directly from the Go application. You can use a proxy such as Nginx or Apache to handle the HTTPS protocol and forward the requests to your Go application. What is important is that your data is secure and encrypted between your user and your server.

All this theory is great, but let's apply some of this to our API project. Let's start adding CORS support to our API.

Adding CORS to our API

Let's imagine we have a web application that needs to access our API. To do it properly, we need to use CORS. If not, we can only have our web application in the same domain as our API, or the browser will block the requests.

For our API, we are going to use the github.com/rs/cors package.

Before we add CORS, we need to modify how we do routing in our API. Instead of registering the handlers directly using http.HandleFunc, we will use a mux variable to register the handlers.

```go
func main() {
  ...
  mux := http.NewServeMux()
  mux.HandleFunc("GET /lists", authRequired(handleListLists))
  mux.HandleFunc("POST /lists", adminRequired(handleCreateList))
  mux.HandleFunc("GET /lists/{id}", authRequired(handleGetList))
  mux.HandleFunc("PUT /lists/{id}", adminRequired(handleUpdateList))
  mux.HandleFunc("DELETE /lists/{id}", adminRequired(handleDeleteList))
  mux.HandleFunc("PATCH /lists/{id}", adminRequired(handlePatchList))
  mux.HandleFunc("POST /login", handleLogin)
  http.ListenAndServe(":8888", mux)
  ...
}
```

As the example shows, we create our mux variable with http.NewServerMux, and now register all the handlers in that mux variable. Instead of passing nil to http.ListenAndServe as the second parameter, we will pass our mux variable. This will serve mux and all the register handlers on port 8888.

With this in place, we can add the CORS middleware to our API. Let's see how we do that:

```go
func main() {
  ...
  corsMiddleware := cors.New(cors.Options{
    AllowedOrigins: []string{"http://localhost:3000"},
    AllowedMethods: []string{
      http.MethodGet,
      http.MethodPost,
```

```
        http.MethodPut,
        http.MethodPatch,
        http.MethodDelete,
        http.MethodOptions,
    },
    AllowedHeaders: []string{
        "Content-Type",
        "Authorization",
    },
    MaxAge: 300,
})
handler := corsMiddleware.Handler(mux)
server.ListenAndServe(":8888", handler)
}
```

We create our CORS middleware with the API domain and port, and pass a list of the allowed methods and headers. Also, we define MaxAge there to allow caching pre-flight requests for 300 seconds. We use the middleware created to wrap our mux variable, adding CORS to all our APIs. Finally, we run http.ListenAndServe with the handler generated by the middleware. Now, everything should be ready to properly handle CORS in our API.

Now, let's check whether the middleware is working correctly, running our API pre-flight calls using curl, and see whether the response includes the correct CORS headers.

```
$ curl -i -X OPTIONS -H "Access-Control-Request-Method: DELETE" -H
"Access-Control-Request-Headers: content-type" -H "Origin: http://
localhost:3000" http://localhost:8888/lists/123
HTTP/1.1 204 No Content
Access-Control-Allow-Headers: content-type
Access-Control-Allow-Methods: DELETE
Access-Control-Allow-Origin: http://localhost:3000
Access-Control-Max-Age: 300
Vary: Origin, Access-Control-Request-Method, Access-Control-Request-
Headers
Date: Mon, 30 Dec 2024 09:45:30 GMT
```

As you can see in the example, now when we ask for the CORS information with an OPTIONS request, we use the Access-Control-Request-Method, Access-Control-Request-Headers, and Origin headers to ask for what we want to do.

In the reply, we can see that our API is now giving the CORS information correctly to determine what is allowed and what is not. But let's see an example of asking for something that is not permitted – for example, another header:

```
$ curl -i -X OPTIONS -H "Access-Control-Request-Method: DELETE" -H
"Access-Control-Request-Headers: x-made-up-header" -H "Origin: http://
localhost:3000" http://localhost:8888/lists/123
HTTP/1.1 204 No Content
Vary: Origin, Access-Control-Request-Method, Access-Control-Request-
Headers
Date: Mon, 30 Dec 2024 09:50:28 GMT
```

In the example, if we send the pre-flight request asking for a header that is not allowed, the API will reply without the CORS headers, so it does not allow the request, and the browser will block it.

Now we have CORS up and running in our API, let's add another essential security feature, HTTPS.

Adding HTTPS to our API

HTTPS used to be painful because you had to get your certificate through a CA, pay for it, and renew it every year, and that was far from ideal, especially for small projects. Hence, the situation was that many projects didn't use HTTPS or they used self-signed certificates, which are not trusted by browsers. But then, Let's Encrypt appeared, and everything changed. Now, you can easily integrate the certificate generation with your application and refresh it when needed without human intervention. The recommended way of using certs is using certbot, but because this is a book about Go, let's add the code-based way to our example.

First, we will need a certs directory to store the certificates generated by Let's Encrypt. Let's create it:

```
$ mkdir certs
```

Once we have the directory, we modify our main function to use the autocert package to generate the certificates for us. Let's see how we can do it:

```
import "golang.org/x/crypto/acme/autocert"

...

func main() {
  ...
```

```
certManager := autocert.Manager{
  Prompt:     autocert.AcceptTOS,
  HostPolicy: autocert.HostWhitelist("ourdomain.com"),
  Cache:      autocert.DirCache("certs"),
}
server := &http.Server{
  Addr:      ":https",
  Handler:   corsHandler,
  TLSConfig: certManager.TLSConfig(),
}
go http.ListenAndServe(":http", certManager.HTTPHandler(nil))
server.ListenAndServeTLS("", "")
}
```

As we can see here, we create the certManager using the autocert library and then generate an HTTP server that includes our previously created corsHandler, and the TLS configuration from the certificate. Pay attention to HostWhitelist. There goes your domain, and in DirCache, the directory you created to store the certificates.

Also, you have probably noticed that we are running http.ListenAndServe, which uses a handler provided by the certManager.HTTPHandler call. This HTTP server is a "challenge" to verify that you own the domain. Let's Encrypt needs to verify that you are the domain owner before giving you the certificate, and it does so by exposing a challenge that Let's Encrypt will verify in port 80.

And finally, we run server.ListenAndServeTLS with the empty strings as the certificate and key because certManager will take care of that for us.

With this, our certificate is created and refreshed automatically, so we should be able to access our API using HTTPS, and the browser will trust the certificate because it is signed by Let's Encrypt.

This example of the code is not going to be used in future changes to the API, for simplicity, because it requires a registered domain and your API to be publicly exposed to the internet to work, so we will use the localhost without HTTPS for the rest of the book. But if you would consider making your API available to the internet, I strongly recommend you use HTTPS and Let's Encrypt or any other CA.

Summary

In this chapter, we explored some essential details about security, the importance of not trusting user input data, and how to sanitize and validate that data to avoid the most common threats, such as SQL injection attacks or XSS attacks. We also explored how to properly handle, store, and safely validate our passwords. Another important topic in API security is the HTTP protocol security features. Some of them are less well known than they should be, such as CSP, CORS, and the importance of the Content-Type header. Finally, we explored HTTPS support using Let's Encrypt, a vital security feature of every API. As in previous chapters, we applied some concepts directly in our API project. In this case, we integrated CORS and Let's Encrypt into our API.

Now you have the fundamental knowledge to understand what to pay attention to in order to avoid dangerous mistakes and the tools needed to make your API more secure, incorporating password hashing, encryption, CSP, and CORS in your API, keeping it safe. Now is the time for another hot topic: performance. So, let's move on to the next chapter and see how we can make our API faster and more efficient.

8

API Performance

Everybody loves performance. The faster, the better, right? Performance is always a hot topic, and for APIs, it is essential. The more performant your API is, the better experience your users will have. You will save money on your infrastructure if your API does not consume many resources. Also, if your API is fast enough, it will be easier to absorb spikes in traffic. The good news for you is that Go is a very fast language, so if you are using Go, you are already in a great position. But there are two things that you need to be clear about. One, you can't optimize without knowing what to optimize, and two, when optimizing, there is something that is always faster than executing highly optimized code, and that is not executing it. For those two reasons, we are going to cover the following in this chapter:

- How we reduce the load on the server with HTTP caching headers
- How we use an **entity tag (ETag)** to reduce bandwidth usage
- How we use the server cache to reduce the load on the server
- How we detect and measure performance bottlenecks
- How to add HTTP headers to your API
- How to add an in-memory cache to your API

One of the most essential tools an API developer can have is the HTTP protocol. The HTTP protocol provides multiple mechanisms to improve the performance of your application, from having better control of the cache to reducing bandwidth usage through compression. We will leverage these capabilities to enhance our API's overall performance. Let's start with one of the most essential parts, the HTTP cache control.

Technical requirements

All the code examples for this chapter are included in this book's GitHub repository: `https://github.com/PacktPublishing/Modern-REST-API-Development-in-Go`. You only need the Go compiler installed on your system to compile and execute the code.

HTTP cache

The API client cache is an excellent mechanism for reducing the load on the server and bandwidth consumption. All browsers have a cache mechanism that stores responses from the server and uses them when the same request is made again. But it is hard for the browser to know exactly what can be cached and for how long. Browsers have their own policy. Sometimes, it can mean requesting again without a need, and sometimes, it means using the cache and missing something that has changed in the server. To help the browser, HTTP provides a set of headers that allow us to control how caching is done from the API. As an API developer, you can leverage those to avoid hitting the API from the client when it is not needed. Let's start exploring how we control the cache.

Cache control

We can use multiple headers to control the cache, but the most important is the **Cache-Control header**. It defines the caching policy for the response sent to the user. It accepts multiple parameters that describe how the cache is stored and shared on the client side and for how long it will be valid.

There are two key parts of cache control that you should know about, and they define how and for how long the data is cached. Let's start by defining how long a cache is going to be valid. For that, we use the `max-age` parameter, which specifies how much time, in seconds, the information provided by the API is valid. For example, if we want our response to be cached for five minutes, we can use the following header:

```go
func myHandler(w http.ResponseWriter, r *http.Request) {
    w.Header().Set("Cache-Control", "public, max-age=300")
    w.Write([]byte("Response content"))
}
```

Now, let's talk about how it is stored. We can pass one of the following parameters: `no-store`, `no-cache`, `private`, and `public`.

The `no-store` parameter means the client shouldn't store the response in any cache. That turns off the caching of the response entirely.

Then, we have the no-cache parameter, meaning the client can store a cached version of the response, but it needs to be revalidated before using it (we will talk about revalidation later in the chapter). I know the name is misleading, and in fact, it is a common mistake to use no-cache when we want to use no-store. Be careful with this.

Another possible value is private, meaning the response can be cached but only in private caches. A private cache is a cache that is not shared between users, such as the browser cache. The other kind of cache is a public cache, a cache shared by multiple users, such as a proxy cache shared by the whole company in the office network or something like a **content delivery network** (**CDN**).

Last but not least, the public parameter; you guessed, it allows private and public caches to store cache information in public caches.

With these parameters, we have a lot of control over the cache. For example, we can decide that the response we send to the client will be valid for the next 5 minutes, but multiple clients shouldn't share it because the data is specific to that user. It would be something like this:

```go
func myHandler(w http.ResponseWriter, r *http.Request) {
  w.Header().Set("Cache-Control", "private, max-age=300")
  w.Write([]byte("Response content"))
}
```

Or you can decide that a specific endpoint shouldn't be cached ever because the data is always changing, so you can use the no-store parameter:

```go
func myHandler(w http.ResponseWriter, r *http.Request) {
  w.Header().Set("Cache-Control", "no-store")
  w.Write([]byte("Response content"))
}
```

Now that we know how to control the cache, let me give you some historical context. Apart from the max-age parameter in the Cache-Control header, we can define another HTTP header to express how long the data is valid. That header is Expires. The Expires header defines a specific date in a human-readable format, which makes it hard to parse for a computer and is error-prone. That was the only mechanism in the past before max-age was added. It is still in use for other things, and if you don't define the max-age parameter, the client will use it to decide when to expire a cache.

We have discussed cache headers focused on the API side, but that is only half of the equation. We can also control the cache on the server side from the client.

The client can also send Cache-Control headers with similar meanings. The no-cache parameter means that the server shouldn't use the server cache to resolve this request, and the no-store parameter means that the server shouldn't store the request/response in the server cache. The client can send the max-age parameter to define how long the cache will be valid on the server side. Of course, all these headers can be handled or ignored; it is up to you as the API developer to respect or discard those instructions from the client. There is one more thing that we should explore before we move on, and that is **cache revalidation**.

Cache revalidation

As we mentioned before, we can use the no-cache parameter to instruct the client that you need to *revalidate* your cache before using it. Revalidating the cache means asking the server if the current cache version is still valid. We have different mechanisms, such as ETag, which we will explore in detail in the next section, or the If-Modified-Since header. With the If-Modified-Since header, we can pass a date of the cache object that I have stored on my client side, and if it hasn't changed in the server, the server can reply with a 304 Not Modified status code so that I can use my cached version of it. If not, the server would reply directly with the most updated data.

An example of this can be as follows:

```
func handler(w http.ResponseWriter, r *http.Request) {
  responseData := getMyData()

  modifiedSince := r.Header.Get("If-Modified-Since")
  if modifiedSince != "" {
    since, err := time.Parse(time.RFC1123, modifiedSince)
    if err != nil {
      w.WriteHeader(http.StatusInternalServerError)
      return
    }
    if responseData.LastUpdateAt <= since {
      w.WriteHeader(http.StatusNotModified)
      return
    }
  }
  data, err := json.Marshal(responseData)
  if err != nil {
    w.WriteHeader(http.StatusInternalServerError)
    return
```

```
    }
  w.Write(responseData)
}
```

In this example, we are getting some data that, in this case, has a very convenient LastUpdateAt field. If I receive the If-Modified-Since header, I compare it to the LastUpdateAt field of my data, and if there hasn't been any modification since that date, I return the 304 Not Modified status.

> Note:
>
> For more details about the HTTP cache, please review the MDN documentation available at https://developer.mozilla.org/en-US/docs/Web/HTTP/Caching.

We have mentioned ETag as a revalidation mechanism. It is an interesting and not-so-well-known topic, so let's talk about it.

ETag

Caching is great and will save you a lot of time and bandwidth, in many cases saving us from the whole round trip, but sometimes that is impossible. For example, if you are dealing with data that can change at any time, you don't know when you can reuse your cache, so you use the no-cache flag, and you need a way to check if your current version of the cache is still valid (revalidation). This is where ETag comes in.

An ETag is a unique identifier for the exact version of the data that you have. For example, it can be a completely random UUID somehow stored in the server, a hash of the data, or any other way that you can uniquely identify that version of the data. Whenever the server sends the data to the client, it includes the ETag header, which is stored as part of the cache information. The client can send the If-None-Match header with the ETag in subsequent requests. Similar to the If-Modified-Since header that we talked about before, if the server detects that the latest version has the same ETag, it will respond with a 304 Not Modified status code and send you the response with an empty body, which means that you should use your already cached version. This can save a lot of bandwidth between the server and the client.

But let's see this with an example:

```
func handler(w http.ResponseWriter, r *http.Request) {
  responseData := getMyData()
  data, err := json.Marshal(responseData)
```

```go
  if err != nil {
    w.WriteHeader(http.StatusInternalServerError)
    return
  }
  etag := fmt.Sprintf(`"%x"`, sha256.Sum256(data))

  if match := r.Header.Get("If-None-Match"); match == etag {
    w.WriteHeader(http.StatusNotModified)
    return
  }

  w.Header().Set("ETag", etag)
  w.Write(responseData)
}
```

In this example, we get the data from the server and store it in an array of bytes. Then, we calculate a sha256 hash of the data and use it as the ETag. The next step is verifying if the request has the If-None-Match header and if it matches the ETag. If the ETag matches, the client can use the cached version, so we return a 304 Not Modified status code. If the ETag doesn't match, we send the ETag in the response and the data.

You don't even need to implement an ETag for every handler. You can use a middleware to do that for you, but consider that not every handler necessarily benefits from ETags. If your data changes for each request, you will invest CPU time calculating the ETag for nothing.

Another interesting concept related to ETags is **Weak ETags**. A regular ETag is a byte-by-byte identical response, and if any byte is different, it shouldn't match. A Weak ETag, on the other hand, is semantically equivalent information. For example, a JSON file can be semantically identical, but the spaces between keys or the indentation can differ, so the Weak ETag can match those responses. Also, you can consider that two different versions of the object can be regarded as equivalent even if there are some changes in fields that you consider irrelevant. With Weak ETags, there is no guarantee that the resource will be identical; it is more about being equivalent in the cache context.

Let's see a Weak ETag example here:

```go
  type Response {
    Message string
    Timestamp time.Time
```

```go
    }

    func handler(w http.ResponseWriter, r *http.Request) {
      responseData := getMyData()
      data, err := json.Marshal(responseData)
      if err != nil {
        w.WriteHeader(http.StatusInternalServerError)
        return
      }

      etag := fmt.Sprintf(`W/"%x"`, sha256.Sum256(responseData.Message))

      if match := r.Header.Get("If-None-Match"); match == etag {
        w.WriteHeader(http.StatusNotModified)
        return
      }

      w.Header().Set("ETag", etag)
      w.Write(responseData)
    }
```

In this example, we only consider the Message string to calculate the ETag because, in terms of the logic of my example, the timestamp is not relevant to the cache (this can not be true depending on the use case). So, if two requests have the same message but a different timestamp, the Weak ETag would still match, and the response would be 304 Not Modified.

So far, we have avoided the client making extra requests when they are unnecessary and saved some bandwidth when the user already has the correct data, but they don't know that. But there is still one more thing we can do to improve the performance of our API, and that is to use a server cache. So, let's talk about that in more detail.

Server cache

One of the problems of API development is that it is very asymmetric regarding resources. The server handles the load for many clients, sometimes thousands of them, so the server has to be very efficient in handling all those requests. Caching in the client is going to save you from handling some requests, but there are many requests that you need to handle anyway. The best way to be efficient is to avoid doing unnecessary things, and that is where server caches come into play.

A server cache is about storing information that you are going to need to reuse in a quickly accessible way. For example, accessing the SQL database server is always slower than accessing the memory of your process, so if you store a copy of the data that is frequently accessible in an in-memory cache, you can save a lot of time accessing the database. It doesn't need to be an in-memory cache. You can use in-memory-oriented databases such as Redis or Memcached. But everything boils down to the same: saving a copy of frequently accessed information in a high-speed medium.

There are multiple things that you have to consider whenever you are building a cache. One of the things is, what are you caching, and what are you not? If you add something to the cache that is rarely accessed, you are wasting memory and not benefiting from it. On the other hand, if you are not caching something that is frequently accessed, you are wasting time and resources.

Another important concept to consider is **cache invalidation**. The cache is a copy of the original version, typically in your main database. Every time you modify that original copy, you should invalidate the cache to avoid using out-of-date data from your application. If you take that into account, any frequently changing resource has the potential to not be a good option for caching because the cache will be constantly invalidated.

Also, it is crucial to consider the cache size and the cache strategy when using caches. You usually can't store a whole database in an in-memory cache, so you have to decide what to cache and what not. There are multiple policies about that, but the most common and well-known strategy is **Least Recently Used (LRU)**. An LRU cache will store a limited amount of data and always discard any data that hasn't been used for a long time.

With all this in mind, let's see how we can use a cache in Go. For that, we are going to use as an example the LRU in-memory cache implementation from HashiCorp:

```
github.com/hashicorp/golang-lru/v2
...
  cache, err := lru.New[string, User](128)
...
```

Somewhere in our code, we can define our LRU cache. In this case, we are defining a cache that stores 128 users. We will use a string for the key; specifically, the user ID. Now, let's see how we store and retrieve from the cache:

```
func GetUser(userID) (*User, error) {
  user, ok := cache.Get(userID)
    if ok {
```

```
      return &user, nil
  }

  user, err = getUserFromDatabase(userID)
  if err != nil {
    return nil, err
  }
  cache.Add(userID, user)
  return &user, nil
}
```

Here, we use a method that gets the user from the database. The first thing that we do is try to get the user from the cache. If we have it, we return it. If we don't have it, we get it from the database and store it in the cache. This is a straightforward example, but it is generally not that simple. Something important is still missing here: cache invalidation. Every time we make a change that makes our data on the cache obsolete, we should invalidate that entry in the cache; otherwise, we can get out-of-date data. So, let's see how it works:

```
func UpdateUser(userID) (*User, error) {
  user, err := updateUserInDatabase(userID)
  if err != nil {
    return nil, err
  }
  cache.Remove(userID)
  return &user, nil
}
```

In this case, we are changing how we update the user. Here, whenever I update the user in the database, I have to remove it from the cache, so the next time somebody tries to get the data from the cache, it is not there, and it has to retrieve the new version from the database and put it in the cache again. You can update the user cache directly here, but because you want to focus on the reading patterns to properly populate the cache, it is not necessarily a good idea (it depends on the workload of your API). For example, if you update some data frequently but it rarely gets read, you keep that alive in the cache, taking the space that could be used for more frequently accessed data.

Another thing you should consider is that cache invalidation needs to be done in any call that makes the cache data obsolete. It is not always that clear, but think about other methods that could lead to that, such as, in this case, the user deletion or maybe a "login" if you store something such as the LastLogin information in your user.

There are other types of caches that you can generate, not only for database access but also for file access, calculated values, or network-accessed information. Anything that would take time to generate or access is a potential candidate for caching.

Now that we have seen how to improve our performance with caching and HTTP headers, let's apply that knowledge to our shopping list project.

Go performance

Another fundamental piece of API performance is to make things work faster, and one of the things that we normally want to go faster is the code we are executing. To be fair, Go is already really fast and is rarely the bottleneck of your API. The most common bottleneck is going to be your database and the access patterns that you have for that, but still, your project can be one of those cases where Go code CPU or memory usage is the place that needs to be optimized. So, let's explore some of the tools Go provides to analyze and improve your performance, starting with the profiling part.

Profiling

As we said before, it is important to know what to optimize, so the first thing we need to know is how to measure the performance of our application. For that, Go comes with its own built-in profiler, named pprof. This allows you to collect CPU and memory profiles in your applications in different ways. Still, one of my favourite ways is exposing an HTTP interface that you can use to consume profiling data. You only need to add some minor changes to your application, and magically, you have access to all your profiling data. Let's see how to incorporate that into the code:

```
...
import (
    "net/http"
    _ "net/http/pprof"
)
...

func main() {
    ...
```

```
    go func() {
      http.ListenAndServe(":6060", nil)
    }()
    ...
  }
```

We need to import the net/http/pprof package, and that will add a new route name, /debug, to the default router (be careful; if you are using your own router, you have to expose that on that router or expose pprof on a different port). We can run our HTTP server once we have that registered in the default router. In this case, we are launching it on port 6060. Suppose your API is already running http.ListenAndServe, which is using the default router; you don't even need to run that.

Consider that this exposes your profile information, so you probably don't want this executed in production or, at least, publicly exposed.

Once you have that, you can start getting profiling information from your application on the fly using the go tool pprof command. But before that, let's explore what is offered through HTTP by pprof. If you go with your browser to http://localhost:6060/debug/pprof/, you will see something like this:

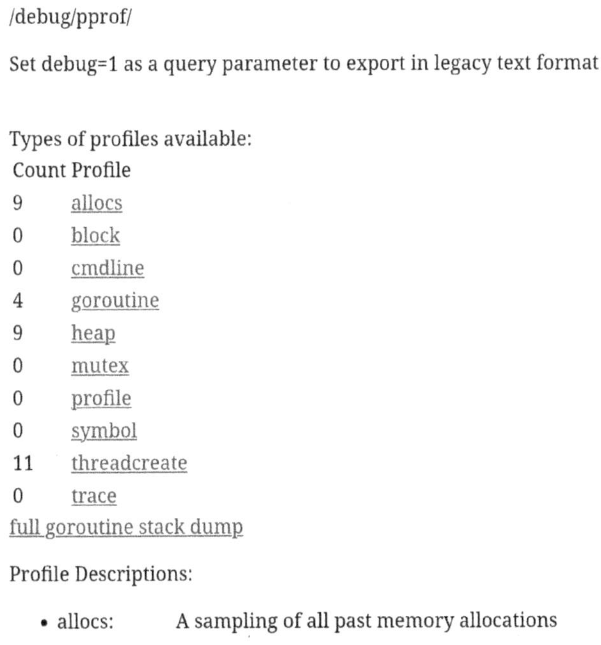

/debug/pprof/

Set debug=1 as a query parameter to export in legacy text format

Types of profiles available:
Count Profile
9   allocs
0   block
0   cmdline
4   goroutine
9   heap
0   mutex
0   profile
0   symbol
11   threadcreate
0   trace
full goroutine stack dump

Profile Descriptions:

- allocs: A sampling of all past memory allocations

Figure 8.1 – pprof index

We can see here some links that point to profiling information; things such as `allocs`, which gives you information about memory allocations; `goroutine` with the stack traces of all current goroutines; `cmdline`, which gives you the current command-line execution with the parameters; `profile`, which provides the CPU usage profile. This is all helpful information, but it is exposed as raw data, so there must be a better way to analyze and visualize it, right? Of course there is. Go comes with go `tool pprof`, which allows you to access this data and get detailed information about what is happening. Let's explore how:

```
$ go tool pprof -http :1234 http://localhost:6060/debug/pprof/profile
```

In this example, pprof will start collecting CPU profile information. Whenever it has collected data for 30 seconds (you can configure it), it will expose the results on port 1234 so that you can see it in a nice web interface in `http://localhost:1234`, as in the following diagram:

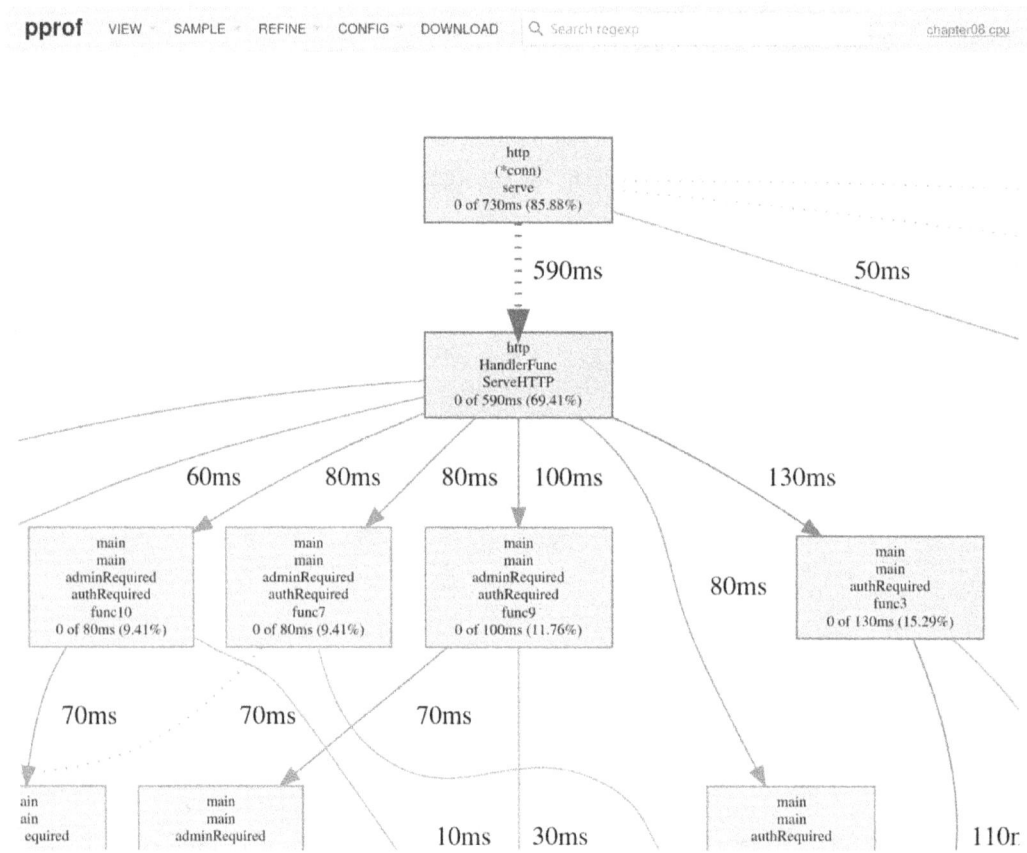

Figure 8.2 – CPU profile graph

🔍 **Quick tip**: Need to see a high-resolution version of this image? Open this book in the next-gen Packt Reader or view it in the PDF/ePub copy.

📖 **The next-gen Packt Reader** and a **free PDF/ePub copy** of this book are included with your purchase. Scan the QR code OR visit `packtpub.com/unlock`, then use the search bar to find this book by name. Double-check the edition shown to make sure you get the right one.

In this diagram, you can see a function call graph and the time consumed at each point. The bigger the block, the more time is consumed there. This view already provides a lot of insights, but others can also be interesting depending on the use case. For example, it also provides a flame graph view of the data, and it looks like this:

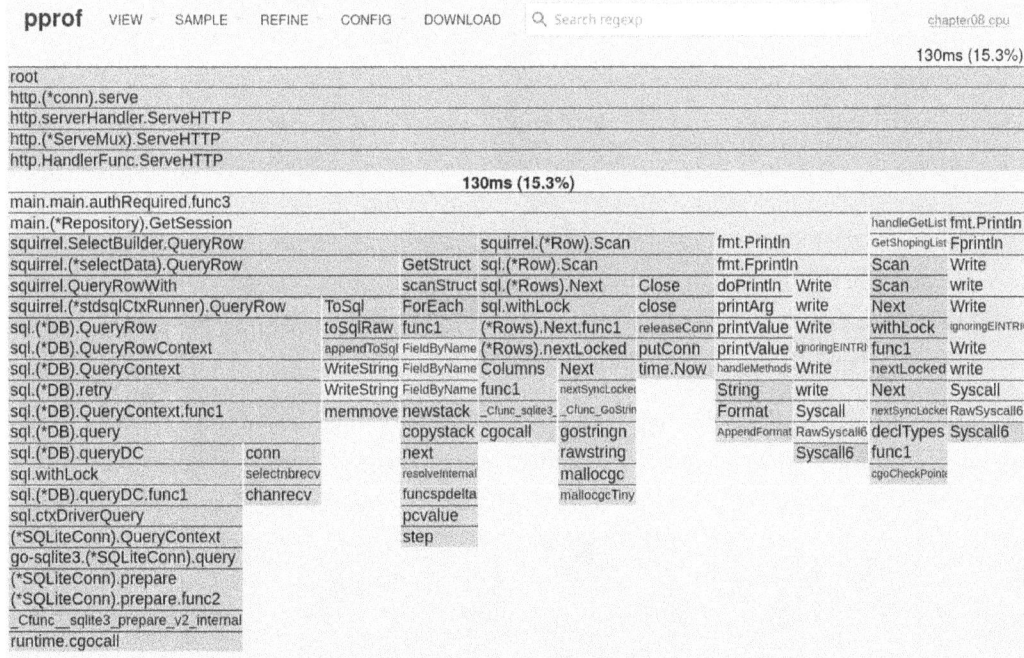

Figure 8.3 – CPU profile flame graph

The flame graph is helpful in identifying areas of the code that consume more time and determining how the time consumed is distributed inside each function. But sometimes, what you need is simply to have a list of the top time-consuming functions, so we can also find a view for that in the pprof UI interface:

		pprof	VIEW	SAMPLE	REFINE	CONFIG	DOWNLOAD	Q Search regexp		chapter08 cpu
Flat	**Flat%**	**Sum%**	**Cum**	**Cum%**	**Name**					**Inlined?**
40ms	4.71%	4.71%	40ms	4.71%	runtime.cgocall					
20ms	2.35%	7.06%	20ms	2.35%	internal/runtime/syscall.Syscall6					
10ms	1.18%	8.24%	10ms	1.18%	time.Time.AppendFormat					
10ms	1.18%	9.41%	10ms	1.18%	time.Now					
10ms	1.18%	10.59%	10ms	1.18%	runtime.step					
10ms	1.18%	11.76%	10ms	1.18%	runtime.memmove					
10ms	1.18%	12.94%	10ms	1.18%	runtime.mallocgcTiny					
10ms	1.18%	14.12%	10ms	1.18%	runtime.chanrecv					
10ms	1.18%	15.29%	10ms	1.18%	runtime.cgoCheckPointer					
0	0.00%	15.29%	10ms	1.18%	time.Time.String					
0	0.00%	15.29%	10ms	1.18%	time.Time.Format					
0	0.00%	15.29%	20ms	2.35%	syscall.write					
0	0.00%	15.29%	20ms	2.35%	syscall.Write					(inline)
0	0.00%	15.29%	20ms	2.35%	syscall.Syscall					
0	0.00%	15.29%	20ms	2.35%	syscall.RawSyscall6					
0	0.00%	15.29%	10ms	1.18%	runtime.selectnbrecv					
0	0.00%	15.29%	10ms	1.18%	runtime.rawstring					(inline)
0	0.00%	15.29%	10ms	1.18%	runtime.pcvalue					
0	0.00%	15.29%	10ms	1.18%	runtime.newstack					
0	0.00%	15.29%	10ms	1.18%	runtime.mallocgc					
0	0.00%	15.29%	10ms	1.18%	runtime.gostringn					

Figure 8.4 – CPU profile table

As you can see in the screenshot, it is very clear that the most time-consuming function in this case is runtime.cgocall, followed by syscall.Syscall6. Both are heavily optimized internal Go methods, so there is no point where you want to try to optimize.

This interface is handy and intuitive, but you may prefer something simpler, such as a **command-line interface (CLI)**. Of course, pprof also comes with a CLI that you can use to answer the same questions that you resolve with the UI. Here is an example of using it in the command line:

```
$ go tool pprof http://localhost:6060/debug/pprof/profile
Fetching profile over HTTP from http://localhost:6060/debug/pprof/profile
File: chapter-08
Build ID: 400192140d5749c33f800c6a924fbef118621443
```

```
Type: cpu
Time: Feb 10, 2025 at 11:45am (CET)
Duration: 30s, Total samples = 240ms (  0.8%)
Entering interactive mode (type "help" for commands, "o" for options)
(pprof)
```

We run the same command we did before, except we are not passing the -http parameter this time. We get a prompt and can now ask for that information using commands. For example, to see the whole top more time-consuming functions, we can run the top command:

```
(pprof) top
Showing nodes accounting for 190ms, 79.17% of 240ms total
Showing top 10 nodes out of 129
      flat  flat%   sum%        cum   cum%
      50ms 20.83% 20.83%       50ms 20.83%  runtime/internal/syscall.
Syscall6
      40ms 16.67% 37.50%       40ms 16.67%  runtime.cgocall
      20ms  8.33% 45.83%       20ms  8.33%  bufio.(*Reader).Peek
      20ms  8.33% 54.17%       20ms  8.33%  runtime.findfunc
      10ms  4.17% 58.33%       10ms  4.17%  database/sql.(*driverConn).
resetSession
      10ms  4.17% 62.50%       10ms  4.17%  github.com/Masterminds/
squirrel.Eq.toSQL
      10ms  4.17% 66.67%       10ms  4.17%  net.(*OpError).Timeout
      10ms  4.17% 70.83%       10ms  4.17%  net.(*netFD).Write
      10ms  4.17% 75.00%       10ms  4.17%  runtime.(*fixalloc).alloc
      10ms  4.17% 79.17%       10ms  4.17%  runtime.futex
```

With this, you know about CPU usage, but profiling also gives you information about other things, such as goroutines or memory usage. For example, you can get profiling information about memory allocations with the following command:

```
$ go tool pprof http://localhost:6060/debug/pprof/allocs
File: chapter-08
Build ID: 400192140d5749c33f800c6a924fbef118621443
Type: alloc_space
Time: Feb 11, 2025 at 4:59pm (CET)
Entering interactive mode (type "help" for commands, "o" for options)
(pprof) top
```

```
Showing nodes accounting for 670.17MB, 50.99% of 1314.22MB total
Dropped 73 nodes (cum <= 6.57MB)
Showing top 10 nodes out of 139
      flat  flat%   sum%         cum    cum%
 132.01MB 10.05% 10.05%    132.01MB 10.05%  github.com/lann/ps.(*tree).
clone (inline)
   77.52MB  5.90% 15.94%     77.52MB  5.90%  net/textproto.readMIMEHeader
   75.54MB  5.75% 21.69%     77.54MB  5.90%  encoding/json.(*Decoder).
refill
   61.01MB  4.64% 26.33%    612.58MB 46.61%  main.(*Repository).
GetUserByUsername
   60.52MB  4.60% 30.94%     60.52MB  4.60%  net/http.Header.Clone
   60.02MB  4.57% 35.51%     60.02MB  4.57%  net/textproto.MIMEHeader.Set
   54.51MB  4.15% 39.65%    265.55MB 20.21%  net/http.(*conn).readRequest
   51.02MB  3.88% 43.53%     51.02MB  3.88%  reflect.packEface
   51.01MB  3.88% 47.42%    291.05MB 22.15%  github.com/Masterminds/
squirrel.SelectBuilder.QueryRow
   47.01MB  3.58% 50.99%     47.01MB  3.58%  encoding/json.NewDecoder
```

This example shows a different view of the profiling: this time around, memory allocations and where the top memory consumers in our code are.

Now, we have a way to investigate where the performance bottlenecks are, but we need to know how to improve them. The first step to being able to improve is to know if there is, in fact, any improvement with your changes. This is where Go provides you with another tool that is key to this process: benchmarks.

Benchmarks

Benchmarks in Go are very similar to tests in Go, but they are focused on performance analysis. The simplest way to understand them is with an example, so let's jump in:

```go
func BenchmarkLongListCreation(b *testing.B) {
  for b.Loop() {
    list := []int{}
    for j := 0; j < 1000; j++ {
      list = append(list, j)
    }
  }
}
```

```
func BenchmarkLongListCreationPreAllocated(b *testing.B) {
  for b.Loop() {
    list := make([]int, 0, 1000)
    for j := 0; j < 1000; j++ {
      list = append(list, j)
    }
  }
}
```

In this example, we are building two benchmarks:

- The first is creating an empty list of integers, which appends 1000 integers to the list
- The second one does the same but creates a list with a pre-allocated capacity of 1000 integers

These two pieces of code have the same behavior and, at first glance, shouldn't be that different in performance, so let's run this and see the result of the benchmarks:

```
$ go test -bench .
goos: linux
goarch: amd64
pkg: chapter-08/benchmark
cpu: Intel(R) Core(TM) i9-10900X CPU @ 3.70GHz
BenchmarkLongListCreation-20                          102332            12285
ns/op
BenchmarkLongListCreationPreAllocated-20            2869825
492.2 ns/op
PASS
ok   chapter-08/benchmark   3.157s
```

We run the benchmark using the go test command because benchmarks are part of the Go testing framework. You can see the benchmark result here. It is very interesting because the benchmark tried to execute the code I shared as many times as possible in a specific time (by default, 1 second). On the one hand, we had the implementation without the pre-allocation; it could execute the code 102332 times, so it took 12285 nanoseconds to perform each operation. On the other hand, you have the pre-allocated version that could execute 2869825 times in 1 second, which means around 492 nanoseconds per operation. In this case, there is a massive difference between the executions.

The reason for this is related to how lists work in Go. Without the pre-allocation, every time the list reaches the already allocated size, it has to grow to double the size, over and over again. In the pre-allocated version, it only allocates the space for the data once, which makes it way faster. However, the key part is to understand how the benchmarking tool works.

This is just an example of how you compare two implementations, but usually, what you want to do is execute your benchmark with the current version of the code, annotate the numbers that you have, make the changes, and rerun the benchmark to verify if you have an improvement or not (or even better, have branches with your improvements in your source control system, and switch between them to compare the performance). Sometimes, you will discover that what you thought was an improvement is a regression, so having the benchmarks in place is necessary.

These tools will allow you to detect and improve bottlenecks in your source code. But how do we optimize our code when we know where to optimize and have our benchmark in place? That question is extensive, and it always depends on your software. Sometimes, it will change the architecture; other times, it is changing how you structure the data; another time, it is about parallelizing; and very rarely is it about micro-optimizations to specific functions in your code. If you want more details about how to improve the performance of your Go application, you should check out the *Hands-On High Performance with Go* book.

Now that we have a general overview of how to improve the performance of our Go application, let's apply some of the things we learned during this chapter to our shopping list project.

Adding HTTP headers to your API

The first thing we can do is add ETags to our APIs. We will change specifically the handleGetList handler and implement the usage of the ETag header. We will use the sha256 hash of the list to generate an ETag. Let's see how we can do that:

```go
func handleGetList(w http.ResponseWriter, r *http.Request) {
  id := r.PathValue("id")
  list, err := repository.GetShopingList(id)
  if err != nil {
    http.Error(w, err.Error(), http.StatusInternalServerError)
    return
  }
  data, err := json.Marshal(list)
  if err != nil {
    http.Error(w, err.Error(), http.StatusInternalServerError)
```

```
      return
  }

  etag := fmt.Sprintf(`"%x"`, sha256.Sum256(data))
  if match := r.Header.Get("If-None-Match"); match == etag {
    w.WriteHeader(http.StatusNotModified)
    return
  }
  w.Header().Set("ETag", etag)
  w.Write(data)
  return
}
```

As you can see, adding ETags to our API is very simple. We just need to calculate the hash of the data we send to the client, and then we can use that as the ETag. Also, we handled the case where the client is sending If-None-Match to avoid sending the data if the client already has the correct version.

The other thing we want to do here is add HTTP Cache-Control headers to our response because we want to be sure that the cache is used the way we want. In this case, we want to pass the Cache-Control: no-cache configuration to ensure the client always revalidates the cache with the server using the recently added ETag header. Let's see the resulting code:

```
func handleGetList(w http.ResponseWriter, r *http.Request) {
  ...

  w.Header().Set("Cache-Control", "no-cache")

  etag := fmt.Sprintf(`"%x"`, sha256.Sum256(data))
  if match := r.Header.Get("If-None-Match"); match == etag {
    w.WriteHeader(http.StatusNotModified)
    return
  }
  w.Header().Set("ETag", etag)

  ...
}
```

We can add it right before the check for the ETag, because we want to be sure that the client always receives the `Cache-Control` header, even if the ETag is the same. With these changes, we ensure that the client will try to reuse the cache but always revalidate it with the server, so we will save some bandwidth, but at the same time, we can be sure that the client is always using the latest version.

This same approach can be used in other handlers that retrieve data, such as `handlerListLists`. There is no point in using it on handlers that modify the data, such as `handlerDeleteList` or `handlerUpdateList`.

Because all the other methods in our API are `POST`, `PATCH`, `PUT`, or `DELETE`, we don't need to add the `Cache-Control` header to them; by default, they are not cacheable. If you add the `Cache-Control` header, the correct header configuration would be `Cache-Control: no-store` unless you have a good reason for changing that.

But we are still hitting the database in every request. We are saving some bandwidth, but not much more. Let's incorporate a server cache into our API to improve performance.

Adding an in-memory cache to your API

We will incorporate an in-memory cache into our API to improve the performance. We will use the HashiCorp LRU cache library we saw earlier in the chapter to implement the store's `handleGetList` method cache.

First of all, we need to define our LRU cache. We will use a global variable because I want to keep it simple, but you probably want to use another struct containing your application state:

```
var (
  repository *Repository
  allData    = []ShopingList{}
  listsCache lru.Cache
)

func main() {
  var err error
  listsCache, err = lru.New[string, ShopingList](128)
  if err != nil {
    fmt.Println("Unable to initialize the lists cache:", err.Error())
    os.Exit(1)
  }
}
...
```

This creates our LRU in-memory cache that we can use in the rest of our API. We need to modify our `handleGetList` method to use the cache. Let's see how we can do that:

```
func handleGetList(w http.ResponseWriter, r *http.Request) {
  id := r.PathValue("id")
  list, ok := listsCache.Get(id)
  if (!ok) {
    var err error
    list, err = repository.GetShopingList(id)
    if err != nil {
      http.Error(w, err.Error(), http.StatusInternalServerError)
      return
    }
    listsCache.Add(id, list)
  }
  ...
```

As you can see, we try to get the cache from the list. If it is there, we use it. If not, we get it from the database and store it in the cache. But this is not all. We still need to be sure that we invalidate the cache whenever we update the list, so let's see how we can do that; for example, in `handleUpdateList`:

```
func handleUpdateList(w http.ResponseWriter, r *http.Request) {
  ...
  updatedList, err := repository.UpdateShopingList(id, &newList)
  if err != nil {
    http.Error(w, err.Error(), http.StatusInternalServerError)
    return
  }
  listsCache.Remove(id)
  ...
}
```

After updating the shopping list in the repository, we can remove the item from the cache so that it can be loaded appropriately again in subsequent requests.

Now, our API can leverage server and client caches to provide a more performant experience.

Summary

In this chapter, we explored the most common approach of optimizing APIs in general, and more specifically in Go, using techniques such as instructing the client's cache to properly store information that is needed, adding a way to properly revalidate caches whenever possible using ETag, and adding server-side caches to avoid database server latencies and processing time. Finally, we went through the tooling provided by Go for performance analysis and bottleneck detections with pprof and Go benchmarks.

Performance is complex, and this is just a glance over some of the techniques that you can follow to improve it in the context of an API, but it always depends on your project and the usage patterns that your users have. This brings us to the next step in our journey. To have users, they need access to your API. To provide access to your API, you need to have it deployed somewhere. In the next chapter, we will cover how to deploy your Go program, exploring options from bare metal to **Function as a Service (FaaS)**.

Unlock this book's exclusive benefits now

Scan this QR code or go to packtpub. com/unlock, then search this book by name.

Note: Keep your purchase invoice ready before you start.

9

Deploying Your API

Go is an ideal language for deployment. Its ability to build a single statically linked binary makes deploying and running in any environment easy. The cross-compilation support is another key feature that makes Go an excellent choice for deployment anywhere. You can build your Go binaries on any platform and deploy them on the destination platform. This suits you incredibly well when running them in other architectures, such as ARM for Raspberry Pi or MIPS for routers. Nowadays, there are a lot of options for deployment, from real hardware to modern orchestration systems such as Kubernetes, and many other things in between, such as Docker, **virtual machines (VMs)**, or serverless functions. Go can be very convenient for any of those deployments, but how should you deploy each of them?

We are going to explore the following in this chapter:

- What kind of deployment options suit your needs
- How I deploy in a bare-metal or virtual server
- How I deploy using Docker
- How I deploy using Kubernetes
- How I deploy using serverless

Technical Requirements

All the code examples for this chapter are included in this book's GitHub repository: https://github.com/PacktPublishing/Modern-REST-API-Development-in-Go. You only need the Go compiler installed on your system to compile and execute the code.

Selecting the correct deployment for you

When it comes to deploying your API, there are several options available, the most common of which are the following:

Bare-metal deployment: Direct installation on physical servers

Virtual server deployment: Direct installation on virtual servers

Container-based deployment: Using Docker or other container technologies

Kubernetes deployment: For complex, scalable deployments

Function as a Service (FaaS) deployment: Serverless deployment options

But what are the advantages and trade-offs of each option? Let's explore them in more detail.

Bare metal

A bare-metal deployment is when you use real hardware to deploy your application, for example, a server in a data center.

Bare-metal deployments have a lot of advantages, especially when you have a small deployment or infrastructure:

- First, you remove many abstraction layers, such as container runtime or orchestration mechanisms, that introduce extra complexity and overhead. If your deployment is small and straightforward, you don't need that additional complexity.
- Second, you can get better performance because you don't have to pay for any abstraction layers you are not using.
- Third, you can configure your hardware and software specifically to your needs.

In general, it is a much simpler deployment with fewer moving parts. But take into account that simpler doesn't mean easier:

- You will have to take care of all the details that are abstracted away in other deployment options.
- When you are using bare metal, it is hard to scale. You must manually add and configure more hardware, which takes time and effort. Also, you will have to take care of everything typically provided by AWS, Azure, or Google Cloud, such as monitoring, logging, security, backups, and so on.

- Another common problem with bare metal is the lack of flexibility whenever you need to downscale. If you have bought a server, you have already paid for it. Stopping it whenever you no longer need it will not save you any money.

In more dynamic environments, where you need to grow and shrink your capacity based on the demand, hardware is not a great option. This is where VMs can provide you with significant savings. Let's talk about this in more detail.

Virtual server

A virtual server is an abstraction of hardware that simulates a whole system running. This allows multiple virtual servers to run inside one physical server.

Virtualization was a revolution when it was introduced in the software industry, tackling some bare-metal problems, such as the lack of flexibility and the need to buy hardware whenever you need to scale up. With virtualization, you can have some physical machines in your data center and host dozens of VMs. Not only that, but most cloud providers also offer virtual servers that you can start and stop whenever you need them, and you will pay only for usage time.

The problem with virtual servers, especially when using a cloud provider, is that they are usually more expensive than bare metal for the same amount of resources. But thanks to virtual servers' flexibility, you can pay less if you use the resources efficiently.

Virtual servers are also a layer of abstraction over bare metal, so if you are using a cloud provider, you are no longer taking care of the hardware part. However, you must still worry about the operating system, dependencies, configurations, and so on.

Containers

Containers are a different abstraction; instead of simulating a whole set of hardware, they encapsulate the software, giving the sensation of an isolated operating system.

Containers are a technology popularized by Docker and a game changer in the industry. For many people, they were like lightweight virtual servers, but the reality is that containers are restricted execution environments.

Containers solved one huge problem: the ability to have consistent execution environments. The containers combine your application and all the dependencies it needs to execute. That drastically simplifies the application's running in different environments.

Containers also have some trade-offs. You must define, build, and distribute containers, which requires extra knowledge and effort. Also, depending on the number of containers you run, it can become a challenging problem. And that is where Kubernetes comes into play.

Kubernetes

Kubernetes is a container orchestration platform. It provides a system that is responsible for running any number of containers. Its responsibility is to keep them running, connected, and working together properly.

Kubernetes has been a big revolution in deploying applications in the last few years. The job of Kubernetes is to abstract the management of containers running in a cluster. If you need to run several replicas of your containers and everything has to be up and running and communicating correctly, Kubernetes is the way to go.

Kubernetes solves some of the problems that containers have, but at the same time, it brings some new challenges. You have to learn how to use and manage Kubernetes properly, and that is not a simple task.

FaaS

Another relatively new option is the idea of FaaS, also known as serverless functions. The idea is to deploy your application in a way that you don't have to worry about the infrastructure. You just deploy your code, and the platform takes care of the rest. This approach is straightforward as a concept, but it limits your control over the infrastructure.

Now that we have a more or less general vision of the pros and cons of each deployment option, we can start exploring how to deploy your API in each of them. Let's start with bare-metal/VM deployment.

Bare-metal/VM deployment

Bare-metal deployment is the kind of deployment option that has always existed. You simply take your program and run it on the server. In terms of the deployment process, there is no difference between deploying on a physical server or a VM – the process is the same.

For a bare-metal deployment, we can use the static linking that Go provides by default in its binaries. That means you can build your binary in your development environment, copy it to the server, and run it.

As an example, we are going to use an elementary Go program:

```go
package main
import (
  "fmt"
  "log"
  "net/http"
)
func main() {
  http.HandleFunc("/hello", func(w http.ResponseWriter, r *http.Request) {
    fmt.Fprintf(w, "Hello, World!")
  })
  fmt.Println("running on port 8080")
  log.Fatal(http.ListenAndServe(":8080", nil))
}
```

○ **Quick tip**: Enhance your coding experience with the **AI Code Explainer** and **Quick Copy** features. Open this book in the next-gen Packt Reader. Click the **Copy** button

(1) to quickly copy code into your coding environment, or click the **Explain** button

(2) to get the AI assistant to explain a block of code to you.

```
                                             Copy      Explain
function calculate(a, b) {
  return {sum: a + b};                        ①          ②
};
```

🔖The next-gen **Packt Reader** is included for free with the purchase of this book. Scan the QR code OR go to packtpub.com/unlock, then use the search bar to find this book by name. Double-check the edition shown to make sure you get the right one.

This program is a very straightforward API that returns a "Hello, World!" string.

Now, we can build it and upload it to the server:

```
$ go build my-api.go
$ scp my-api my-server.example.com:/opt/my-api
```

Here, we are building an API named my-api and copying it to the server; in this case, to the /opt/my-api path. Depending on your project, you may need to copy other files, such as configuration files or assets, but let's suppose here that the only file needed is the binary.

Once we have that in the server, we can access the server and run the API:

```
$ /opt/my-api
running on port 8080
```

This execution starts the server in the foreground. That is not a good idea for a production server because if the program crashes, it will not restart automatically.

A better approach is to use a process manager, such as systemd. It is specific to your operating system or your distribution, but the rough idea is to set up a service that the system will manage for you. Let's see an example of how to set up a systemd service in Ubuntu.

The first thing that we need to do is create a service file. In this case, it could be /etc/systemd/system/my-api.service with the following content:

```
[Unit]
Description=My API Service
After=network.target

[Service]
User=your-user
Group=your-group
ExecStart=/opt/my-api
WorkingDirectory=/opt
Restart=on-failure

[Install]
WantedBy=multi-user.target
```

This defines how the service is going to be executed and when. It defines what needs to be executed after the network is up, and it also describes the user and group that executes the service, the command to execute, the working directory, and if it needs to restart in case of failure.

The user and the group are very important to ensure your service is running with the correct permissions, so creating a specific user and group for your service and running it with that user is a good idea. That user would have permission to read and write the files that the service needs.

Also, we define that we need to run this as part of the `multi-user` target, which is the default target in Ubuntu. This means running the services when the system starts (if the service is activated).

Once we have the service file defined, we need to reload the `systemd` configuration and start the service:

```
$ sudo systemctl daemon-reload
```

With this, the `systemd` service will detect the new service file, and we can start the service:

```
$ sudo systemctl start my-api
```

This starts our service. We can check it by trying to access it:

```
$ curl http://localhost:8080
Hello World!
```

And it works! The service is running, but it is not "activated" yet. An active service in `systemd` is a service that will be started when the system starts. To activate the service, we need to run the following:

```
$ sudo systemctl enable my-api
```

We now have our service running and activated, so we can be sure that `systemd` will try to keep our service running all the time.

But sometimes, things go wrong, and the service crashes. For those cases, we need to explore the logs. Depending on how you log things, it can end up in the standard output. If that is the case, you can see the logs with the following command:

```
$ journalctl -u my-api
```

With this, we have a clear vision of the need to deploy your Go API in a bare-metal or virtual server. But what about if you want to deploy your API in a container? Let's explore that in the next section.

Container deployment

Multiple container technologies are available, but Docker is the most popular one, so I will focus my examples on that (the concepts apply to other container systems too).

When you build a container, you have to think about it as an application with all the dependencies included. It is possible to include multiple applications in a container, but it is a common consensus that the good practice is to include only one application per container. That means you don't need any configuration, such as systemd or any other process manager. When you run the container, you are running the application.

Whenever we want to build a container, we need to define a Dockerfile. A Dockerfile is a file containing the instructions to create an image that will be used to run the container. An image is the blueprint of your container, defining what is in the filesystem, what to execute, and so on. The file starts with a base image, adding modifications, installing the dependencies, copying files, and so on.

Let's see that with an example:

```
FROM ubuntu:latest
WORKDIR /opt
COPY my-api .
RUN chmod +x my-api
EXPOSE 8080
CMD ["./my-api"]
```

The first thing we see here is the FROM ubuntu:latest line that defines the base image. In this case, we are using Ubuntu in the latest LTS version. I selected Ubuntu here to ensure compatibility with the application. You can use Alpine to get an even smaller image, but you need to be sure that your application doesn't require glibc, because Alpine uses musl libc (a smaller implementation of libc).

Then, we define the working directory. In this case, we have selected /opt. Next, we add our binary file to the image with COPY my-api ., which effectively copies the my-api binary file into the /opt directory in the image.

Then, we run the command to set the correct permissions to the binary file – in this case, granting execution permissions; define which ports will be exposed with EXPOSE 8080; and finally, we define the command that will be executed when my container runs, which is the my-api binary.

With this, we have the definition of the image, but we need to build it. Here is how you do it:

```
$ docker build -t my-api .
```

We run docker build to create the container, passing the -t my-api parameter defining the container's name. The . instance at the end is the path to the project that contains the Dockerfile, which, in this case, is the current directory.

At this point, the container is built and stored in the local Docker registry. Now, we can see it with the following command:

```
$ docker images
REPOSITORY TAG      IMAGE ID       CREATED        SIZE
my-api      latest cab92bda238f   2 minutes ago  94.6MB
```

This command lists all the images stored in the local Docker registry. You should see the my-api image, and probably others if you have used Docker before.

Now that we have our image built and ready to use, we can run it:

```
$ docker run -p 8080:8080 my-api
running on port 8080
```

This will take our my-api image, and based on that, we will start a new container and execute what is in the image; in this case, our API. The -p 8080:8080 parameter maps port 8080 from the container to port 8080 in the host. That means you can access the API on the host machine on port 8080.

We can verify that the container is running by asking Docker:

```
$ docker ps
CONTAINER ID  IMAGE   COMMAND      CREATED
8a78669a2b8f  my-api  "./my-api"   31 seconds ago
STATUS          PORTS
Up 30 seconds   0.0.0.0:8080->8080/tcp, [::]:8080->8080/tcp
NAMES
optimistic_keldysh
```

Here, the container runs with the port open and mapped to the host port. Also, we can see that it has a randomly generated name.

Now, we can access `http://localhost:8080` and see the API running in our container. From now on, to run your API, you can use that image to generate a new container, and you will be ready to go. The only missing thing is how you share the image. Multiple options exist:

Create the imageon the server where you want to run it

Upload it to a registry using the `docker push` command, which is the most common one

Export and import the image using the `docker save` and `docker load` commands

As you can see, Docker is a great way to deploy your API. But what if your application is more complex and you need to run hundreds of containers? Maybe your API is not just an API; it is a set of microservices that need to be orchestrated and managed. In that case, Kubernetes is the way to go. Let's explore that in the next section.

Kubernetes deployment

Kubernetes is a container orchestration platform that runs your containers in a cluster of machines. Kubernetes is a very complex system, but usually, you don't need to set it up yourself. You typically rely on cloud providers that offer managed Kubernetes services, or your company has a Kubernetes cluster that you can use. If you want to learn and test it locally, you can use tools such as `kind` or `minikube`, which are designed to run a local Kubernetes cluster for development purposes.

Here, let's explain the more straightforward concepts to deploy our API in Kubernetes. The first thing is understanding that Kubernetes is a declarative system, meaning that you define the state where you want the system to be, and Kubernetes makes that happen. Those declarations are named "resources". For our API, we must understand five different resources: pods, deployments, services, ConfigMaps, and secrets.

- A **pod** is a group of one or more containers that are executed together. Typically, you will have one container per pod, but that is not a restriction.
- A **deployment** is a resource that defines how we want to run our pods. It defines how many replicas we want to run, how we check if the pods are healthy, what Docker image we want to run, and so on.
- A **service** is a way of defining how, from a networking perspective, a deployment will be accessed. It gives consistent and stable access to the deployment pods. It doesn't matter if the pods are being restarted or one is down for whatever reason. The service will be the same even if the pods are changing.

- A **ConfigMap** is a way to store configuration data in Kubernetes. It is a key-value store that we can use to store our API configuration, such as a database connection string.

- And finally, similar to ConfigMaps, **secrets** are designed to store sensitive data, such as passwords or API keys.

Now that we know the basic concepts we need, let's see how we work with an example.

For this, we will use the HashiCorp `http-echo` Docker image, a straightforward API that returns `hello-world` whenever you send it a request. For that, we are going to need pods and a deployment. You rarely need to define pods directly. You usually define the deployment and let Kubernetes create pods for you.

So, let's start defining the deployment:

```
apiVersion: apps/v1
kind: Deployment
metadata:
  name: http-echo
spec:
  replicas: 2
  selector:
    matchLabels:
      app: http-echo
  template:
    metadata:
      labels:
        app: http-echo
    spec:
      containers:
        - name: http-echo
          image: hashicorp/http-echo:latest
          ports:
            - containerPort: 5678
          livenessProbe:
            httpGet:
              path: /
              port: 5678
            initialDelaySeconds: 3
            periodSeconds: 10
```

In this example, we see that we are defining our deployment with different attributes:

- The `apiVersion` attribute for Kubernetes, which is always needed for any resource and defines the Kubernetes API version to use when creating a resource.

- The `kind` attribute is the type of resource. In this case, it is a deployment.

- The `metadata` attribute used in Kubernetes to know the resource better. In this case, we are adding a name to identify the deployment pods associated with it.

- Finally, the `spec` attribute, the most crucial part of the deployment, defines how we want to run our pods.

In the deployment `spec` field, we are defining that we want two replicas, meaning we will have two pods running the `http-echo` application in parallel. Here, we define `selector`, which determines how to find the pods related to this deployment. Then, we have `template`, which defines the labels we can use to find the pods of this deployment, as we did in the selector.

To finish, we have `containers`, which represents the containers that are going to be executed inside each pod; in our case, `hashicorp/http-echo`. We also export the port that we are using for this container. Because we are exposing an API, it is good practice to add a `livenessProbe` instance that checks that the HTTP is responding on the corresponding port (which helps Kubernetes understand whether the pod is healthy).

Once we have our deployment defined (for example, in the `deployment.yaml` file), we have to apply the YAML file to the Kubernetes cluster. For that, we use the `kubectl` command:

```
$ kubectl apply -f deployment.yaml
```

This will send that YAML file to Kubernetes and create the resource. Then, Kubernetes will take care of doing everything needed to reach the state where that deployment is running, which means, in this case, pulling the Docker image, creating pods, and so on.

Now, we should have a deployment and a couple of pods running. Let's check it:

```
$ kubectl get pods
NAME                          READY  STATUS    RESTARTS  AGE
http-echo-5644f56d8b-h74l5    1/1    Running   0         1m
http-echo-5644f56d8b-ph28c    1/1    Running   0         1m
```

Here, we have two pods running from the `http-echo` deployment.

Next, let's check the deployment itself:

```
$ kubectl get deployments
NAME        READY   UP-TO-DATE   AVAILABLE   AGE
http-echo   2/2     2            2           1m
```

There is the deployment, with the expected number of pods running, and the time it has been running. But we still can't access it outside the cluster; for that, we need a service. Let's define a service for our deployment:

```
apiVersion: v1
kind: Service
metadata:
  name: http-echo-service
spec:
  selector:
    app: http-echo
  ports:
    - protocol: TCP
      port: 8000
      targetPort: 5678
      nodePort: 30000
  type: NodePort
```

In this case, we define the service as a NodePort type that exposes the service mentioned as a port on the Kubernetes node. I'm using that because I'm using kind, which doesn't provide a load balancer, but for production environments, you should use the LoadBalancer type. To get the kind node IP, we have to use the following command:

```
$ docker inspect kind-control-plane | grep \"IPAddress\"
  "IPAddress": "",
  "IPAddress": "172.19.0.2",
```

This will give us IPAddress information that we can use to hit our http-echo service, like this:

```
$ curl http://172.19.0.2:30000
hello-world
```

With this, we already have our http-echo server running in a Kubernetes cluster with two replicas fully managed by Kubernetes. This is an elementary example, but essentially, from the application perspective, this is what you usually expect to do as part of the deployment.

Also, suppose you are developing in a Kubernetes environment. In that case, it is healthy to have your application deployed in a Kubernetes environment as part of the development process to ensure everything is working as expected.

However, Kubernetes is not the only way of abstracting a big part of the administration process; there is another option that we can explore. In this case, we are talking about FaaS. Let's jump into that.

FaaS

FaaS, also known as serverless, is an interesting concept that abstracts away the infrastructure. The idea is simple: you implement a function that is executed whenever something happens; in our case, we are building APIs, which can react to an HTTP request. When that HTTP request occurs, your function gets called, and the result is returned to the user. And that's all you have to worry about: your function.

FaaS implementations can vary from one to another, but the idea is the same. In this case, I will use AWS Lambda as an example, but you can also use others, such as Google Cloud Functions, Azure Functions, or OpenFaaS.

Whenever you are using AWS Lambda, you have to define the function that you want to execute, so let's start there:

```go
package main
import (
  "github.com/aws/aws-lambda-go/events"
  "github.com/aws/aws-lambda-go/lambda"
)

func handler(request events.APIGatewayProxyRequest) (events.
APIGatewayProxyResponse, error) {
  return events.APIGatewayProxyResponse{
    Body:      "Hello, World!",
    StatusCode: 200,
  }, nil
}
func main() {
  lambda.Start(handler)
}
```

Chapter 9 155

As you can see, the function can be straightforward. Here, we are defining a handler that receives an `events.APIGatewayProxyRequest` instance and returns an `events.APIGatewayProxyResponse` instance. In this case, we are returning a `"Hello, World!"` string and a `200 OK` status.

At this point, we are ready to build and deploy our function in AWS Lambda. Let's start building the function:

```
$ GOOS=linux GOARCH=amd64 go build -o bootstrap main.go
$ zip function.zip bootstrap
```

The compilation is a standard Go compilation process, but we must put the binary into a ZIP file. That is the one that we are going to deploy.

You can deploy your lambda function through the AWS console interface (following the instructions here: https://docs.aws.amazon.com/lambda/latest/dg/configuration-function-zip.html) or the command line. I prefer the command line, so let's use that. Your AWS command-line tool must be installed and configured with your credentials. Also, you need a role set up with permissions to create lambda functions and invoke function URLs. Once you have that, you can run the following command to create the lambda function:

```
$ aws lambda create-function \
--function-name my-function-lambda \
--runtime provided.al2 \
--handler bootstrap \
--zip-file fileb://function.zip \
--role arn:aws:iam::123123123123:role/your-lambda-role
{
    "FunctionName": "my-function-lambda",
    "FunctionArn": "arn:aws:lambda:us-east-1:123123123123:function:my-
function-lambda",
    "Runtime": "provided.al2",

    ...
}
```

With this command, we create a new lambda function named `my-function-lambda` that uses the `provided.al2` runtime, which is the runtime used for Go. We declare the handler and the ZIP file to upload, and the role to use for that.

Once we execute that, we get the JSON definition of the newly created serverless function, which is currently inaccessible. To make it accessible, we need to generate a URL for the function. To do that, we will use the following command:

```
$ aws --profile mm-loadtest lambda create-function-url-config --function-
name my-function-lambda --auth-type NONE
{
    "FunctionUrl": "https://v5blee4gzzoz22nl5z57evr4ra0jled1.lambda-url.
us-east-1.on.aws/",
    "FunctionArn": "arn:aws:lambda:us-east-1:122059300807:function:my-
function-lambda",
    "AuthType": "NONE",
    "CreationTime": "2025-02-25T19:18:37.025365921Z"
}
```

This is telling AWS that we want to make our function publicly available. It is important to note that `--auth-type NONE` sets the URL as public. You can make it private using `AWS_IAM` as the authorization type. Once we have this, we can use our function by using `curl`:

```
$ curl "https://v5blee4gzzoz22nl5z57evr4ra0jled1.lambda-url.us-east-1.
on.aws/"
Hello World!
```

Isn't it great? We are 100% abstracted from the hardware and the execution flow. We only have to define our function and deploy it. But there are some limitations that you have to take into account whenever you work with FaaS. Things such as the limit of execution time or the limit in resources, the extra complexity when you need multiple functions collaborating, or the need to persist any state that you want to preserve between calls can make FaaS the wrong option, depending on the project.

Summary

This chapter explored multiple ways of deploying your API, from the traditional bare-metal approach to advanced systems such as FaaS and Kubernetes. Every deployment method has its strengths and weaknesses, so there is no one right or wrong approach. There are just different options, and you must select them based on your needs.

We have presented the pros and cons of each system and explored the process to get a Go application running in those different environments. We went through each step of the process to understand what we were doing and why.

Being able to deploy your application sounds excellent, but before you make it publicly available, you probably want to ensure that everything works as you wish. That is where testing comes into play, and we will explore it in the next chapter. So, stay with me, and let's explore how Go solves testing elegantly.

Unlock this book's exclusive benefits now

Scan this QR code or go to `packtpub.com/unlock`, then search this book by name.

Note: Keep your purchase invoice ready before you start.

10

Testing

Testing is one of the fundamental aspects of software development. You can decide to write tests before the code (**test-driven development**, or **TDD**) or after the code, but you have to write tests of your code to ensure your project remains maintainable as it grows. The Go team knows that. That is why the Go language incorporates a testing tool into the Go distribution.

Go comes with everything you need to write tests for your code, but it doesn't stop there. There are also a lot of other testing tools and libraries provided by the ecosystem, such as **testify** for assertions, **gomock** for mocking, and **testcontainers-go** for integration testing.

In this chapter, we will cover how you test your Go API using the three main types of testing, and we will learn about the following:

- How to test your API
- Using unit testing and mocks
- Creating integration testing using **testcontainers**
- **End-to-end** (E2E) testing of our API using an HTTP client
- Incorporating testing into our API project

But before we jump into the code, let's first understand the different types of testing.

Technical requirements

All the code examples for this chapter are included in this book's GitHub repository: https://github.com/PacktPublishing/Modern-REST-API-Development-in-Go. You only need the Go compiler installed on your system to compile and execute the code.

How do you test your API?

Testing software is not a trivial task. It requires a good understanding of the code intentions, an understanding of some theory around testing, and the skills to set the system up for testing. That is why building your test in parallel to your application is essential:

1. First, the code's intentions are fresh and clear in your mind

2. Second, you design the code to be testable

3. Third, you can be sure that everything is working as expected before moving on, which reduces the mental burden of the project and the accidental introduction of bugs in thast code in the future

But how do you test your API? There are three main kinds of tests that are well known and recognized by software developers:

*   Unit tests

*   Integration tests

*   E2E tests

Let's explore each one in detail, starting with unit tests.

Unit tests

Unit tests are tests that only test one specific thing at a time; for example, one specific function or one specific method. The idea is to test the smallest piece of code possible and avoid any side effects – a good example is testing a function that does a mathematical operation or a transformation in a string. That is a good example because it always has the same output for the same input.

But it is not always that easy. There are a lot of cases where your functions need to rely on a side effect, such as accessing the database. In those cases, we use mocks if we want to keep the test only testing the function code instead of the whole system. A **mock** is a fake implementation of something. For example, if we need to call the database to do an action, we create a mock that simulates doing that action and gives us the expected result. This way, we can test the function code in isolation; not only that, but we can also easily simulate situations such as error handling when the database crashes for whatever reason. That is not so easy without mocks.

However, testing in isolation has some problems. You can have two functions that work perfectly well in isolation, but when you put them together, they do not do what you expect. For example, if I'm using a mock for the database, and I pass something that is not acceptable in the database, the mock will accept that when we test it, but it will not work when we put the whole system together. That is why we need the following kind of test: an integration test.

Integration tests

Integration tests are a higher level of testing than unit tests. We are no longer testing the correct behavior of a specific function; we are now testing functionality in a system. For example, we are no longer mocking the database or I/O. We are no longer testing only specific functions but all the execution chains that any function can trigger.

Integration testing is achieved by testing things with the systems in place, such as databases, filesystems, networks, third-party services, and so on. If any system pieces are not real, you are not doing "integration testing" for that part. This directly makes these kinds of tests slower and more brittle than unit tests, because they require more systems working and interacting properly.

This kind of test is fundamental for understanding how your system works and how the different parts of your system operate together. But you can go higher in abstraction and test the whole system like a black box. In that case, we are doing E2E testing, so let's talk more about it.

E2E testing

E2E testing consists of testing your application like a black box. It connects your application using the client and operates on the application like a regular user. For APIs, it can be a web interface that uses the API or a client library that hits the API. It depends on your application and your needs. However, the key part of E2E testing is testing the whole system from the outside.

This idea of testing from outside makes these kinds of tests slower than integration tests and also more brittle, because any change in the application behavior can break some E2E tests.

Sometimes, it is a bit blurry where one testing method starts and where it finishes, but I think it is going to be more evident during the chapter when we begin exploring the different kinds of tests. Let's start with unit testing to understand how testing generally works in Go.

Unit testing and mocks

As we explained, a unit test is about verifying one specific part of the code in isolation. In Go, we have a testing framework built in, so we don't need to do anything to actually start testing.

Let's begin with an elementary example:

```go
func Add(a, b int) int {
  return a + b
}

func TestAdd(t *testing.T) {
```

```
  got := Add(1, 2)
  want := 3
  if got != want {
    t.Errorf("Add(1, 2) = %d; want %d", got, want)
  }
}
```

In this case, we define an **Add** function that adds two numbers and returns the result. Right after the **Add** function, we define the **TestAdd** function, responsible for testing the **Add** function. In Go, there is a well-known pattern for testing: the **got/want** pattern – we set a **want** variable to the value that we expect to happen on the function execution, then we execute the function and store the result in the **got** variable. Then, we check if they match. If they don't, we will use **t.Errorf** to report the error in the test.

With this simple pattern, we can test many things, but we haven't actually tested anything yet. We therefore need to run tests. To do this, we use the **go test** command:

```
$ go test .
ok myapi 0.004s
```

The **go test** command allows us to run tests, which, in this case, are all the tests in the current directory. This will find any file that has the **_test.go** suffix and run the tests in that file. A test function is a regular function that starts with the **Test** prefix and receives ***testing.T** as the only argument.

But what happens if I change **want** to **4**? Let's see:

```
$ go test .
--- FAIL: TestAdd (0.00s)
myapi_test.go:13: Add(1, 2) = 3; want 4
FAIL
FAIL myapi 0.004s
FAIL
```

As you can see, the tests are failing now, and the output tells you which test failed and how it failed.

This test is straightforward – we are just checking one possible value – but it is common to want to test multiple values for a function, right? One of the best ways to do that is by using subtests and table-driven tests. Let's start talking about subtests.

Subtests

Subtests allow us to group related tests. For example, I can have a test for **Add** with subtests for checking different behaviors, such as checking the sum of positive numbers, negative numbers, zero, and so on. Let's see an example:

```go
func TestAdd(t *testing.T) {
  t.Run("positive numbers", func(t *testing.T) {
    got := Add(1, 2)
    want := 3
    if got != want {
      t.Errorf("Add(1, 2) = %d; want %d", got, want)
    }
  })

  t.Run("negative numbers", func(t *testing.T) {
    got := Add(-1, -2)
    want := -3
    if got != want {
      t.Errorf("Add(-1, -2) = %d; want %d", got, want)
    }
  })
}
```

Here, we have **TestAdd** with two subtests, one for positive numbers and one for negative ones.

Now, we have to execute it. In this case, we are going to pass the **-v** parameter to the **go test** execution to get extra details about the test execution:

```
$ go test -v .
=== RUN TestAdd
=== RUN TestAdd/positive_numbers
=== RUN TestAdd/negative_numbers
--- PASS: TestAdd (0.00s)
--- PASS: TestAdd/positive_numbers (0.00s)
--- PASS: TestAdd/negative_numbers (0.00s)
PASS
ok myapi 0.004s
```

Here, we can see that we are now running **TestAdd**, but also, as part of **TestAdd**, we have **positive_numbers** and **negative_numbers** subtests.

Now that our tests are grouped, let's explore the idea of table-driven testing.

Table-driven tests

Instead of defining a set of subtests, when you use table-driven tests, we define a table with the inputs and the expected outputs and then run the subtests based on those values. There is nothing fundamentally different between table tests and any other subtests. It is a very convenient pattern widely used in the Go community. Here is the code for that:

```go
func TestAdd(t *testing.T) {
  tests := []struct {
    name string
    a int
    b int
    want int
  }{
  {"positive numbers", 1, 2, 3},
    {"zero", 0, 0, 0},
    {"negative numbers", -1, -1, -2},
  }

  for _, tt := range tests {
    t.Run(tt.name, func(t *testing.T) {
      got := Add(tt.a, tt.b)
      if got != tt.want {
        t.Errorf("Add(%d, %d) = %d; want %d", tt.a, tt.b, got, tt.want)
      }
    })
  }
}
```

Here, we are defining a list of tests we want to execute, looping over those examples, and running subtests for each one. This way, we can test multiple values for the same function and keep them organized.

If we execute these table tests, we can see the results:

```
$ go test -v .
=== RUN  TestAdd
=== RUN  TestAdd/positive_numbers
=== RUN  TestAdd/zero
=== RUN  TestAdd/negative_numbers
--- PASS: TestAdd (0.00s)
--- PASS: TestAdd/positive_numbers (0.00s)
--- PASS: TestAdd/zero (0.00s)
--- PASS: TestAdd/negative_numbers (0.00s)
PASS
ok myapi 0.004s
```

Everything is working as expected, and you can see my three test cases for positive numbers, zero, and negative numbers.

Another good thing about this approach is how easy it is to add more test cases. For example, I can simply add {"mixed numbers", -1, 3, 2} to the list, which would add that test case. Simple.

But everything is straightforward with these kinds of small functions. Let's explore functions that have side effects, such as accessing the database. For that, we will need mocks.

Mocks

To understand mocks, we need to have a clear vision of the problem we are trying to solve. Suppose we have the following function:

```
func (app *App) Login(username, password string) (string, error) {
  user, err := app.db.GetUserByUsername(username)
  if err != nil {
    return "", err
  }

  if user.Password != password {
    return "", errors.New("invalid password")
  }

  return user.SessionToken, nil
}
```

We have an application with a **Login** method that receives the username and password and uses a **db** attribute (using the repository pattern) to get the user's information. Then, it compares the password passed and the password of the user – if they match, it returns the session token; otherwise, it returns an error.

It is straightforward, but testing this has one big problem. For **db**, I would need to generate a **db** service, ensure there are users that I want to test, and ensure the database is up and running. That is not a unit test anymore. As I want to keep it simple and test only the **Login** function and not the database, I need to avoid calling **db** methods. That is where mocks come to the rescue.

Suppose that **DB** is an interface, and we have a mock implementation for that interface. Let's see how we can test the **Login** function using a mock:

```go
func TestLogin(t *testing.T) {
  app := NewApp()
  ctrl := gomock.NewController(t)
  m := mocks.NewMockDB(ctrl)
  app.db = m


  m.EXPECT().GetUserByUsername("invalid-username").Return(
    nil, errors.New("invalid user"))
  _, err := app.Login("invalid-username", "password")
  if err == nil {
    t.Errorf("Login(invalid-username, password) error = %v; want not nil",
             err)
  }
}
```

In this scenario, we are creating a new test. First, we initialize the mock using **NewMockDB** and then define **EXPECTS** functions. The **EXPECTS** functions are functions that the mock can answer and define the response that is going to be returned. If any function in the mock is called without a corresponding **expect**, the test is going to fail. By defining **EXPECTS** functions, we can generate the behavior we need for the test; in this case, we can see that we are generating an error. We could create a result or anything that we want to drive the test in the path of executions that we wish.

We are missing other tests here, such as whenever everything goes well, or the user password does not match correctly. You can use that as an exercise if you want. But before that, we need to know how to create the **MockDB** instance we have there.

To create mocks, we use the **gomock** library, which is officially maintained by the Uber team. It allows us to create mocks for interfaces and then use them, as we saw in the example. In this case, we had an interface that is of the **DB** type, defined like this:

```
type DB interface {
    GetUserByUsername(username string) (*User, error)
}
```

Next, we need to generate a mock from this interface to make it work in our code, but first, we need to install the **mockgen** code generator from the **gomock** package. We can do that using the **go install** command:

```
$ go install go.uber.org/mock/mockgen@latest
```

Once we have **mockgen** installed, we can generate our mocks using this command, for example:

```
$ mockgen -source myapi.go -package mocks -destination mocks/db.go
```

So, we can now mock any interface to ensure we are only testing the parts of our code that we want to test. This is ideal for unit testing and will give you confidence in your code.

If you want to know more about **gomock**, you can explore the documentation at https://github.com/uber-go/mock.

It is important to notice that this same pattern can be achieved by a simple fake implementation of the interface that has the behavior that you need for the testing. Depending on the interface and the degree of complexity, you can prefer this approach instead of using **gomock** or another mocking library.

We have a good set of tools to test our code, but probably some of you are used to richer assertions. In the Go world, the common practice is to use the **got**/**want** approach explained before and fundamental assertion primitives such as **t.Error** or **t.Fatal**, but some libraries can provide richer assertions. One of those libraries is **testify**, so let's explore it a bit.

The testify library

The **testify** library is an assertion library that provides many assertion functions, and it is divided into two packages: **assert** and **require**. Both contain the same assertions, but the difference is that the **assert** package is going to log the error and continue the test execution, while the **require** package is going to log the error and stop the current test execution.

Let's see how we can use it:

```go
func TestExample(t *testing.T) {
  err := createSampleData()
  require.NoError(t, err)

  user, err := getUser("username")
  require.NoError(t, err)

  assert.Equal(t, "username", user.Username)
  assert.Equal(t, "username@example.com", user.Email)
}
```

In the example, we can see that we are doing specific initializations with the **createSampleData** function. We require no error because if that fails, there is no point in continuing to check the rest of the test. In that case, I use the **require** package. Then, I try to get the user. Again, there is no point in checking anything if there is an error. Finally, I start checking the returned user data. In that case, I want to check every field independently, so I use **assert** to check all of them and report if any or both are incorrect.

Another good thing about **testify** is that it provides more complex assertions, such as checking if a slice contains a specific element, a map includes a specific key, or a string contains a particular substring, or even checking something over and over again until it is **true**.

Also, you can provide a text to define why the assertion is failing, but by default, it offers a good message; for example, for **assert.Equal**, the error would be something like this:

```
--- FAIL: TestExample (0.00s)
    main_test.go:69:
        Error Trace: main_test.go:69
        Error:       Not equal:
                     expected: "username@example.com"
                     actual  : "otheremail@example.com"

                     Diff:
                     --- Expected
                     +++ Actual
                     @@ -1 +1 @@
                     -username@example.com
```

```
                    +otheremail@example.com
        Test:       TestExample
```

As you can see in the error, **testify** provides a better description of why the test is failing.

Some people prefer the standard library, whereas others prefer to use **testify** assertions, but that is up to you.

If you want to know more about **testify**, you can explore the documentation at `https://github.com/stretchr/testify`.

I think this is enough for unit testing, but you want to be sure that all the pieces of your software are working together as you expect. So, let's jump into integration testing.

Integration testing

In Go, the main difference between integration testing and unit testing is what you test, but there is no real difference between the tools you use. You can use the same testing package and similar testing code, but instead of testing a small chunk of isolated code, you test parts of the system together.

For example, we can test the **Login** function again, but this time, we will use the real thing instead of mocking the database. Let's see how we can do that:

```go
func TestLogin(t *testing.T) {
  app := NewApp()
  user := User{Username: "user", Password: "password", SessionToken:
"123123"}
  app.db.InsertUser(user)
  defer app.db.DeleteUser(user.Username)

  t.Run("invalid user", func(t *testing.T) {
    _, err := app.Login("invalid-username", "password")
    if err == nil {
      t.Errorf("Login(invalid-username, password) error = %v;
              want not nil", err)
    }
  })

  t.Run("invalid password", func(t *testing.T) {
    ...
```

```
    })

    t.Run("valid login", func(t *testing.T) {
    ...
    })
}
```

This way, we are testing the same function but are using the actual database under the hood; instead of defining what the mock does, we are just initializing the database with the data needed for the integration tests. That gives us the confidence that in a real-world scenario, the function will work as expected and the database will be used correctly.

But we are talking about APIs here, right? So, one of the best testing points for this kind of integration testing is the API itself! Go also helps us here with the **net/http/httptest** package, which allows us to create requests and analyze responses easily. Let's see how we can test an API using this package:

```
func handler(w http.ResponseWriter, r *http.Request) {
  w.WriteHeader(http.StatusOK)
  w.Write([]byte(`{"message": "hello world"}`))
}
```

This is a simple handler that returns a JSON string with a **"hello world"** message.

Let's see how we test that handler:

```
func TestMyHandler(t *testing.T) {
  req := httptest.NewRequest("GET", "/", nil)
  w := httptest.NewRecorder()
  handler(w, req)
  resp := w.Result()
  defer resp.Body.Close()
  data, err := io.ReadAll(res.Body)
  if err != nil {
    t.Errorf("Failed to read response body: %v", err)
  }
  if data != `{"message": "hello world"}` {
    t.Errorf("Expected message 'hello world'; got '%s'", data)
  }
}
```

As you can see, we are creating a fake request using the **httptest.NewRequest** function, as well as a response object with **httptest.NewRecorder**, which will allow me to explore the response generated. With that, we call the handler that we want to test and analyze the response result. This way, we can simulate requests that come from the outside directly inside our testing code, but we still have a good amount of control over the execution state because we are still in the same code base.

Integration testing is great, but there is a common problem with having integration tests that are repeatable and isolated. For example, if all the tests use the same database, one test can interfere with other tests, and you end up having flaky tests that sometimes fail and pass other times. That can become a massive pain in the long run, but there are interesting solutions, such as using **testcontainers**.

The testcontainers library

The **testcontainers** library allows you to spin up Docker containers on the fly during testing. That way, you can have your own PostgreSQL database server for each specific test or set of tests. Let's see how we can use **testcontainers** to test an API with a PostgreSQL database:

```
import "github.com/testcontainers/testcontainers-go/modules/postgres"

func TestAPIWithPostgres(t *testing.T) {
  ctx := context.Background()
  pgContainer, err := postgres.Run(ctx,
    "postgres:16-alpine",
    postgres.WithDatabase("test"),
    postgres.WithUsername("user"),
    postgres.WithPassword("password"),
  )
  defer testcontainers.TerminateContainer(pgContainer)
  connStr, _ := pgContainer.ConnectionString(ctx, "sslmode=disable",
                                            "application_name=test")

  app.db = store.New(connStr)

  app.db.InsertUser(user)
  defer app.db.DeleteUser(user.Username)

  t.Run("invalid user", func(t *testing.T) {
    _, err := app.Login("invalid-username", "password")
```

```
    if err == nil {
      t.Errorf("Login(invalid-username, password) error = %v;
                  want not nil", err)
    }
  })
}
```

This test is very similar to the one that we did for integration testing, but this time, whenever we run the test before it gets executed, it spins up a containerized Postgres instance with a database and uses it for the test. Once the test is done, the container is cleaned up. This way, we know that the test will not be affected by anything external because the database is dedicated exclusively to this test.

This is what it looks like when running:

```
2025/02/28 18:39:31 🐳 Creating container for image postgres:16-alpine
2025/02/28 18:39:39 🐳 Creating container for image testcontainers/
ryuk:0.11.0
2025/02/28 18:39:39 ✅ Container created: f91cb509a75d
2025/02/28 18:39:39 🐳 Starting container: f91cb509a75d
2025/02/28 18:39:39 ✅ Container started: f91cb509a75d
2025/02/28 18:39:39 ⏳ Waiting for container id f91cb509a75d image:
testcontainers/ryuk:0.11.0. Waiting for: &{Port:8080/tcp timeout:<nil>
PollInterval:100ms skipInternalCheck:false}
2025/02/28 18:39:39 🔔 Container is ready: f91cb509a75d
2025/02/28 18:39:39 ✅ Container created: c19a068d41ca
2025/02/28 18:39:39 🐳 Starting container: c19a068d41ca
2025/02/28 18:39:39 ✅ Container started: c19a068d41ca
2025/02/28 18:39:39 🔔 Container is ready: c19a068d41ca
=== RUN   TestAPIWithPostgres/invalid_user
2025/02/28 18:39:39 🐳 Stopping container: c19a068d41ca
2025/02/28 18:39:50 ✅ Container stopped: c19a068d41ca
2025/02/28 18:39:50 🐳 Terminating container: c19a068d41ca
2025/02/28 18:39:50 🚫 Container terminated: c19a068d41ca
--- PASS: TestAPIWithPostgres (72.43s)
    --- PASS: TestAPIWithPostgres/invalid_user (0.00s)
```

As you can see here, the **testcontainers** library creates a container in Docker and removes it when it is finished. It also spins up a different container named **ryuk**, which is responsible for removing any container that is no longer used there. It is like a garbage collector if your tests are not finishing in the container properly.

In **testcontainers**, you can spin up Postgres and many other systems, such as Redis, YugabyteDB, Kafka, MariaDB, MongoDB, OpenSearch, and many others. If you need a module that doesn't exist, you can easily create your module or simply run a new container with the **GenericContainer** function. If there is a Docker image for that, you can use it in your tests through **testcontainers**.

If you want to know more about **testcontainers**, you can check out the documentation at https:// golang.testcontainers.org/.

Integration testing focuses on system integration and how subsystems work together, but there is another kind of test that we haven't explored yet: E2E testing.

E2E testing

E2E testing focuses on the system as a whole and is more focused on use cases and scenarios than on specific functions or subsystems working together. For example, if you have an API, you can test the API like a black box, sending requests that make sense for specific use cases, such as registration and first login, or creating, updating, listing, and deleting a shopping list.

The most common case for E2E testing is using a web browser to consume a web application that sends requests to the server. In those scenarios, you use tools such as Selenium, Playwright, Cypress, or similar tools to simulate user interactions. However, you can use a simple HTTP client to send requests and analyze the responses for APIs. Let's see how we can do that:

```
func TestRegisterAndLogin(t *testing.T) {
  resp1, err := http.Post("http://localhost:8080/register",
    "application/json", strings.NewReader(`{"username": "user",
      "password": "password"}`))
  defer resp1.Body.Close()
  if resp1.StatusCode != http.StatusOK {
    t.Errorf("Expected status code 200; got %d", resp1.StatusCode)
  }

  resp2, err := http.Post("http://localhost:8080/login",
    "application/json", strings.NewReader(`{"username": "user",
      "password": "password"}`))
```

```
    defer resp2.Body.Close()
    if resp2.StatusCode != http.StatusOK {
      t.Errorf("Expected status code 200; got %d", resp2.StatusCode)
    }


    ...

  }
```

In this case, we expect that the API is already running on port **8080** of **localhost**, and we are sending a request to register and log in as the user. After registering and logging in to verify that everything went well, I could do more things, such as trying to get the user itself or trying to clean up the created user.

You can combine some of the previously used techniques here, such as using **testcontainers**, this time to spin up the API itself. Also, you can use a created client for your API instead of direct HTTP requests. But all that is up to you.

Now that we have a general understanding of the different types of tests, let's see how we can incorporate testing into our API project.

Adding tests to our shopping list API

Now that we have a clear vision of how tests work, let's apply it to our project: our API for shopping lists. We'll start with unit tests, then integration testing, and finally, E2E testing using an HTTP client.

Unit tests

Let's start by creating a simple unit test. One of the things that we can test in isolation for our application is, for example, the cache middleware. It is a great example of unit tests because it does not require any external dependencies, so it is isolated and doesn't need any mocks. So, let's start there:

```
func TestAddCacheHeaders(t *testing.T) {
  testHandler := http.HandlerFunc(func(w http.ResponseWriter,
    r *http.Request) {
    w.WriteHeader(http.StatusOK)
  })
  req := httptest.NewRequest("GET", "/lists", nil)
  rec := httptest.NewRecorder()
```

```
    handler := addCacheHeaders(testHandler)
    handler(rec, req)
    if rec.Header().Get("Cache-Control") != "public, max-age=300" {
      t.Errorf("Not valid Cache-Control found, got %v, want %v",
        rec.Header().Get("Cache-Control"), "public, max-age=300")
    }
    if rec.Header().Get("Expires") == "" {
      t.Errorf("Not valid Expires, got %v, want not empty",
        rec.Header().Get("Expires"))
    }
  }
```

Here, we are creating a test of the middleware. We make a fake handler that returns a **200** status code, then generate a fake request and response, and wrap my fake handler with **addCacheHeaders** middleware. Then, when I execute the handler, I can check that the behavior of **addCacheHeaders** is the expected one.

This simple test is good, but I also want to check that I'm correctly handling the inputs on my API. For example, I want to check that the login works as expected. But for that, I need to use the repository, and we are still working on the unit testing part.

Before we can start testing the API handlers, we need to create a mock for the repository, and for that, we need to make the repository an interface to replace the actual implementation with the mock. Let's create an interface inside the **store.go** file:

```
  type RepositoryInterface interface {
    GetUserByUsername(username string) (*User, error)
    GetSession(token string) (*Session, error)
    AddSession(username string) (*Session, error)
    GetShopingList(id string) (*ShopingList, error)
    GetShopingLists() ([]*ShopingList, error)
    AddShopingList(list *ShopingList) (*ShopingList, error)
    UpdateShopingList(id string, list *ShopingList) (*ShopingList, error)
    PatchShopingList(id string, patch *ShopingListPatch) error
    DeleteList(id string) error
  }
```

With this, we have a repository interface and can use **mockgen** to generate a mock for that interface. Here is how you do it:

```
$ mockgen -source store.go -package main -destination repository.go
```

Finally, we changed our code to use a **RepositoryInterface** repository instead of the actual repository by changing the variable type in the **main.go** file, like this:

```
var (
  repository RepositoryInterface
)
```

Once that is done, we can add tests that use this mock. Let's start with the **handleLogin** function:

```
func TestHandleLogin(t *testing.T) {
  ctrl := gomock.NewController(t)
  mock := NewMockRepositoryInterface(ctrl)
  repository = mock
  mock.EXPECT().GetUserByUsername("testuser").Return(
    &User{"user", "testuser", "password"},
    nil
  )
  mock.EXPECT().AddSession("testuser").Return(
    &Session{"test-token", time.Now().Add(time.Hour), "testuser"},
    nil
  )
  req := httptest.NewRequest("POST", "/login",
    strings.NewReader(`{"username":"testuser","password":"password"}`))
  req.Header.Set("Content-Type", "application/json")
  rec := httptest.NewRecorder()
  handleLogin(rec, req)
  if rec.Code != http.StatusOK {
    t.Errorf("handleLogin() status = %v, want %v", rec.Code,
      http.StatusOK)
  }
}
```

Here, we are testing for login while mocking the two methods in the repository. In this case, we can verify that we are getting the right username and password from the inputs because they are the ones passed to the mock, and also, we see that the behavior is the expected one whenever we send the correct data.

So, we can now write good unit tests in our application, not depending on the behavior of services such as, in this case, the database. But we want to test that the database is behaving correctly, right? So, let's jump into integration testing.

Integration tests

Now that we have incorporated unit testing into our API, we can start writing integration tests to ensure the API works correctly with the database. In our case, we are using SQLite, so we don't need anything such as **testcontainers**, but we would still need to make a temporary database for the tests. Here, SQLite is ideal because we can run it in an in-memory database. Let's see how we can do this in our project:

```go
func TestLoginAPI(t *testing.T) {
  var err error
  repository, err = NewRepository("file::memory:?cache=shared")
  if err != nil {
    t.Errorf("NewRepository() error = %v", err)
  }
  repository.Init()

  req := httptest.NewRequest("POST", "/login",
    strings.NewReader(`{"username":"admin","password":"admin"}`))
  req.Header.Set("Content-Type", "application/json")
  rec := httptest.NewRecorder()
  handleLogin(rec, req)
  if rec.Code != http.StatusOK {
    t.Errorf("handleLogin() status = %v, want %v", rec.Code,
      http.StatusOK)
  }
}
```

As we can see in the example, I initialize the repository with an in-memory database and then initialize that database. Then, I simply run my handler and expect that the result is the right one. This way, we can verify that the handler works correctly with the database.

Here, we are only testing one case; we would need to add more tests here, such as cases where the user doesn't exist, so the login fails because of that, or the case where the user exists, but the password is wrong.

We now have a basic example of writing integration tests for our API. We can replicate this in other system parts, such as API endpoints or **authRequired** middleware.

Now that our application has integration tests, let's jump into E2E testing.

E2E testing

Finally, we have reached E2E testing. Here, we are going to handle our API as a black box, and we are going to send requests to the API and analyze the responses, but always as an external agent.

You can do this kind of E2E testing, which looks very similar to integration testing, but when I'm working on E2E testing, I prefer to focus on the use cases, not on integrating the different pieces of the system. For example, in our case, we want to be sure you can log in, create a new list, and list your shopping lists. So, let's explore that scenario:

```go
func makeRequest(method, url string, body io.Reader, token string) (*http.
Response, error) {
  req, err := http.NewRequest(method, url, body)
  if err != nil {
    return nil, err
  }
  req.Header.Set("Content-Type", "application/json")
  if token != "" {
    req.Header.Set("Authorization", "Bearer "+token)
  }
  return http.DefaultClient.Do(req)
}
```

In this code, we create a simple **makeRequest** helper function that allows us to make requests to the API. This way, we can reuse this function for all the tests. If I have an API client already created, we could use that client instead. But for this case, we are going to use this helper function.

Now, we need to make the test itself and start doing the login process:

```go
func TestLoginAndList(t *testing.T) {
  baseURL := "http://localhost:8888"

  reqBody := strings.NewReader(`{"username":"admin","password":"admin"}`)
  resp, err := makeRequest("POST", baseURL+"/login", reqBody, "") // Reset
the database
    if err != nil {
```

```
      t.Fatalf("Failed to make a request: %v", err)
   }
   defer resp.Body.Close()

   var response map[string]string
   json.NewDecoder(resp.Body).Decode(&response)
   token := response["token"]
   if token == "" {
      t.Fatal("No token returned from login")
   }
   ...
}
```

At this point, we are executing the login process like a regular user of the API would do. We run the request by passing the username and password to the login endpoint, and then we get the token from the response.

Now, with that token, we can create a new shopping list with another request:

```
func TestLoginAndList(t *testing.T) {
   ...
   listName := fmt.Sprintf("Test List %d", rand.Int())
   reqBody = strings.NewReader(fmt.Sprintf(`{"id": "", "name": "%s",
         "items": []}`, listName))
   resp2, err := makeRequest("POST", baseURL+"/lists", reqBody, token)
   if err != nil {
      t.Fatalf("Failed to make a request: %v", err)
   }
   defer resp2.Body.Close()

   if resp2.StatusCode != 201 {
      t.Errorf("Expected status 201, got %d", resp.StatusCode)
   }
   ...
}
```

This part of the code calls the API needed to create a new shopping list in the application. We need it to be able to verify whether we can get the shopping lists.

Finally, I can get the lists of shopping lists and verify that the list I made is there:

```go
func TestLoginAndList(t *testing.T) {
    ...

    resp3, err := makeRequest("GET", baseURL+"/lists", nil, token)
    if err != nil {
        t.Fatalf("Failed to make a request: %v", err)
    }
    defer resp3.Body.Close()

    var lists []ShoppingList
    json.NewDecoder(resp3.Body).Decode(&lists)

    found := false
    for _, list := range lists {
        if list.Name == listName {
            found = true
        }
    }
    if !found {
        t.Errorf("Unable to find list with name '%s'", listName)
    }
}
```

And now, we can run these tests. We need to have our application up and running because the test is "external" to the application. You can put any mechanism you want in place to spin up the server, but at the end of the day, the test connects to a running instance and tries to do what is expected. That mechanism can clean up the database between tests or do whatever you consider necessary for your tests.

With this, we have covered everything you need to get up and running with testing in Go.

Summary

In this chapter, we explored the fundamentals of testing in Go, going through how the built-in testing framework provides everything needed to ensure your API works as expected. We covered the three main ways of testing your application, with unit tests for localized and isolated code testing, integration tests for verifying the correct interaction between components, and E2E tests for validating complete workflows from a user's perspective as a black box.

We also explored testing patterns such as table-driven tests and mocking. We explored libraries for helping in the testing process, such as **testify** for assertions, **gomock** for mocking, and **test-containers** for integration testing. We also explored applying all these concepts in our API project, adding all kinds of tests, from unit to E2E tests.

Testing is essential when developing an API to prevent your users from experiencing problems when using your API. Still, there is another tool that complements testing in that regard, and that is documentation. The next chapter will explore how to document your API using tools such as OpenAPI and Swagger.

Unlock this book's exclusive benefits now

Scan this QR code or go to `packtpub.com/unlock`, then search this book by name.

Note: Keep your purchase invoice ready before you start.

11

Documenting with OpenAPI

Documentation is a critical part of any API development process. Good documentation makes your API more accessible and easier to use. In a world where APIs are increasingly the primary interface between systems, having clear, accurate, and comprehensive documentation is no longer optional; it's essential. For documenting REST APIs, the de facto standard is OpenAPI, and how it works and integrates with Go is what we will explore in this chapter. For that, we are going to learn about the following concepts:

- What OpenAPI is and why it's important
- How to document your endpoints with OpenAPI
- Tools for working with the **OpenAPI Specification (OAS)**
- Publishing your API documentation
- Adding OpenAPI documentation to our shopping list API

In this chapter, we'll use some applications that require node, npm, and npx to be installed on your system. Ensure that you have them installed if you want to follow all the examples.

Technical requirements

All the code examples for this chapter are included in this book's GitHub repository: https://github.com/PacktPublishing/Modern-REST-API-Development-in-Go. You only need the Go compiler installed on your system to compile and execute the code.

What is OpenAPI?

OpenAPI (formerly known as Swagger) is a specification for describing RESTful APIs. It is written in **YAML Ain't Markup Language (YAML)** or **JavaScript Object Notation (JSON)**, both structured and machine-readable formats, but simultaneously human-readable. This way, your API can be documented so that humans and machines can understand without needing the source code. Also, OpenAPI is language agnostic. It is not tied to Go or any other language, which makes it great for interoperability between different systems.

An OpenAPI document describes an API, its endpoints, operations, **input/output (I/O)** parameters, authentication methods, and other details. Let's see a simple example of it:

```
openapi: 3.0.0
  info:
    title: Sample API
    description: A sample API to illustrate OpenAPI concepts
    version: 1.0.0
  paths:
    /users:
      get:
          summary: Returns a list of users
        responses:
            '200':
             description: A JSON array of user names
            content:
               application/json:
                 schema:
                   type: array
                 items:
                     type: string
```

This simple document describes an API named `Sample API`, with a single endpoint (`/users`) that responds to `GET` requests and returns an array of strings with usernames. As you can see, I don't need to read any code to understand what this API does and what to expect regarding requests and responses.

There are several reasons why OpenAPI has become so widely adopted and you should care about it:

- **Standardization**: OpenAPI fixes one of the main complaints about RESTful APIs: the lack of consensus about specific practices. Properly documenting your API with OpenAPI makes it easier for other developers to understand and integrate it.

- **Tooling**: The OpenAPI tooling ecosystem is excellent. From code generators to documentation generators, it makes your API automatically easier to understand and integrate with almost zero effort.

- **Machine-readable**: Being machine-readable enables automation. With OpenAPI, you can create integration or load testing entirely or partially automated.

- **Human-readable**: The YAML or JSON format is readable by humans, and you can easily understand it. Also, OpenAPI contains a lot of metadata focused on human understanding of the API behavior, such as descriptions and examples.

The OpenAPI format

OAS is very rich and extensive. Still, I want to explain some commonly used parts to give extra context to the examples we will see later in this chapter.

First of all, we already saw in our first example two essential sections. Firstly, there is openapi, which defines the version of the format; for example, 3.0.0. Following that is the info section, which gives us general information about the API, such as the name of the API, the version, or what the API is for.

Next, we can talk about what I think is the most crucial section of the whole OpenAPI document: the paths section. This section allows us to define every endpoint in our system, defining the URL path, and, under that, all possible cases, the different methods that the URL accepts, what parameters with what responses, and so on. Of course, it also explains what the API endpoints do. We will see more examples later in the chapter, but let's discuss reusability.

One problem you will find sooner rather than later is that you don't want to define every single time you return a specific entity; for example, a user or the whole entity there. So, there must be a way to not repeat yourself; that is where the components section comes into play. The components section allows us to define different types of objects that you can reference from other parts of the OpenAPI document. For example, you can define responses, schemas, parameters, headers, and others. Let's see that in action to understand it better:

```
...
paths:
  /users/{id}:
```

```yaml
    get:
      summary: Returns a user
      responses:
        '200':
          description: A JSON array of user names
          content:
            application/json:
              schema:
                $ref: '#/components/schemas/User'
components:
  schemas:
    User:
      type: object
      properties:
        id:
          type: integer
        name:
          type: string
        email:
          type: string
    ...
```

In this example, we can see that the definition of the User entity is in the components section, and then we can reference it from different paths in my application. Defining components is very convenient for reducing code duplication and avoiding errors from modifying only some copies of the same entity.

You can investigate other sections, such as the security section, which allows you to define authentication, or the tags section, which enables you to group your endpoints. But for now, I think this is enough to understand the basics of OpenAPI. So, let's jump into how we document our API endpoints.

Documenting your endpoints

As I said before, OpenAPI is language agnostic, so you can document your API endpoints individually, write that OpenAPI document yourself, and generate your Go code from that. Also, you can write your code, including some comments, and use a tool that produces an OpenAPI document from your source code.

The third option would be generating both and manually keeping them in sync. All the approaches have interesting benefits and drawbacks, so let's explore them.

Writing code and OpenAPI documents

Writing both code and OpenAPI documents is a way that some people prefer because it gives us fine-grained control over the OpenAPI document generated and the code generated. Also, it doesn't require any extra dependencies to get this working. However, as often happens, with more control comes more responsibility. This approach requires you to keep code and OpenAPI documents in sync, which can be challenging. This approach eventually requires some process to check consistency, such as a linter.

But there is a more straightforward way to maintain consistency: generating API code from the OpenAPI document, so let's talk about that.

Generating code from your OpenAPI document

One standard option is to have the OpenAPI document as the source of truth and, from there, generate API code. Of course, you are not generating all the API code, only the parts related to the API handlers. We need to implement our business logic, but we no longer have to care about API-related code here.

Multiple libraries can help you with this, such as openapi-generator, ogen, oapi-codegen, and others. We will explore ogen, but any of the other tools will also do a good job. Let's start defining our OpenAPI document:

```
openapi: 3.0.0
info:
  title: Sample API
  description: A sample API to illustrate OpenAPI concepts
  version: 1.0.0
paths:
  /users:
    get:
      summary: Returns a list of users
      responses:
        '200':
          description: A JSON array of user names
          content:
            application/json:
```

```
    schema:
      type: array
      items:
        type: string
```

Here, we are using the same code we used as an example before, but this time, we will generate source code to execute our API. To do that, we need to install the ogen library:

```
$ go install -v github.com/ogen-go/ogen/cmd/ogen@latest
```

With the ogen library installed, we can start generating code:

```
$ ogen sample.yml
```

Running this command will generate a Go module named API that contains all the code related to the API. There is a lot of generated code, but the vital part in our case is the one that defines what we need to implement: the Handler interface. The generator defines the interface we need to implement to have our API working in the api/oas_server_gen.go file. For our example, the interface looks like this:

```
type Handler interface {
  // UsersGet implements GET /users operation.
  //
  // Returns a list of users.
  //
  // GET /users
  UsersGet(ctx context.Context) ([]string, error)
}
```

As you can see, it is a simple interface that requires us to implement what we need to implement the logic that you can expect from the OpenAPI document. So, let's write a trivial implementation of it:

```
type API struct {}
func (_ API) UsersGet(ctx context.Context) ([]string, error) {
  return []string{"user1", "user2"}, nil
}
```

With this, we have an API that always returns the user1 and user2 users. Now, one last thing that we need to do is to create a main function that will start the server and register our API handler:

```
package main
import (
```

```
    "net/http"
    "simpleapi/api"
)

func main() {
  srv, err := api.NewServer(API{})
  if err != nil {
    panic(err)
  }
  if err := http.ListenAndServe(":8080", srv); err != nil {
    panic(err)
  }
}
```

With this, we have implemented our simple OpenAPI document, and we can run itand start making requests.

The cool part is that you can simply keep changing the OpenAPI document and regenerating the code, and you will only need to implement the new methods in the Handler interface. This way, everything is consistent, including your API documentation and code implementation.

But this is not necessarily always the best solution. In some cases, you want to do it all the way around. You want to write the code and generate an OpenAPI document from it, so let's explore that option.

Generating an OpenAPI document from your code

Multiple reasons exist for wanting to generate an OpenAPI document from the code. One of them is that you prefer not to have automatically generated code that you don't have complete control of, or maybe you already have your API code and want to document it.

Generating code from an OpenAPI document is way more common, and multiple tools allow you to do that in Go, but generating an OpenAPI document from Go is not yet mature. There are options to generate older versions of OpenAPI (OpenAPI 2.0, also known as Swagger), such as swaggo or go-swagger. So, in this case, we will explore swaggo to generate OpenAPI 2.0, and then we will use a tool to convert OpenAPI 2.0 to OpenAPI 3.0.

All these tools are based on the use of "annotated code," meaning that you will add a set of defined comments to your code, and then the tool will read those comments and generate an OpenAPI document from them. I think an example would be more explicit:

```
...
// @title Hello World API
// @description An API that returns "Hello, World!"
// @version 0.1
func main() {
  http.HandleFunc("/", Handler)
  http.ListenAndServe(":8080", nil)
}

// @Summary Get a greeting
// @Description Returns a greeting message
// @Success 200 {string} string "Hello, World!"
// @Route / [get]
func Handler(w http.ResponseWriter, r *http.Request) {
  fmt.Fprintf(w, "Hello, World!")
}
...
```

This example here shows some basic annotations before the `main` function and my API handler. We can see things such as the title and the description of the API on the `main` function comments, as well as the return in case of the handler's success, and the path to which the handler will respond. Now, we need to install the swag tool from `swaggo`, which we will use to generate an OpenAPI document. We can do it with this command:

```
$ go install github.com/swaggo/swag/cmd/swag@latest
```

Now that we have the swag tool installed, we can run it to generate an OpenAPI document using the following command:

```
$ swag init
```

This command will generate a `docs` folder containing the OpenAPI document in JSON and YAML format, as well as a go package that we can use to access the OpenAPI documentation programmatically.

The resulting generated YAML OpenAPI document would be the following:

```
info:
  contact: {}
  description: An API that returns "Hello, World!"
  title: Hello World API
  version: "0.1"
paths:
  /:
    get:
      description: Returns a greeting message
      responses:
        "200":
          description: Hello, World!
          schema:
            type: string
      summary: Get a greeting
swagger: "2.0"
```

As you can see, this document is `swagger: "2.0"`, and the rest of the data is correctly generated from source code annotations. So, we next need to use a tool to convert the OpenAPI 2.0 document into an OpenAPI 3.0 document. For that, we can use a tool called `swagger2openapi`, which is a command-line tool that allows us to convert OpenAPI 2.0 documents into OpenAPI 3.0 documents. So, let's use it. I will use `npx` for that. So, the command would be the following:

```
$ npx -p swagger2openapi swagger2openapi --yaml --outfile docs/openapi.
yaml docs/swagger.yaml
```

The `swagger2openapi` tool will read the original OpenAPI 2.0 document in `docs/swagger.yaml` and generate an OpenAPI 3.0 document in `docs/openapi.yaml`. The resulting OpenAPI 3.0 document would look like this:

```
openapi: 3.0.0
info:
  contact: {}
  description: An API that returns "Hello, World!"
  title: Hello World API
  version: "0.1"
paths:
  /:
```

```
    get:
      description: Returns a greeting message
      responses:
        "200":
          description: Hello, World!
          content:
            "*/*":
              schema:
                type: string
    summary: Get a greeting
```

As you can see, it is now a valid and properly formatted OpenAPI 3.0 document.

With this, we have different ways of generating our OpenAPI document and code: editing the code and the OpenAPI document ourselves, or building only one and generating the other. All the options are valid; you can choose the one that best suits your needs and your preferred workflow.

Now that we have a good definition of our API using OpenAPI, what can we do with it? The first and most obvious answer is to generate good documentation for our API that we can expose out there, so let's explore that.

Publishing your API documentation

OpenAPI contains a lot of very valuable information about your API for very different usages. Of course, the main one is documentation, and we will explore it, but there are other usages, such as client code generation or API testing, which we will explore here. But let's start with documentation.

Using OpenAPI for documentation

There are multiple ways to publish your OpenAPI documentation, but one of the simplest ones is to generate a static HTML page that contains the OpenAPI documentation. Various tools can help you with that, such as Swagger UI, ReDoc, or others. These tools allow you to generate a static HTML page that contains the OpenAPI documentation in a human-friendly format.

Let's see an example running Redoc with npx, like this:

```
$ npx @redocly/cli build-docs docs/openapi.yaml
```

Redoc has generated a static HTML page in the redoc-static.html file. You can open this file in your browser and see the OpenAPI documentation, which looks like this for our case:

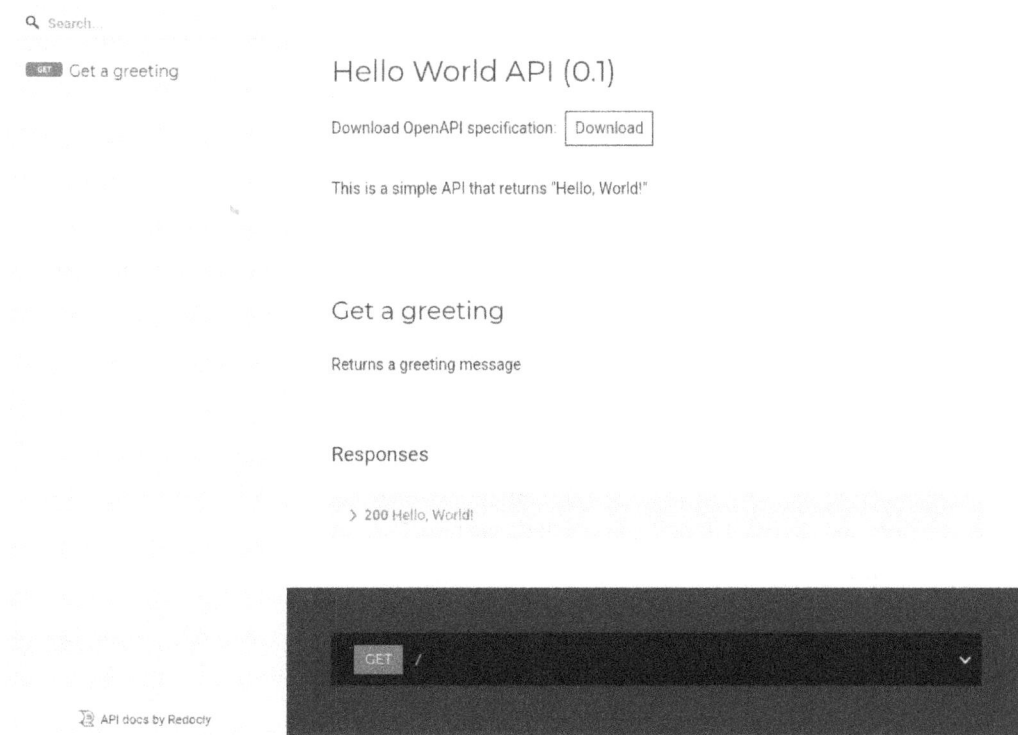

Figure 11.1 – Redoc-generated documentation

As you can see, you now have usable API documentation to share with your users. This redoc-static.html file can be published anywhere because it is just a static HTML file.

But sometimes, you don't want to worry about hosting the documentation and prefer that others do that. For that, OpenAPI is still great. You can use services such as SwaggerHub, ReadMe.io, Postman, and so on. These services allow you to import your OpenAPI document and generate and host documentation for you, and usually much more. Let's talk about another use case: API testing.

API testing

The first kind of testing you will want for your API is to allow the developers to test the API endpoints and check how they behave. As we saw in *Chapter 2*, Postman can be a great tool for this. The good news is that Postman and similar tools, such as SwaggerHub, support OpenAPI, so you can import your OpenAPI document directly into those services. With that, you are ready to start manual testing of the API.

Tools such as Postman and SwaggerHub also provide tooling for generating integration tests for your API. This way, you can interact manually with your API comfortably and rest assured that your API is not breaking because some changes were not correctly reflected in the OpenAPI document. Automated testing is great for keeping your API documentation up to date and honoring the actual implementation of the API.

However, we also mentioned another exciting case: client code generation. So, let's talk about it.

Client code generation

We have explored the server-side code of the API being automatically generated from the OpenAPI document, but that is only half of the story. The other half is the client. You need to have clients to connect to your API, but... You don't know your API user's preferred language, right? Maybe it is Go, but perhaps it is Python, JavaScript, Haskell, or any other. One of the more interesting things that OpenAPI provides is the ability to generate client code for OpenAPI in almost any language.

The de facto standard for code generation is OpenAPI Generator, a project that allows you to generate client code in many languages. So, let's see how I can use it to generate a client for our OpenAPI document by running the following command:

```
$ npx @openapitools/openapi-generator-cli generate -i docs/openapi.yaml -g
go -o client
```

This command will generate a Go client for our OpenAPI document in the client folder, including all the code needed and documentation about how to use it. For example, we could use it like this:

```
...
configuration := client.NewConfiguration()
apiClient := client.NewAPIClient(configuration)
resp, r, err := apiClient.DefaultAPI.RootGet(
  context.Background()).Execute()
if err != nil {
  panic(err)
}
fmt.Printf("Response from the API: %v\n", resp)
...
```

As you can see here, it is a very easy-to-use Go client for our API, but we talked about other languages, right? Let's generate a different client, this time for Python:

```
$ npx @openapitools/openapi-generator-cli generate -i docs/openapi.yaml -g
python -o pythonclient
```

We just changed the language to Python and the output directory to pythonclient, and now we have a Python client for our API that we can start using. Here is an example of the code to use it:

```
cfg = client.Configuration(host="http://localhost")
with client.ApiClient(cfg) as api_client:
  api_instance = client.DefaultApi(api_client)
  api_response = api_instance.root_get()
  print("Response from the API: %s\n" % api_response)
```

With this, we can use Python to access our API without worrying about implementing the client code ourselves.

At this point, I think you are already convinced of the huge benefits of properly documenting your API with OpenAPI, so let's jump into our practical example and apply this to our existing API code.

Adding OpenAPI documentation to your API

Because we already have most of our API defined, I think the right approach here is to generate an OpenAPI document for our code, so let's do that.

We will incorporate the swaggo library annotations into our previous code, and then we will generate an OpenAPI document from it. So, let's start with general details of the API. For that, we will add annotations to our main package with all the important information about the API, such as the title, the version, the description, and so on. So, let's see what it looks like:

```
// @title Shopping List API
// @version 0.1
// @description An API for managing shopping lists
// @host my-shopping-lists.com/api
// @BasePath /

// @securityDefinitions.apikey BearerAuth
// @in header
// @name Authorization
// @description Type "Bearer" followed by a space and the JWT token
package main
```

At this point, I'm already providing a lot of information about the API, including more general metadata such as the title and the description, and important security details such as the authentication method.

If we use swaggo to generate an OpenAPI document with the swag init command, we are going to get a document that looks like this:

```
basePath: /
host: my-shopping-lists.com/api
info:
  contact: {}
  description: An API for managing shopping lists
  title: Shopping List API
  version: "0.1"
paths: {}
securityDefinitions:
  BearerAuth:
    description: Type "Bearer" followed by a space and the JWT token
    in: header
    name: Authorization
    type: apiKey
swagger: "2.0"
```

We can see all the information we put in the annotations there, but this is far from enough. We need to annotate the endpoints and the data we are exposing, so let's start annotating a type; for example, the ShoppingList type. For that, we can use struct tags. Here is an example:

```
// ShoppingList represents a shopping list with items
// @Description Shopping list with items
type ShopingList struct {
  ID string `json:"id" example:"123e4567-e89b-12d3-a456-426614174000"`
  Name string `json:"name" example:"Grocery List"`
  Items []string `json:"items" example:"milk,eggs,bread"`
}
```

With this, we have information about the struct exposed. Still, no endpoint has been annotated for using it, so if we generate an OpenAPI document now, we will not see any of this information. So, let's add an endpoint that uses this struct, such as the ListLists endpoint. For that, we can use the following annotations:

```
// handleListLists get all the shopping lists
// @Summary List all shopping lists
// @Description Get all shopping lists for the authenticated user
```

```
// @Tags lists
// @Accept json
// @Produce json
// @Security BearerAuth
// @Success 200 {array} ShoppingList
// @Failure 401 {string} string "Unauthorized"
// @Router /lists [get]
func handleListLists(w http.ResponseWriter, r *http.Request) {
   ...
}
```

Now, we have an endpoint that is exposed, and it uses the struct that we defined before. If we generate an OpenAPI document, we will see two blocks of YAML, one for the struct and one for the endpoint. Let's start by seeing the one for the struct:

```
...
definitions:
  main.ShoppingList:
    description: Shopping list with items
    properties:
      id:
        example: 123e4567-e89b-12d3-a456-426614174000
        type: string
      items:
        example:
        - milk
        - eggs
        - bread
        items:
          type: string
        type: array
      name:
        example: Grocery List
        type: string
    type: object
...
```

As we can see in the YAML here, it defines a struct with all the data that we annotated, including the description and the example values. Now, let's see the endpoint definition:

```yaml
  ...
paths:
  /lists:
    get:
      consumes:
      - application/json
      description: Get all shopping lists for the authenticated user
      produces:
      - application/json
      responses:
        "200":
          description: OK
          schema:
            items:
              $ref: '#/definitions/main.ShoppingList'
            type: array
        "401":
          description: Unauthorized
          schema:
            type: string
      security:
      - BearerAuth: []
      summary: List all shopping lists
      tags:
      - lists
  ...
```

Again, the endpoint definition is generated based on the annotations, and we can see how ShoppingList references the struct we defined before. As you can see, everything gets appropriately associated and organized in the OpenAPI document. We only need to keep adding structs and endpoint annotations to the code, and swaggo will keep our API correctly documented.

Once we finish annotating our endpoints and the structs, we will be ready to build and share our API documentation. In this case, I will use Redoc to generate a static HTML page, but you can use any of the tools we have discussed, including services such as SwaggerHub or Postman.

Redoc supports OpenAPI 2.0 and 3.0, so we can use it to generate documentation for our API with the swaggo-generated YAML, but for completeness, I will include the step converting it from 2.0 to 3.0. So, now that we have our whole API documented with OpenAPI 2.0 and we have run our swag init command to get files generated, we can run swagger2openapi with the following command:

```
$ npx -p swagger2openapi swagger2openapi --yaml --outfile docs/openapi.
yaml docs/swagger.yaml
```

The output file, openapi.yaml, is now in OpenAPI 3.0 format, and we can use Redoc to generate a static HTML page. For that, we can run the following command:

```
$ npx @redocly/cli build-docs docs/openapi.yaml
```

This command generates our static HTML page in the redoc-static.html file. Now, you can open it and see the complete documentation of our API with all the endpoints that you have annotated.

Summary

In this chapter, we explored how to document APIs using OAS. We saw how, using OpenAPI, we can provide accurate and extensive documentation of our REST API, making it easier to understand, test, and consume. We looked at the structure of OpenAPI documents and the different building blocks that compose them, such as components, paths, and general API information.

We also explored some tools in the ecosystem that allow us to build our OpenAPI document from the code or our code from the OpenAPI document, including the server and client sides.

Finally, we explored how to add OpenAPI documentation to our shopping list API by annotating our existing Go code and using the swaggo tool.

Good documentation is a critical part of a successful REST API. OpenAPI is the industry standard for that, so we have an excellent new tool to include in our REST API development process.

Now that we have helped API users by providing detailed documentation, let's jump into our next chapter and help the developers of the API, providing them with observability over the API and allowing them to get insightful information through metrics, logs, and traces.

Unlock this book's exclusive benefits now

Scan this QR code or go to packtpub.
com/unlock, then search this book by
name.

Note: Keep your purchase invoice ready
before you start.

12

Metrics, Logs, and Traces

A good understanding of what is going on in your system is the foundation of performance, security, and reliability. Helping to build that understanding is where observability and instrumentation come into play. This chapter will explore the three pillars of software observability: logs, metrics, and traces. Each of them provides a different perspective on the system's behavior. The logs are a registry of relevant things that have happened in the system. Monitoring is more about the big picture of what is going on in your system. Traces are a way to get fine-grained details about your system behavior, as profound as the level of function executions. The observability of your system is key to any production environment to allow you to detect, understand, and fix any problem, such as performance bottlenecks, system instability, or even security hazards.

In this chapter, we are going to explore the following:

- Why do we need logs, metrics, and traces?
- Logging the relevant information of our API
- Using metrics to understand the state and evolution of our system
- Including tracing to analyze bottlenecks or memory consumption properly
- Using OpenTelemetry for doing it in distributed environments

But let's start by talking about the why of all this.

Why do we need logs, metrics, and traces?

In modern software systems, particularly those running in distributed environments, understanding what's happening can be challenging. The bigger the project and the more distributed it is, the harder it is to understand what is happening in the system.

Traditionally, software developers have relied on logs to understand the application's state. Logs are a great tool; we will keep using them, but sometimes we need other information. Sometimes, we need a general overview of how the system evolves. For example, is memory consumption growing over time? Is the number of goroutines stable? Is the average response time ramping up? Where is the time spent when we call a specific endpoint?

There are a lot of questions that logs can't respond to, or at least not in a simple way. To answer those questions, we need tools such as metrics and traces.

We are going to explore logs, metrics, and traces in detail during the following sections, but let's summarize the differences between them:

- **Logs** give you detailed records of what happened in your application when it happened
- **Metrics** provide aggregated values over time, allowing you to understand trends and the global state of your system
- **Traces** show you the path of a specific request and the fine-grained detail of what has happened to this particular request

These tools allow you to monitor, troubleshoot, and optimize your application effectively without guessing.

Now that we understand what they are and why we need them, let's get into the details, starting with logs.

Logs

Logs are chronological records of events that happen throughout your application. For REST APIs, they can provide you with information about serving what API endpoints have been called, authentication attempts, errors that have occurred because the system is misbehaving or the user is giving wrong data, or events that you want to track to better understand what your system is doing.

But how does it work in Go? Go provides a built-in logging package in the standard library, but many third-party libraries offer more advanced features. This section will explore the standard library and some popular third-party libraries for logging in Go. So, let's start with a simple example using the standard library:

```
...
func myHandler(w http.ResponseWriter, r *http.Request) {
  log.Printf("Received request: %s %s from %s", r.Method, r.URL.Path,
          r.RemoteAddr)
...
```

♀ **Quick tip:** Enhance your coding experience with the **AI Code Explainer** and **Quick Copy** features. Open this book in the next-gen Packt Reader. Click the **Copy** button (**1**) to quickly copy code into your coding environment, or click the **Explain** button (**2**) to get the AI assistant to explain a block of code to you.

```
                                                        Copy      Explain
function calculate(a, b) {                               1          2
  return {sum: a + b};
};
```

📖 **The next-gen Packt Reader** is included for free with the purchase of this book. Scan the QR code OR go to packtpub.com/unlock, then use the search bar to find this book by name. Double-check the edition shown to make sure you get the right one.

In this example, we can see the most straightforward approach to this. Every time the handler is called, we log the request information. Because we are using the log.Printf function from the log package directly, we use the default logger, which writes to the standard output. But we can make it a bit more complex. Let's see:

```
...
var errorLogger *log.Logger

func init() {
    file, _ := os.OpenFile("error.log", os.O_APPEND|os.O_CREATE|os.O_WRONLY,
                           0666)
    errorLogger = log.New(file, "ERROR: ",
                          log.Ldate|log.Ltime|log.Lshortfile)
}

func myHandler(w http.ResponseWriter, r *http.Request) {
```

```
errorLogger.Printf("Received request: %s %s from %s", r.Method,
                   r.URL.Path, r.RemoteAddr)
...
```

In this case, we use a custom logger that writes to a file called error.log. Also, when we define the logger, we're passing the "ERROR: " prefix, which means all the messages passed to that logger will be prefixed with that. This kind of pattern is beneficial to have deep control over how and where we generate our logs. Also, it is worth mentioning that the log.Ldate|log.Ltime|log.Lshortfile flags add the date, time, and filename to the log message.

The log package allows us to write the logs, but the whole point of the logs is about reading them. Something to consider here is that we are not the only ones reading the logs. Actually, in big systems, we rarely read the logs directly. We use tools to read and analyze them. The problem is that we are putting out simple text that interpolates key information. That is not easy for machines to read. That's why we need to talk about a specific way of logging: structured logging.

Structured logging

Plain text is excellent for humans and can get you very far in the process, but as soon as your logs are big enough, you cannot scan through them quickly. Then, you need to start thinking of tools to assist you. For that, you need to make your logs readable for machines. This is where structured logging comes in. Structured logging organizes log data into a format (typically JSON) that is machine-readable, which allows tools such as Elasticsearch to index your log, and you can search and filter the information in the logs.

In Go, multiple libraries provide structured logging, but let's first explore the one from the standard library: the log/slog package. Let's see an example of how it works:

```go
...
var logger *slog.Logger

func init() {
    logger = slog.New(slog.NewJSONHandler(os.Stdout, &slog.HandlerOptions{
        Level: slog.LevelDebug,
    }))
}

func myHandler(w http.ResponseWriter, r *http.Request) {
    logger.Debug("Received request",
        slog.String("method", r.Method),
```

```
      slog.String("path", r.URL.Path),
      slog.String("remote", r.RemoteAddr),
   )
)
...
```

Here, we now have way more structure in the logs. We are not building a string. We are expressing what data and information we are logging, so the output is not just a string. Our output is a well-defined JSON object that a machine can read and understand. The output of this code would look like this:

```
{
   "time": "2025-04-13T15:00:05Z",
   "level": "DEBUG",
   "msg": "Received request",
   "method": "GET",
   "path": "/",
   "remote": "127.0.0.1:52903"
}
```

As mentioned, the standard library is great and provides a lot of functionalities, but it is not the only option. You can use many other libraries for logging, so let's look at the two most popular ones: logrus and zap.

The previous examples using logrus would look like this:

```
...
var logger = logrus.New()

func init() {
  logger.SetFormatter(&logrus.JSONFormatter{})
  logger.SetLevel(logrus.DebugLevel)
}

func myHandler(w http.ResponseWriter, r *http.Request) {
  logger.WithFields(logrus.Fields{
    "method": r.Method,
    "path": r.URL.Path,
    "remote": r.RemoteAddr,
```

```
    }).Debug("Received request")
  )
  ...
```

As you can see, the API is very different, but the concepts are the same. So, let's see what it looks like with zap:

```
...
var logger *zap.Logger

func init() {
  var err error
  logger, err = zap.NewProduction()
  if err != nil {
    panic(err)
  }
}

func myHandler(w http.ResponseWriter, r *http.Request) {
  logger.Debug("Received request",
    zap.String("method", r.Method),
    zap.String("path", r.URL.Path),
    zap.String("remote", r.RemoteAddr),
  )
)
...
```

In this case, zap has a way more similar API to the standard library, but again, this will generate a JSON object that machines will be able to read.

So, when selecting a logging library, you should consider multiple things, such as the ergonomics of the library, the performance, the features you need, and the burden of adding a new dependency to your project. Depending on all that, you can go with zap, logrus, zerolog, slog, or any other that fits your needs.

Now that you know what it looks like to log in Go, let me show you something interesting: **Open-Telemetry** (also known as **OTel**) for logging.

OTel logging

OTel provides a standardized approach to observability (including logging) across different services and languages. More importantly, it not only gives you logs, metrics, and trace libraries, but it also makes all of them correlate together so you can understand the relationship between, for example, a log entry and a trace. But let's see how it differs from our current logging.

Here's an example of using OTel for API logging in Go:

```go
...
func init() {
  exporter, err := stdoutlog.New(stdoutlog.WithPrettyPrint())
  if err != nil {
    panic(err)
  }
  provider := sdklog.NewLoggerProvider(sdklog.WithBatcher(exporter))
  global.SetLoggerProvider(provider)
}

func myHandler(w http.ResponseWriter, r *http.Request) {
  logger := global.Logger("my-api")
  logger.Emit(context.Background(), log.Record{
    Severity: log.SeverityDebug,
    Body: "Received request",
    Attributes: []log.KeyValue{
      log.String("method", r.Method),
      log.String("path", r.URL.Path),
      log.String("remote", r.RemoteAddr),
    },
  })
}
...
```

As you can see, the API is a bit different, but the concepts are the same. We initialize the logger, in this case, using the standard output, and create a log provider based on that. Then, we register that provider as the global log provider. Finally, whenever we want to use the logger, we ask for the logger and use it.

OTel shines in distributed systems, where you want to correlate logs, metrics, and traces from different services and associate all the information together. For example, if you have a request that requires access to three microservices to provide the final response, with OTel, you can associate a `request_id` with all the logs. Then, you can access all the logs related to that `request_id` associated with all the microservices, giving you understandable logs across all your microservices.

If you are building distributed systems, OTel is an excellent option for logging.

I think that is enough about logging. Now, we are going to jump into another interesting topic: metrics.

Metrics

As we said before, metrics are about the big picture of our system. When you do monitoring, you want to keep track of things in absolute numbers or averages over time. For example, is your CPU consumption at a sane level over time? How much time is it taking your API endpoints to reply on average? How well or not are you leveraging the cache?

There are multiple tools and services that you can use to add metrics to your application, but the most popular one is **Prometheus**. Prometheus is a robust, open source monitoring and alerting toolkit widely used for collecting metrics. So, whenever you want to add metrics to your application, it is probably one of the first names you will find.

Before adding metrics to your application, you need to understand the kind of data that you are collecting and the format it will be in. There are three main formats—counters, gauges, and histograms:

- A counter is a number that only goes up and represents a total value, such as the number of requests your API has received
- A gauge is a number that can go up and down and represents a value at a specific time, such as the number of goroutines running in your API
- A histogram is a set of values representing the distribution of a value, such as the time your API takes to reply to a request

With these three types of values (and variations of them), we can build a whole set of metrics for our API, but what kind of metrics should we track? It always depends on our specific case, but some of the most common are as follows:

- API response times (per endpoint)
- CPU usage
- Memory usage

- Network bandwidth
- Cache hit ratio
- Number of goroutines

Another critical concept to understand is the concept of **labels**. Labels are key-value pairs you can attach to your metrics to provide additional context. For example, you can add labels to your API response time metrics to indicate the endpoint, HTTP method, and status code. This allows you to filter and group your metrics more meaningfully. Understanding how labels work is crucial for effectively using Prometheus because the abuse of labels can lead to inefficiencies. Let me explain why with an example.

Imagine that you have a counter that counts the number of hits to your endpoints. Over time, it would look like this:

```
...
endpoint_hits 100
...
```

That means that your endpoints have been hit 100 times, but it doesn't tell you which endpoint has been hit. You can add an endpoint label to your metric, so now, it would look like this:

```
...
endpoint_hits{endpoint="/api/users"} 23
endpoint_hits{endpoint="/api/teams"} 72
endpoint_hits{endpoint="/api/login"} 5
...
```

In this case, what is happening now is that we're seeing one metric for each endpoint. If we have three, that is not a big deal. If we have 100 endpoints, that means we're tracking 100 metrics, but you know what? It doesn't stop there because now, we don't know whether the endpoint is being hit with a GET, POST, DELETE, or any other method, so we need to add another label to our metric. Now, it would look like this:

```
...
endpoint_hits{endpoint="/api/users", method="GET"} 21
endpoint_hits{endpoint="/api/users", method="POST"} 2
endpoint_hits{endpoint="/api/teams", method="GET"} 65
endpoint_hits{endpoint="/api/teams", method="POST"} 7
endpoint_hits{endpoint="/api/login", method="POST"} 5
...
```

Now it is getting bigger, and depending on the number of endpoints and methods, it is growing again. Having a few thousand metrics is not necessarily a problem, but what would happen if we wanted to add a label for the `request-id`? That would lead to one metric per request, which probably would quickly lead to millions of different metrics, generating a problem in our metrics system.

Now that we understand what metrics and labels are, let's see a code example of Prometheus working in Go:

```go
...
var myHandlerRequests = prometheus.NewCounterVec(
  prometheus.CounterOpts{
    Name: "my_handler_requests_total",
    Help: "Total number of requests to my handler",
  },
  []string{"method", "status"},
)

func init() {
  prometheus.MustRegister(myHandlerRequests)
}

func myHandler(w http.ResponseWriter, r *http.Request) {
  ...
  myHandlerRequests.WithLabelValues(r.Method, "200").Inc()
}
...
```

This allows us to define the metric, including the different labels to use, register it with Prometheus, and then use it in our handler. As you can see here, you can track the metric of how many times this handler has been called and know the method and the status code that it returned.

Still, something is missing. Whenever you use Prometheus, you need to expose the metrics of your application, because the Prometheus server will scrape the metrics from your application from time to time. For that, you need to add the following code to your application:

```go
...
http.Handle("/metrics", promhttp.Handler())
...
```

Wherever you expose your API, you can expose your metrics using the `promhttp.Handler`. If you go to that `/metrics` endpoint, you will see your metrics in the text format that Prometheus expects. It would look something like this:

```
my_handler_requests_total{method="GET", status="200"} 23
```

Another useful thing about the Prometheus library is a set of metrics collectors that allow you to collect metrics from the Go runtime, getting you information such as the number of goroutines, memory usage, CPU usage, and so on. You can use it like this:

```
prometheus.MustRegister(collectors.NewGoCollector())
```

With this simple line, we get a lot of metrics from the Go runtime.

If you are already using OTel because it works better for your use case, you can use the OTel library instead of the Prometheus one. Still, it is common to use OTel to expose Prometheus metrics. Let's see an example of that:

```
...
var myHandlerRequests metric.Int64Counter

func init() {
  prometheus.MustRegister(myHandlerRequests)
  exporter, err := prometheus.New(prometheus.WithoutUnits())
  if err != nil {
    panic(err)
  }
  provider := metric.NewMeterProvider(metric.WithReader(exporter))
  otel.SetMeterProvider(provider)

  meter := otel.Meter("myHandler")
  requestCounter, err = meter.Int64Counter(
    "my_handler_requests_total",
    metric.WithDescription("Total number of requests to my handler"),
  )
  if err != nil {
    panic(err)
  }
}
```

```
func myHandler(w http.ResponseWriter, r *http.Request) {
  ...
  myHandlerRequests.Add(context.Background(), 1,
    attribute.String("method", r.Method),
    attribute.String("status", "200"),
  )
  ...
}
```

As you can see from the example, the code is slightly more complex for the initialization process, but the idea is the same: tracking the metrics and exposing them to Prometheus.

For now, we have shown how we publish metrics in our system, but how do we collect and visualize them? Let's talk about that.

Visualizing the metrics

Before the visualization part, we must understand that a Prometheus server will collect our metrics. The Prometheus server will access the /metrics endpoint that our application exposes and store that information in a specialized (time series) database. Still, we are not visualizing any data. We are storing it. We can query the data using a language named **PromQL** and get the information out that way. But still, not visualizing, right? For visualization, we need to talk about the most common tool used to visualize Prometheus data: Grafana.

Grafana allows us to create dashboards and visualize the data in a more user-friendly way. It allows us to create graphs, tables, and other visualizations that can help us understand the data better. But a picture is worth a thousand words, so let me show you an example of a Grafana dashboard:

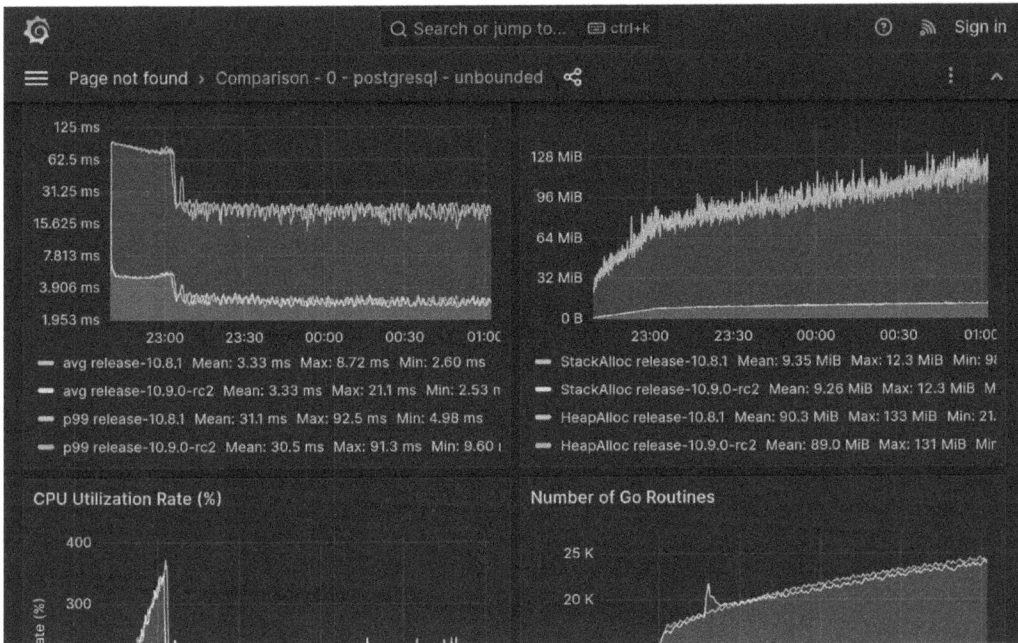

Figure 12.1 – Grafana

🔍 **Quick tip:** Need to see a high-resolution version of this image? Open this book in the next-gen Packt Reader or view it in the PDF/ePub copy.

🔖 **The next-gen Packt Reader** and a **free PDF/ePub copy** of this book are included with your purchase. Scan the QR code OR visit packtpub.com/unlock, then use the search bar to find this book by name. Double-check the edition shown to make sure you get the right one.

As you can see in *Figure 12.1*, we can have a lot of metrics and see how they evolve.

Now that we know how to monitor our API and have a global overview of the health of our system, let's see how we can get into the details by tracing.

Traces

While logs provide a detailed record of events and metrics offer aggregated numbers about system performance, traces give you insights into the execution path of requests through your system. This is particularly important for REST APIs, where a single client request might touch multiple internal services, databases, and external APIs. It becomes even more important in distributed systems such as microservices, where a single request can span various services.

Traces can allow you to identify performance bottlenecks, understand execution flows, and debug complex issues by providing a detailed view of what happened during the execution of a request.

The de facto standard for distributed tracing is OTel, which provides the APIs needed to instrument your code and generate the traces sent to the backend you like. The most common backends are **Jaeger**, **Zipkin**, and **Grafana Tempo**. However, you can also use other tools such as **Datadog** or **New Relic**.

But what exactly is a trace in OTel? A trace is a collection of spans, each representing a single operation within the trace—for example, calling a handler or executing a SQL query. Each span has a start time, an end time, and a set of attributes that provide additional context about the operation. For example, a span can have the name `GET /api/users` when you run the handler for that. Also, you can add attributes such as the status code or the query parameters.

Another essential concept of spans is that they have a parent-child relationship. That way, you can associate different operations together. For example, if the handler accesses the database, the database access can be a child span of the handler execution span. Therefore, you know the relationship between the different operations/spans that happen in your trace.

The other key concept is the **Trace ID**, a unique identifier for the trace, which is used to correlate all the spans that are part of the same trace.

I think this can be made more explicit with a graphical representation:

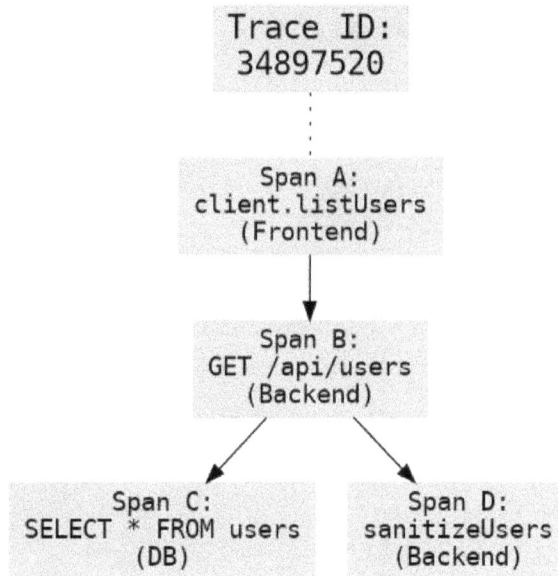

Figure 12.2 – Trace representation

This graph represents a trace that starts on the client side, the web application that connects to your API, and from there, calls the API. The API receives the information needed to keep adding spans to the trace. The first trace added is that you are calling the handler, and the handler also calls the database. After calling the database, the handler continues the execution and calls the sanitezeUser function (also traced). This is the kind of granularity that you can have with distributed tracing, giving you times, execution information, and metadata that you expose there.

This tool is powerful, but how can we incorporate it into our Go project? Let's see an example:

```
...
var tracer trace.Tracer

func init() {
  exporter, err := jaeger.New(jaeger.WithCollectorEndpoint(
    jaeger.WithEndpoint("http://localhost:14268/api/traces")
  ))
  if err != nil {
    panic(err)
  }
}
```

```
  tp := tracesdk.NewTracerProvider(
    tracesdk.WithBatcher(exporter)
  )

  otel.SetTracerProvider(tp)
  tracer = tp.Tracer("my-api-server")
}
...
```

With this, we initialize the tracer, and in this case, we set up a Jaeger server to store the traces. Now, we need to start using the tracer to send traces:

```
func myHandler(w http.ResponseWriter, r *http.Request) {
  ctx, span := tracer.Start(r.Context(), "myHandler")
  defer span.End()

  span.SetAttributes(
    attribute.String("http.method", r.Method),
    attribute.String("http.url", r.URL.String()),
  )
  users, err := getUsersFromDB(ctx)
  if err != nil {
    span.RecordError(err)
    span.SetStatus(codes.Error, err.Error())
    http.Error(w, "Failed to get users", http.StatusInternalServerError)
    return
  }
  ...
}
```

In this example, we create a span from the request context. Right after that, we defer the span. End() call to ensure this span is closed when the function finishes. After that, we add some attributes to the span and do what is needed. In case of an error, we also record the error information in the span. Now is the time to go deeper. We already have one span, but what about having a child span for the database access?

That can be very useful during debugging, so let's add it:

```go
...
func getUsersFromDB(ctx context.Context) ([]User, error) {
  ctx, span := tracer.Start(ctx, "getUsersFromDB")
  defer span.End()

  span.SetAttributes(
    attribute.String("db.system", "postgresql"),
    attribute.String("db.statement", "SELECT * FROM users"),
    attribute.Int("db.results.count", 2),
  )
  ...
}
```

In the previous example, we called the getUserFromDB, passing the context returned by the tracer. Start function, and now we use that context to create the new span. This generates a child span that we can start populating with the desired data. As in the previous example, we are deferring the span.End() to ensure it gets properly closed whenever the function ends.

With this simple pattern, we can generate complex traces including all kinds of information, and keep track of the relationships between the spans.

Now we can collect and store the traces in our Jaeger server, but we are missing the most crucial part, accessing those traces, so let's explore that together.

Visualizing traces

To make sense of traces, we need a way to visualize them. We have used Jaeger in our examples, so let's see what our traces look like in the Jaeger interface. For demo purposes, we're using the demo application provided by Jaeger, named **HotROD**, but the concepts are the same.

You can find the instructions to get this working in the Jaeger documentation: https://www.jaegertracing.io/docs/2.5/getting-started/

So, let's see what the traces look like in Jaeger.

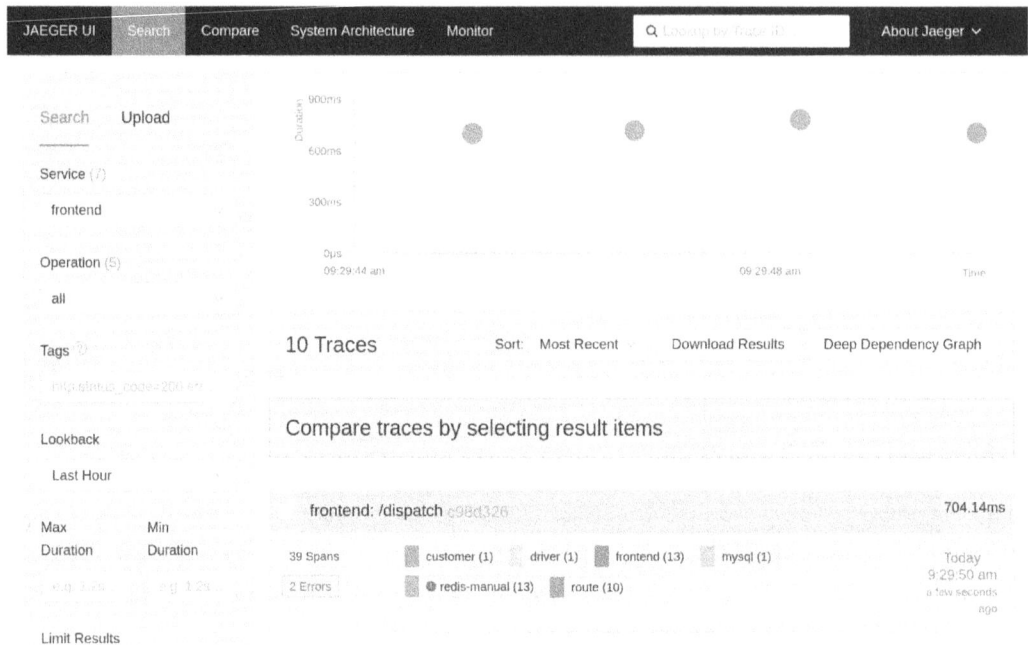

Figure 12.3 – The Jaeger list of traces

As we can see in *Figure 12.3*, we have a list of traces that interact with different components of the application. These include MySQL, the frontend, Redis, the customer, and so on. Also, we can see information such as the number of spans and errors in each trace and the time it takes to execute. But now, let's explore a bit more about the details of what a specific trace looks like (see *Figure 12.4*).

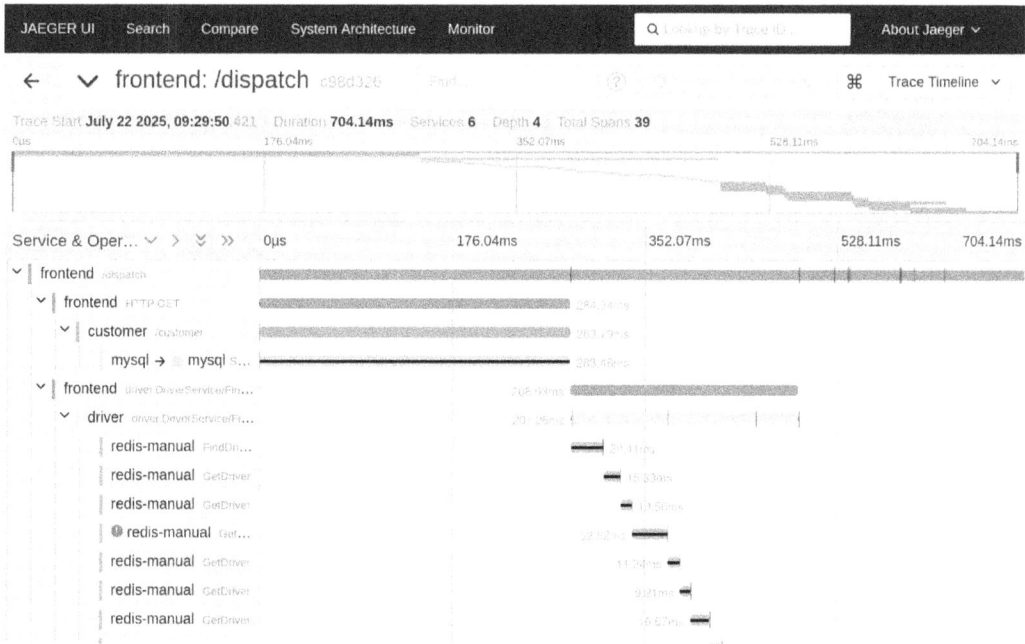

Figure 12.4 – Jaeger trace details

When you open a trace, you can see all the spans with the information of each span, such as the duration of the span and when it started compared to the other spans. You can even enter into the details of a span and see all the metadata associated with it, such as, in this case, the SQL query executed in the MySQL span.

All this information can lead to a better understanding of your system and the problems that happen in it, which makes bugs, bottlenecks, and performance issues easier to solve. So, now is the time to explore how to add all this observability to your project.

Adding observability to our project

For simplicity, we will use slog for logging, Prometheus for metrics, and OTel for tracing. This way, we will explore multiple approaches and add all the observability tools we have seen in this chapter. However, it is up to you to select the tools you consider the best option for your project; for example, you could use OTel for everything.

So, let's start adding some logging to our application.

Logging

One of the typical cases where we want to have logging is whenever there is an error, so let's add some logging to our handleCreateList function:

```
func handleCreateList(w http.ResponseWriter, r *http.Request) {
  var list ShoppingList
  defer r.Body.Close()
  err := json.NewDecoder(r.Body).Decode(&list)
  if err != nil {
    slog.Info("Invalid request body", slog.Any("error", err))
    http.Error(w, err.Error(), http.StatusBadRequest)
    return
  }
  newList, err := repository.AddShoppingList(&list)
  if err != nil {
    slog.Error("Failed to create new shopping list", slog.Any("error",
                                                            err))
    http.Error(w, err.Error(), http.StatusInternalServerError)
    return
  }
  w.WriteHeader(http.StatusCreated)
  json.NewEncoder(w).Encode(newList)
}
```

As you can see here, we can add logs and simply pass the message with the values we want to log. We can provide extra information for debugging, as per the following example:

```
func handleCreateList(w http.ResponseWriter, r *http.Request) {
  slog.Debug("Creating new shopping list",
    slog.String("ip", r.RemoteAddr),
    slog.String("user", r.Header.Get("X-User")),
```

```
      slog.String("request_id", r.Header.Get("X-Request-ID")),
  )
  ...
}
```

As you can see, we can pass handy information to the logs to figure out what is happening in our system, allowing us to determine the root cause of the problems.

Now that we have logging, let's jump into metrics.

Metrics

Let's see how we incorporate metrics into our project. We'll start by defining a metrics package. For that, we need to define our metrics and register them with Prometheus:

```
type Metrics struct {
  RequestCounter prometheus.CounterVec
  RequestDuration prometheus.HistogramVec
}

func NewMetrics() *Metrics {
  metrics := Metrics{}
  metrics.RequestCount = prometheus.NewCounterVec(
    prometheus.CounterOpts{
      Name: "http_requests_total",
      Help: "Total number of HTTP requests received",
    },
    []string{"method", "path"},
  )
  metrics.RequestDuration = prometheus.NewHistogramVec(
    prometheus.HistogramOpts{
      Name: "http_request_duration_seconds",
      Help: "Histogram of response durations",
      Buckets: prometheus.DefBuckets,
    },
    []string{"method", "path"},
  )
  prometheus.MustRegister(metrics.RequestCount)
  prometheus.MustRegister(metrics.RequestDuration)
}
```

As you can see, we are just defining the metrics for counting the number of requests and the duration of those requests, but we are adding some labels there to have a clear vision of the metrics per endpoint. Now, we have to initialize that in our `main` function:

```
var metricsService metrics.Metrics

func main() {
  metricsService = metrics.NewMetrics()
  ...
}
```

We've defined a global variable that holds the metrics and initialized it in the `main` function. Now, we need to add the metrics to our handlers, so let's see how we can do that in one of the handlers:

```
func handleCreateList(w http.ResponseWriter, r *http.Request) {
  start := time.Now()
  defer func() {
    duration := time.Since(start).Seconds()
    metricsService.RequestDuration.WithLabelValues(r.Method,
        r.URL.Path).Observe(duration)
    metricsService.RequestCount.WithLabelValues(r.Method,
                                    r.URL.Path).Inc()
  }()
  ...
}
```

Here, we calculate the time used to process the request and then use this to update the metrics. But this chunk of code is going to be repeated in all the handlers, so instead of doing this, let's create a middleware that does that for us:

```
func MetricsMiddleware(next http.Handler) http.Handler{
  return http.HandlerFunc(func(w http.ResponseWriter, r  *http.Request) {
    start := time.Now()
    next.ServeHTTP(w, r)
    duration := time.Since(start).Seconds()
    metricsService.RequestDuration.WithLabelValues(r.Method,
        r.URL.Path).Observe(duration)
    metricsService.RequestCount.WithLabelValues(r.Method,
        r.URL.Path).Inc()
  }
}
```

In this middleware, we are applying the same approach to the handler, but this time, we can apply it to all our handlers without repeating ourselves over and over again. Now we only need to wrap each of our handlers with the middleware, and it will have metrics, as per the following example:

```
http.HandleFunc("POST /lists",
    MetricsMiddlware(adminRequired(handleCreateList)))
```

With this, we can now put metrics in any endpoint, or, if we want to add another metric somewhere to measure something specific, we can do it directly in the handler or any other part of the code. However, we have not yet gotten the data from Prometheus. We need to expose the / metrics endpoint, so let's add that to our main function:

```
func main() {
  ...
  http.Handle("/metrics", promhttp.Handler())
  ...
}
```

With this, we've finished the implementation of the metrics in our project. Now, it's time for traces.

Traces

As we said before, we will use OTel for traces, so let's start generating a tracer package that helps us generate the traces. We need to define a tracer and initialize it with the backend we want to use. In this case, we will use Jaeger, but you can use any other backend you like. So, let's see how we can do that:

```
func InitTracer(serviceName string) (io.Closer, error) {
  cfg := &config.Configuration{
    ServiceName: serviceName,
    Sampler: &config.SamplerConfig{
      Type: "const",
      Param: 1,
    },
    Reporter: &config.ReporterConfig{
      LogSpans: true,
      LocalAgentHostPort: "127.0.0.1:6831"
    },
  }
```

```
  tracer, closer, err := cfg.NewTracer(config.Logger(jaeger.StdLogger))
  if err != nil {
    return nil, err
  }


  opentracing.SetGlobalTracer(tracer)
  return closer, nil
}
```

This code connects to the Jaeger server and sets the **OpenTracing** global tracer to use it. With that, we only need to run this function and add traces. Let's initialize the tracer in the main function:

```
func main() {
  ...
  closer, err := tracer.InitTracer("my-api")
  if err != nil {
    log.Fatalf("Could not initialize the tracer: %v", err)
  }
  defer closer.Close()
  ...
}
```

Easy, right? We initialize the tracer, and whenever the program finishes, we close it. Now, we need to add the tracing to our handlers, so let's see how we can do that with an example:

```
func handleCreateList(w http.ResponseWriter, r *http.Request) {
  ...
  parentSpan := opentracing.GlobalTracer().StartSpan("handleCreateList")
  defer parentSpan.Finish()
  ext.HTTPMethod.Set(parentSpan, r.Method)
  ext.HTTPUrl.Set(parentSpan, r.URL.Path)

  newList, err := repository.AddShoppingList(parentSpan, &list)
  if err != nil {
    http.Error(w, err.Error(), http.StatusInternalServerError)
    return
  }
  ...
}
```

In this case, we are using the global tracer to create a new span, then adding relevant data to that span. In this case, we're using the github.com/opentracing/opentracing-go/ext package that declares a lot of common spans, such as http.method and http.url, which are the ones that we are using here. Also, after populating our span, we passed it to the repository function, allowing us to create a child span inside the repository function so the trace can have multiple spans. Let's see what it would look like in the AddShoppingList repository method:

```
func (r *Repository) AddShoppingList(parentSpan opentracing.Span,
    newList *ShoppingList) (*ShoppingList, error) {
    span := opentracing.StartSpan("AddShoppingList",
              opentracing.ChildOf(parentSpan.Context()))
    defer span.Finish()
    span.LogKV("my-custom-data", "relevant data in the trace")
    ...
}
```

As you can see, we are creating a child span for the repository method, and in this case, we're also logging some custom data that we want in the trace—which is nothing extraordinary, only requests made to the OpenTracing library.

With that, we have finished talking about observability in the book itself, but if you want to explore more, I invite you to check out *Chapter 13* to learn about the Gorm Go ORM and *Chapter 14* to learn about the Echo framework. We will explore both and how to incorporate them into our API project.

Summary

In this chapter, we explored what observability involves in Go and how to leverage the existing libraries and tools to provide logs, metrics, and traces. We explored the different kinds of logs (regular logs and structured logs) and the libraries we can use for them. We explored the importance of metrics, how to incorporate them into our projects, and the different kinds of interesting metrics. Finally, we analyzed the traces in systems such as OTel and how we can leverage them to better understand our system's behavior and performance.

Observability is a key part of any modern production-ready API. I encourage you to try including it as early in the process as possible to ensure your system is ready whenever problems start.

With this, we we'll explore the next chapter on GORM, an Object Relational Mapper (ORM) for Go that provides a more abstract and object-oriented approach to database interactions.

Unlock this book's exclusive benefits now

Scan this QR code or go to packtpub.
com/unlock, then search this book by
name.

Note: Keep your purchase invoice ready
before you start.

13

Using GORM

In the previous chapters, we explored how to interact with databases using Go's standard database/sql package and how to enhance our experience with SQL query builders such as SQuirrel. Both approaches give us great control over the SQL queries we execute, but they require us to handle the conversion between Go structures and database data manually. In this chapter, we'll explore **Go Object Relational Mapper (GORM)**, an **object-relational mapper (ORM)** for Go that offers a more abstract, object-oriented alternative for working with databases.

Throughout this chapter, we'll learn about the following:

- What an GORM is and why you might want to use one
- How to set up GORM for your project
- How to define models in GORM
- How to perform **Create, Retrieve, Update, Delete (CRUD)** operations with GORM
- Working with relationships
- How to migrate our shopping list API to use GORM

Technical requirements

All the code examples for this chapter are included in this book's GitHub repository: https://github.com/PacktPublishing/Modern-REST-API-Development-in-Go. You only need the Go compiler installed on your system to compile and execute the code.

What is GORM?

GORM is a popular ORM library for Go. It provides an abstraction over the database, removing the need to write or understand SQL to store and retrieve data from the database. Instead of running queries, we use regular Go structs and methods on those structs to access the database.

Some of the interesting features that GORM provides include automatic database migrations, managing relationships between models (one-to-one, one-to-many, and many-to-many), and hooks, which allow you to run custom code before or after certain operations (such as creating, updating, or deleting records).

All this sounds great, but it doesn't mean using an ORM is always the best option. ORMs have lights and shadows, so let's examine when using GORM will help you or get in your way.

When to use GORM

While GORM can be very convenient, this is not always the case. Here are some advantages of GORM:

Less boilerplate code for database operations

- Simplified handling of relationships between entities
- Automatic schema migrations
- Database agnostic code (works with PostgreSQL, MySQL, SQLite, and SQL Server)
- Reduced risk of SQL injection

But there are also some drawbacks:

- Lack of fine control over the SQL queries that are built
- Extra runtime overhead
- Harder to debug queries
- Hard to use database-specific features

All these characteristics make ORMs such as GORM particularly useful in scenarios where you need to quickly develop applications or abstract the underlying database because you need to allow your application to run on different databases. Also, if your team is not experienced with SQL, GORM provides an interface that abstracts you from the complexities of writing SQL queries. It also takes care of common mistakes, such as SQL injection, by default.

So, if your project requires rapid development, you don't know the database you are going to use, or your team is not experienced with SQL, GORM can be a great choice. But be careful. There are situations where ORMs will get in your way very quickly, so let's talk about those cases.

ORMs are an abstraction layer, and like every abstraction layer, they come with their assumptions, limitations, and trade-offs. ORMs abstract you from the SQL construction, but it still happens under the hood, so it needs to find a way to transform your calls to methods into SQL queries. This decoupling usually leads to less control over the exact SQL queries, making it hard to do things such as performance tuning or writing complex queries that don't map well to the ORM's abstraction. Sometimes, ORMs don't expose all the features the underlying databases provide, only the most common ones, so you are also limited in capabilities.

So, if your project requires complex queries, high performance, and the use of advanced database features, using an ORM can generate many problems. You may fight against abstraction to achieve straightforward things with raw SQL. Consider using raw SQL or a query builder such as SQuirrel in those cases.

Now that we understand GORM and when to use it, let's see how to set it up in our project.

Setting up GORM

The first thing we need to do with GORM is to instantiate it and open the database connection. GORM uses the standard Go SQL package under the hood to open the connection, so let's see how we connect to a database using GORM:

```
package main

import (
  "gorm.io/driver/sqlite"
  "gorm.io/gorm"
  "log"
)

func main() {
  db, err := gorm.Open(sqlite.Open("my-project.db"), &gorm.Config{})
  if err != nil {
    log.Fatal("Failed to connect to database:", err)
  }
}
```

In the example, we open the database connection using the `sqlite` package and pass that connection to GORM's `Open` function. It gets us to our GORM `db` instance, where we can use it. But before we start, we need to define and register our models. Let's see how to do that.

Creating models in GORM

In GORM, a model is a regular Go struct that represents a table in your database. We use `struct` tags to have more control over how struct fields map to database columns. These tags allow us to define constraints, relationships, and other properties of the fields in our model.

Let's define a couple of example models:

```
type User struct {
  Username string `gorm:"uniqueIndex;not null"`
  Password string `gorm:"not null"`
  Role string `gorm:"not null;default:'user'"`
  Sessions []Session
}

type Session struct {
  Token string `gorm:"uniqueIndex;not null"`
  Expires time.Time
  UserID uint
  Username string
}
```

We now have two models, `User` and `Session`, but a few interesting things are happening here. First, we define structs with fields that end up being tables and columns in our database. Also, we are establishing restrictions with `struct` tags, such as setting some fields to not null, some fields to give default values, or creating indexes. Third, we define relationships between models, such as the `Sessions` field in the `User` model, which indicates that a user can have multiple sessions.

Another thing that we can do is add gorm.`Model` as an embedded struct in our models. This struct provides common fields such as `ID`, `CreatedAt`, `UpdatedAt`, and `DeletedAt` (for soft deletes). Here's how we can use it:

```
type User struct {
  gorm.Model
  Username string `gorm:"uniqueIndex;not null"`
  Password string `gorm:"not null"`
```

```
    Role string `gorm:"not null;default:'user'"`
    Sessions []Session
}
```

But for now, we only have a couple of structs that have nothing to do with GORM except the struct tags. So, we need a way to tell GORM to manage these structs as models and create corresponding tables in the database. Let's see how to register the models:

```
...
  err = db.AutoMigrate(&User{}, &Session{})
  if err != nil {
    return nil, err
  }
...
```

The AutoMigrate function will create or update the tables in your database based on the models you defined. If the tables already exist, it will update them to match the current model definitions, adding new columns or indexes as needed. If they don't exist, it will create them. So, I can make changes in the models and run the application again, and everything will be automatically updated for me.

Now that we have our models up and running, we can use our ORM to perform database operations. It's time to learn how to do CRUD operations with GORM.

CRUD operations with GORM

In previous chapters, whenever we wanted to create an entry in the database, we had to write a SQL statement that inserts the data into the table, but that is no longer needed; GORM takes care of all that for us. Let's start creating a new user using our GORM model.

Creating a user

To create a new user, we simply create an instance of our model and call the Create method:

```
user := User{
  Username: "johndoe",
  Password: "password123",
  Role: "user",
}
result := db.Create(&user)
```

```
if result.Error != nil {
  log.Fatal(result.Error)
}
```

With this simple Create call, we are inserting our User model into the database, but not only that; because we add the gorm.Model embedding, GORM, after creating the record, also automatically sets the ID, CreatedAt, and UpdatedAt fields.

It is very cool, isn't it? Now, we don't need all that SQL and the extra boilerplate code; we just create a struct and ask GORM to insert it. But there is more: we also want simplified reads, right? Let's take a look at that.

Reading records

GORM provides different ways to retrieve records from the database. It similarly builds the query to how we did with SQuirrel, but we no longer need to deal with the extra steps of executing the SQL and transforming the results into structs. Instead, we get our results directly as the Go structs we defined as models.

For example, we can retrieve the first 10 users who have the admin role with something like this:

```
var users []User
db.Where("role = ?", "admin").Limit(10).Find(&users)
```

With this code, GORM generates a query needed for that and puts the results directly into the users variable, which is already a slice of User.

It also has convenient methods to retrieve a single record, such as First or Last. For example, if we want to get the first user with the username "johndoe", we can do the following:

```
var user User
db.Where("username = ?", "johndoe").First(&user)
```

So far, there is less boilerplate code, but it's not that different from the SQuirrel examples. Let's try something cooler – let's retrieve the sessions in the same query:

```
var users []User
db.Preload("Sessions").Where("role = ?", "admin").Limit(10).Find(&users)
```

With this query, I'm asking GORM to preload the users' sessions while I'm retrieving them. This will generate a single QUERY operation with a JOIN operation to get the users' sessions, and GORM will automatically map the results into the Sessions field of each User structure. Very convenient, right? Let's jump into updating records now.

Updating records

GORM is very flexible with updates, allowing you to update your models using different approaches. For example, you can do a complete update of the whole row, using the db.Save method. Let's see how:

```
var user User
db.First(&user)
user.Role = "admin"
user.Username = "admin"
db.Save(&user)
```

This code solves the complete update of the user, but you may only want to update a single field. For those cases, we use the Update method, which is going to be very clear with an example:

```
db.Model(&user).Update("role", "admin")
```

In this example, we only update the user's role field, leaving the remaining fields unchanged. But sometimes, you want to modify multiple fields at once, so we use the Updates method. To call this method, we can pass an instance of the model with the fields we want to update, or a map with the pairs of key values of the fields we want to modify. Consider this a partial update, so the Go struct will only update the fields with nonzero values. If you want to update a field to its zero value, use the Update or Updates method with a map. But let's see it in code:

```
db.Model(&user).Updates(User{
  Role: "admin",
  Password: "newpassword",
})

db.Model(&user).Updates(map[string]interface{}{
  "role": "admin",
  "password": "",
})
```

In this example, we are updating the role and the password two times. The second time, because I'm giving an empty string to the password field, and the zero value of a string is the empty string, I must use the map to update it.

Now, the last operation we need to cover is deleting a record.

Deleting records

Deleting records with GORM is also very straightforward, but there are some details that you need to take into account. Let's start by deleting a single record:

```
db.Delete(&user)
```

This code deletes the user record from the database (it will use the ID in the user struct to find the record). But we can also pass the ID directly; for example, like this:

```
db.Delete(&User{}, 1)
```

This example deletes the user with ID 1 directly without loading the user first. This is useful when you don't need to know the data inside the structure to determine whether you must delete it.

Sometimes, you want to delete multiple records simultaneously, generally based on some condition. Let's see an example of that:

```
db.Where("role = ?", "guest").Delete(&User{})
```

In this case, we are deleting all the users with the guest role. This is very similar to how we select records, but instead of using Find, we use Delete.

An important thing to consider is that GORM implements "soft delete" by default for models with a DeletedAt field (which gorm.Model added). The "soft delete" behavior means that when you call Delete, it doesn't remove the record from the database; instead, it sets the DeletedAt field to the current time, marking the record as deleted without actually removing it. So, if you want to delete a record permanently, you need to use the Unscoped method:

```
db.Unscoped().Delete(&user)
```

We now have a good understanding of how to perform CRUD operations with GORM. However, the other big part that is interesting about GORM is how it handles relationships between models. Let's explore that now.

Working with relationships

Relational databases are powerful because they allow us to model complex relationships between different entities. GORM makes it easy to define and work with these relationships using struct tags and methods.

So, let's see some examples of how you deal with relationships in GORM, starting with the creation of related records:

```
user := User{
  Username: "johndoe",
  Password: "password123",
  Role: "user",
  Sessions: []Session{
    {
      Token: "abc123",
      Expires: time.Now().Add(24 * time.Hour),
    },
  },
}
db.Create(&user) // Creates both user and session
```

In this case, we are not only creating a user but also, in the same operation, making a session associated with that user. Then, we retrieve that session, as we saw before:

```
var user User
db.Preload("Sessions").First(&user)
```

As we saw before, we can automatically populate the user Sessions field using Preload. But we can handle the relationships more explicitly, too, as in the following example:

```
session := Session{
  Token: "xyz789",
  Expires: time.Now().Add(24 * time.Hour),
}
db.Model(&user).Association("Sessions").Append(&session)
```

This example creates a new session and adds it to the user. However, maybe you want to remove a specific session from the user. Here's how to do that:

```
db.Model(&user).Association("Sessions").Delete(&sessionToDelete)
```

This code deletes the session for that user, but maybe you want to remove all sessions for the user; in that case, you can run Clear like this:

```
db.Model(&user).Association("Sessions").Clear()
```

This call removes all user-related sessions. So, handling relationships in GORM feels natural, like how you would handle them in an **object-oriented programming** (**OOP**) language.

Before we migrate our shopping list API to GORM, let's examine some interesting features that GORM provides that you might need.

Interesting GORM features

Transactions are a fundamental part of database operations. They let you make sure that all SQL operations that are part of the transaction are performed, or none of them are. Of course, GORM allows you to handle them elegantly. You only need to call the Transaction function and make all your calls inside the function passed as a parameter. Let's see an example:

```
err := db.Transaction(func(tx *gorm.DB) error {
  user := User{
    Username: "johndoe",
    Password: "password123",
    Role: "user",
  }
  if err := tx.Create(&user).Error; err != nil {
    return err
  }


  session := Session{
    Token: "xyz789",
    Expires: time.Now().Add(24 * time.Hour),
    UserID: user.ID,
  }

  if err := tx.Create(&session).Error; err != nil {
    return err
  }

  return nil
})
```

This code starts a transaction and executes different operations as part of the transaction. You can use db.Begin(), db.Rollback(), and db.Commit() manually to handle transactions, but this approach is very convenient because it automatically rolls back the transaction if any error occurs and commits it if everything goes well.

Another interesting feature is the ability to use raw SQL queries. You usually are not going to need it. Still, whenever you need it, it's going to be a lifesaver; sometimes it's going to be a query performance issue, and sometimes it's going to be a specific feature that you want to leverage from the database, but having this option is key. Let's see an example of running raw queries in GORM:

```
var users []User
db.Raw("SELECT * FROM users WHERE role = ?", "admin").Scan(&users)
```

The Raw call allows you to execute raw queries; in this case, one that gets users who have the admin role. Also, sometimes you want to perform a query that doesn't return any results, such as an update or delete. For those cases, you can use the Exec method like this:

```
db.Exec("UPDATE users SET role = ? WHERE id = ?", "admin", 1)
```

In this case, we are updating the user's role with ID 1.

The last thing that can help a lot in your projects is custom hooks. GORM allows you to define hooks executed before or after certain operations, such as creating, updating, or deleting records. These hooks can help implement custom logic, such as validation or logging. Let's see a simple example:

```
func (u *User) BeforeCreate(tx *gorm.DB) error {
  hashedPassword, err := bcrypt.GenerateFromPassword([]byte(u.Password),
    bcrypt.DefaultCost)
  if err != nil {
    return err
  }
  u.Password = string(hashedPassword)
  return nil
}
```

This hook executes before creating any new user and hashes the password before storing it in the database.

With this, I think we have covered enough from GORM to use it and integrate it into our shopping list API, so, without further ado, let's see how we can do that.

Integrating GORM into our shopping list API

As we have seen, introducing GORM requires us to initialize the database connection, define our models, and register them with GORM. But we already have a repository pattern, so we want to abstract that away inside our repository.

We should use the GORM initialization as part of our repository setup, and modify our repository structure to use GORM. Let's start with updating our structs:

```
type ShoppingList struct {
  gorm.Model
  Name string `gorm:"not null"`
  UserID uint `gorm:"not null"`
  Items []string
}


type Session struct {
  gorm.Model
  Token string `gorm:"uniqueIndex;not null"`
  Expires time.Time `gorm:"not null"`
  UserID uint `gorm:"not null"`
}

type User struct {
  gorm.Model
  Role string `gorm:"not null"`
  Username string `gorm:"uniqueIndex;not null"`
  Password string `gorm:"not null"`
  Sessions []Session
  ShoppingLists []ShoppingList
}
```

With this, we have updated our main models to be used by GORM. More specifically, we have modified the User model to have a one-to-many relation with Sessions, and the same for shopping lists. Also, we have added gorm.Model to all of them to include common fields such as ID, CreatedAt, UpdatedAt, and DeletedAt. Finally, we added gorm:"not null" and gorm:"uniqueIndex" tags to fields we want to enforce as not nullable or unique in the database.

With this, we are ready to start initializing our GORM repository. Let's update the repository definition and initialization:

```
type Repository struct {
  db *gorm.DB
}
```

```go
func NewRepository(database string) (*Repository, error) {
  db, err := gorm.Open(sqlite.Open(database),  &gorm.Config{})
  if err != nil {
    return nil, err
  }

  err = db.AutoMigrate(&User{}, &Session{}, &ShoppingList{})
  if err != nil {
    return nil, err
  }

  return &Repository{db}, nil
}
```

As you can see, we have replaced the raw `sql.DB` attribute of the repository with the new rich `*gorm.DB` one, and we have updated the `NewRepository` function to include the creation of the GORM connection, executing the `AutoMigrate` function with the structs we defined as models. The `AutoMigrate` function will ensure that our database schema is updated with our models every time we start the application. So, you no longer need the old `Init` method of the repository, which we created for initializing the database and creating tables, which the `AutoMigrate` method has already done.

Now, let's see how we can implement some repository methods using GORM. We can start with something simple, such as getting a user by username:

```go
func (r *GormRepository) GetUserByUsername(username string) (*User, error)
{
  var user User
  result := r.db.Where("username = ?", username).First(&user)
  if result.Error != nil {
    return nil, result.Error
  }
  return &user, nil
}
```

In this case, we have simply built the query that we want to send to GORM, and without any effort or boilerplate code, we have our user back. Let's now see an example of creating something in the database; for example, a session:

```go
func (r *GormRepository) AddSession(userID uint) (*Session, error) {
  token := strconv.Itoa(rand.Intn(100000000000))
  session := Session{
    Token: token,
    Expires: time.Now().Add(7 * 24 * time.Hour),
    UserID: userID,
  }

  result := r.db.Create(&session)
  if result.Error != nil {
    return nil, result.Error
  }

  return &session, nil
}
```

In this case, we define our model and run the Create method with the session data. Again, it is straightforward. It is unclear here, but we are also already generating a relationship between the session and the user, establishing a UserID field in the Session model.

Let's take an example of something that is drastically simplified with GORM, such as getting all shopping lists for a user:

```go
func (r *Repository) GetShoppingLists() ([]*ShoppingList, error) {
  var results []*ShoppingList
  result := r.db.Find(&results)
  if result.Error != nil {
    return nil, result.Error
  }
  return results, nil
}
```

Here, we simply use Find without conditions to get all records, and GORM automatically fills our slice of pointers to ShoppingList.

Now, we can explore something more complex, such as partial updates of our shopping lists:

```
func (r *Repository) PatchShoppingList(id uint, patch *ShoppingListPatch)
error {
  result := r.db.Model(&ShoppingList{}).Where("id = ?", id).Updates(patch)
  if result.Error != nil {
    return result.Error
  }
  return nil
}
```

As we can see, GORM also makes this easy. We simply pass our patch to the GORM `Updates` method, and it determines whether to update the fields based on the zero values in the struct.

In the sake of completeness, let's also implement a method to delete a shopping list:

```
func (r *Repository) DeleteList(id uint) error {
  result := r.db.Where("id = ?", id).Delete(&ShoppingList{})
  if result.Error != nil {
    return result.Error
  }
  return nil
}
```

Again, this is very straightforward. Remember – as we mentioned earlier, if our model includes `gorm.Model`, this would be a soft delete by default.

With this, you are ready to start using GORM and implement it into your projects. However, there is still a lot to learn about GORM, so I encourage you to explore the GORM documentation (`https://gorm.io/docs/`) for more advanced features and best practices.

Summary

In this chapter, we explored GORM, a powerful ORM for Go. We learned where an ORM can be an advantage and where it can be a problem, leaving us prepared to decide what trade-offs we want to accept. We also explored how to use GORM in our projects, from defining models and performing CRUD operations to working with relationships and using advanced features such as transactions and hooks. We also migrated our shopping list API to GORM, simplifying our repository code.

GORM is an amazing tool for simplifying database interactions in Go, especially for projects requiring rapid development or teams that don't have strong SQL skills. It abstracts away much of the boilerplate and complexity that comes with raw SQL and allows us to focus on our application's business logic. However, it is important to understand that simplicity comes with a cost, and GORM may not be the best fit for every project.

As part of this book, I also want to replace another piece that we have been using during the build of our project—the HTTP package to build our API—with a popular framework for building APIs in Go, the Echo framework. So, let's dive into that in the next chapter.

Unlock this book's exclusive benefits now

Scan this QR code or go to `packtpub.com/unlock`, then search this book by name.

Note: Keep your purchase invoice ready before you start.

14

Using the Echo Framework

In the previous chapter, we explored how to incorporate GORM into our shopping list project. In this chapter, we will use the Echo framework to handle routing, middleware, and request handling. As in the case of GORM, this is not necessarily an improvement over the standard library; it is more a matter of taste and convenience. We will see how a framework such as Echo can reduce boilerplate code and quickly get you up to speed when building REST APIs.

Throughout this chapter, we'll explore the following topics:

- What Echo is and why you might want to use it (or not)
- How to set up Echo for your project
- Working with Echo's routing system
- Using Echo's middleware
- Migrating our shopping list API so that it uses Echo

What is Echo?

Echo is a high-performance, minimalist Go web framework that provides us with the tools to quickly build a REST API. But what does "quickly" mean? If we use Echo, it already implements many things for us. For example, CORS, JWT authentication, and logging are already there for us. We can also marshal and unmarshal to different formats, such as JSON or XML, integrate with Let's Encrypt, and much more.

All these features make Echo a powerful tool for building REST APIs, removing much of the burden of implementing and testing everything from scratch. However, it is essential to note that Echo is not a silver bullet. It is a framework that provides a lot of convenience, but as with any framework, it comes with a set of trade-offs.

When to use Echo

Echo shines in scenarios where you need to build REST APIs quickly and want to leverage pre-built solutions for common problems. Some interesting scenarios are outlined here:

- You're building REST APIs that need standard features, such as CORS, authentication, and logging
- You want to reduce boilerplate in your project
- You're working on a team that benefits from standardized patterns

Echo's abstractions and the pieces that are already included are very convenient, but there are also scenarios where you don't want to use a framework:

- If you need complete control over what happens at every layer
- If you're building straightforward applications where the standard library is sufficient
- If you want to avoid third-party dependencies
- When you need to implement special, non-standard behaviors

Every abstraction hides you from the underlying implementation details, so frameworks can get in the way whenever you need complete control. If you don't need full power, Echo can be a great choice for speeding up development. But let's see how Echo can help us in practice.

Setting up Echo

Getting started with Echo is straightforward. Let's build a simple Hello World API using Echo to see how it works:

```go
package main

import (
  "net/http"

  "github.com/labstack/echo/v4"
)

func main() {
  e := echo.New()

  e.GET("/", func(c echo.Context) error {
    return c.JSON(http.StatusOK, map[string]string{"hello": "world"})
```

```
    })

    e.Logger.Fatal(e.Start(":8080"))
}
```

This is all the code we need to build a Hello World API. Here, we have created a new instance of the Echo framework and registered a `GET` type handler, which returns a JSON response and starts the server. As you can see, it is straightforward and convenient. Methods such as `c.JSON` and the simplicity of the handler interface make the code easy to read and write.

Let's talk more about this simplicity and the power of Echo handlers.

Echo handlers

One of the first things that stands out when using Echo handlers is the `echo.Context` interface. We no longer receive the standard `http.ResponseWriter` and `*http.Request` parameters in our handler functions. Instead, we receive `echo.Context`, which, under the hood, uses `ResponseWriter` and `Request` but provides us with a lot more power. The context allows us to return JSON responses directly based on data structures or handle the incoming requests' data more conveniently by using tools such as data binding or validation. Let's see this in action:

```
e.GET("/hello/:name", func(c echo.Context) {
    name := c.Param("name")
    return c.JSON(http.StatusOK, map[string]string{"hello": name})
})
```

Here, we are registering another `GET` endpoint, but this time, we are getting some data from the URL path. We need something for our API to pass the resource IDs. With `c.Param`, we can get the parameter by name and use it directly. But we also need to receive data from users and entire entities in APIs. For that, Echo provides data binding. Here is how that looks in action:

```
type User struct {
    Name string `json:"name" validate:"required"`
    Email string `json:"email" validate:"required,email"`
}

e.POST("/users", func(c echo.Context) error {
    user := new(User)
    if err := c.Bind(user); err != nil {
        return echo.NewHTTPError(http.StatusBadRequest,
```

```
                              "Invalid request body")
    }
    if err := c.Validate(user); err != nil {
      return echo.NewHTTPError(http.StatusBadRequest, "Validation failed")
    }
    ...
    return c.JSON(http.StatusCreated, user)
})
```

As you can see, we have defined User struct with the necessary JSON struct tags, but in this case, we have also added new struct tags, such as validation tags. These tags allow Echo to know how to validate the data we receive from the user.

Of course, Echo can do more with handlers and routing, such as accessing URL query parameters:

```
query := c.QueryParam("q")
limit := c.QueryParam("limit")
```

Echo can also access cookie data:

```
cookie := c.Cookie("my-cookie")
fmt.Println(cookie.Value)
```

Additionally, it can access grouping routes:

```
api := e.Group("/api")
v1 := api.Group("/v1")
v1.GET("/users", getUsers)
v1.POST("/users", createUser)
v2 := api.Group("/v2")
v2.GET("/users", getUsersV2)
v2.POST("/users", createUserV2)
```

These are just a few examples; there are more options available. Next, we'll talk about another key part of Echo: its middleware system.

Echo middleware

Echo's middleware works similarly to the regular Go HTTP middleware, but Echo makes it easier to build and use. In Echo, middleware is simply a function that takes echo.HandlerFunc and returns another echo.HandlerFunc function. Echo provides a vast amount of power with this simple abstraction, but let's start by looking at something simple:

```
e := echo.New()
e.Use(middleware.Logger())
```

Here, we are adding a logger to our requests that returns something like this for each request:

```
{"time":"2025-07-03T22:55:44.848741244+02:00","id":"","remote_
ip":"127.0.0.1","host":"localhost:8080","method":"GET","uri":"/","user_
agent":"Mozilla/5.0 (X11; Ubuntu; Linux x86_64; rv:139.0) Gecko/20100101
Firefox/139.0","status":200,"error":"","latency":54753,"latency_
human":"54.753μs","bytes_in":0,"bytes_out":18}
```

With just one line, we have an up-and-running logger for our API. But there are more powerful pieces of middleware that we can use, such as the CORS middleware:

```
e := echo.New()
e.Use(middleware.CORS())
```

By running this code, CORS is enabled for all our routes, allowing cross-origin requests. But be careful: if you don't configure CORS, it automatically allows all origins, which is not recommended for production environments. So, let's fix that:

```
e := echo.New()
e.Use(middleware.CORSWithConfig(middleware.CORSConfig{
    AllowOrigins: []string{"https://example.com"},
    AllowMethods: []string{echo.GET, echo.POST},
    AllowHeaders: []string{echo.HeaderOrigin, echo.HeaderContentType, echo.
        HeaderAccept},
}))
```

Now, we have a more secure CORS configuration that only allows valid domains, methods, and headers, something we implemented with minimal effort using the Echo CORS middleware.

We could continue looking at all of the available options, but I think it's better to write our own middleware. For this, we only need to define a function. Let's see how we can do this:

```
func TimeLogger() echo.MiddlewareFunc {
    return func(next echo.HandlerFunc) echo.HandlerFunc {
        return func(c echo.Context) error {
            start := time.Now()

            err := next(c)
```

```
    duration := time.Since(start)
    fmt.Printf("%s %s - %v\n", c.Request().Method, c.Request().URL.Path,
                duration)


    return err
  }
 }
}
```

Here, we are creating middleware that logs the time it takes to process a request. As you can see, the middleware receives a handler function, which is the next one in the chain. It could be another piece of middleware or a final handler, but that doesn't matter – we just call it and put the code that we want to execute before and after it. In this case, we start the timer beforehand, then call the next handler, and finally take the total duration and print it.

Now, it is time to use our middleware and see the result:

```
e.Use(TimeLogger())
```

As with any other middleware, we can register it with the Use method. Now, whenever we call an endpoint, our middleware will be executed. The output will look like this:

```
GET / - 115.662µs
```

We get this simple output that provides the duration of the handler's execution. Nice, right?

Now that we know about Echo's middleware and handlers, I want to show you how you can easily handle different kinds of errors.

Error handling

Error handling is one of the things that you must do in your API. What happens if something fails, there is a panic, or a route is not found?

In Echo, the policy is to have a centralized point for handling errors: HTTPErrorHandler. This handler allows any error in your API to be handled in the same place. By default, this behavior is ideal for API developers. It just returns some JSON with a message field. Here's an example:

```
e.GET("/user/:id", func(c echo.Context) error {
  return echo.NewHTTPError(http.StatusNotFound, "User not found")
})
```

The generated error would be as follows:

```
{"message": "User not found"}
```

However, even though this is very convenient, it doesn't necessarily work for everybody, so you can decide how you want to handle your errors. Maybe you want to have custom errors and use extra information in the errors you return, such as an error code. In those cases, you can build an error handler and configure the system with it. For example, we can define our error type like so:

```
type APIError struct {
  Message   string `json:"message"`
  ErrorCode string `json:"error_code"`
  HTTPCode  int    `json:"http_code"`
}
func (e *APIError) Error() string {
  return fmt.Sprintf("%s (code=%s, http=%d)", e.Message, e.ErrorCode,
        e.HTTPCode)
}
```

With this, we have a custom error. We can now emit that error in our handler:

```
e.GET("/user/:id", func(c echo.Context) error {
  return &CustomError{
    HTTPCode: http.StatusNotFound,
    Message: "User not found in the system",
    ErrorCode: "user-not-found",
  }
})
```

Now that we can use our custom error in our handler, we need to take advantage of this by creating an error handler:

```
func customHTTPErrorHandler(err error, c echo.Context) {
  var code = http.StatusInternalServerError
  var resp = map[string]interface{}{
    "message":   "Internal server error",
    "errorCode": "internal_error",
  }

  if cErr, ok := err.(*CustomError); ok {
    code = cErr.HTTPCode
```

```
        resp["message"] = cErr.Message
        resp["errorCode"] = cErr.ErrorCode
    }
    c.JSON(code, resp)
}
```

With this, we have a custom error handler that, by default, is going to return an internal server error that specifies the new error format that we want. Apart from this, the error handler is going to detect our CustomError type. If the error that's received is of that type, the error handler is going to populate the right fields and return the right JSON response with errorCode set. The only thing we need to do now is register our error handler. For that, we just need to add an extra line:

```
    e.HTTPErrorHandler = customHTTPErrorHandler
```

With this, every single error in our application will be handled through this specific point. But there is still a problem: panics. Panics are not regular errors, so HTTPErrorHandler doesn't catch them by default. But don't worry – Echo also has that under control. You only have to add this middleware:

```
    e.Use(middleware.Recover())
```

With this line, Echo will capture every panic that occurs as part of a handler, convert it into a 500 Internal Server Error response, and hand that to your custom handler.

With this, we have covered everything we need to know about error handling. Now that we have a general understanding of Echo and what it can do for us, let's see how we can migrate our existing shopping list API to Echo so that it can use it.

Migrating our shopping list API to Echo

Echo is easy to set up and use, so it won't be hard to incorporate it into our existing shopping list API. We only need to initialize our echo instance and register our handlers. Of course, we will also need to update our handlers so that they use echo.Context instead of the standard http. ResponseWriter and *http.Request parameters, but that is not a big deal. It's time to jump right into it.

Setting up Echo

The first thing we need to do is prepare our Echo instance and update our router so that it uses Echo's routing system in our main.go file:

```
func main() {
  e := echo.New()

  api := e.Group("/api")
  api.Use(authRequired)

  ...

  e.POST("/api/login", handleLogin)
  api.GET("/lists", handleGetLists)
  api.POST("/lists", adminRequired(handleCreateList))
  api.GET("/lists/:id", handleGetList)
  api.PUT("/lists/:id", adminRequired(handleUpdateList))
  api.PATCH("/lists/:id", adminRequired(handlePatchList))
  api.DELETE("/lists/:id", adminRequired(handleDeleteList))
  e.Logger.Fatal(e.Start(":8080"))
}
```

The first thing we need is our echo instance; after that, we can start building everything. Here, we can follow the previous pattern, creating a router group called /api. Then, we can register some middleware, authRequired, to protect our API (we will learn how to implement the authRequired middleware later). We can also keep using adminRequired, which is also middleware; we'll explore this later. After that, we can handle anything the application requires, such as the database connection, repository initialization, and more. Then, we can register our handlers using the e.POST, e.GET, and e.PUT methods. Finally, we can start our Echo server with e.Start(":8080"). With this, we have an Echo application. The only problem is that it will not compile because we need to update our handlers. Let's look at a couple of examples of how to migrate our handlers so that they can use Echo's context.

Migrating handlers

Migrating our handlers should be easy, and it can be done by using less code than we did previously. Let's start by migrating the GetList handler since it is a simple one to implement:

```
func handleGetList(c echo.Context) error {
  id := c.Param("id")

  list, err := repository.GetShoppingList(id)
  if err != nil {
```

```
        return echo.NewHTTPError(http.StatusNotFound, "List not found")
    }

    return c.JSON(http.StatusOK, list)
}
```

Notice how much shorter this is compared to our previous implementation. We get ID from the path and the objects from the repository and return them as JSON. Here, explicit marshaling is performed, and the correct status and content type are set appropriately. Also, this code is slightly more readable, in my opinion. Now, let's look at an example of using data binding with the CreateList handler:

```
func handleCreateList(c echo.Context) error {
    var list ShoppingList
    if err := c.Bind(&list); err != nil {
        return c.JSON(http.StatusBadRequest, map[string]string{
                    "error": "Invalid request body"})
    }
    newList, err := repository.CreateShoppingList(&list)
    if err != nil {
        return echo.NewHTTPError(http.StatusInternalServerError,
                            "Failed to create list")
    }
    return c.JSON(http.StatusCreated, newList)
}
```

In this example, we can see that Echo is cleaner. There is no more reading the body, no more explicit marshalling and unmarshalling, and no more explicitly setting the content type. Echo provides us with a simpler interface and is less explicit in general. But this is not only true for the handler; our middleware also becomes more straightforward to read.

Migrating middleware

Before migrating our middleware, I want to mention that we should prefer to use Echo's built-in middleware for things such as logging, CORS, and rate limiting. Also, you may be interested in the **JSON Web Token (JWT)** middleware, which allows you to authorize users using JWT by adding a single line of code. However, because we can write our own middleware, I will use our authentication and authorization middleware as an example of migrating them.

The key benefit of using Echo for middleware compared to built-in Go is ergonomics; in this case, it is easy to pass information to the handlers using echo.Context. This is going to be very useful for our authentication middleware, so let's see how we would implement it:

```go
func authRequired(next echo.HandlerFunc) echo.HandlerFunc {
  return func(c echo.Context) error {
    auth := c.Request().Header.Get("Authorization")
    if !strings.HasPrefix(auth, "Bearer ") {
      return echo.NewHTTPError(http.StatusUnauthorized,
                               "Missing or invalid token")
    }

    token := auth[7:]
    session, err := repository.GetSession(token)
    if err != nil {
      return echo.NewHTTPError(http.StatusUnauthorized, "Invalid token")
    }

    c.Set("session", session)

    return next(c)
  }
}
```

As in our previous version, we get the authorization header, check whether that is correct, get the session from that token, and, in this case, set the session in the Echo context, allowing all the handlers to know which user is making the request very easily. Not only that, but we can also use that session from other middleware that comes later, such as our adminRequired middleware:

```go
func adminRequired(next echo.HandlerFunc) echo.HandlerFunc {
  return func(c echo.Context) error {
    session := c.Get("session").(*Session)

    user, err := repository.GetUser(session.UserID)
    if err != nil {
      return echo.NewHTTPError(http.StatusForbidden, "Access denied")
    }

    if user.Role != "admin" {
```

```
        return echo.NewHTTPError(http.StatusForbidden,
                                 "Admin access required")
    }

    return next(c)
  }
}
```

As you can see, we already know that there is a session in the context, so we can get it directly and use it to verify whether the user is a valid admin.

To finish, let's explore some things we can add to our application with minimal effort using Echo.

Additional features with Echo

Let's start with something that we have already implemented: CORS. We used a library to do this previously, but CORS comes built-in with Echo, so we can just add it to our application with a single line of code:

```
...
e.Use(middleware.CORS())
...
```

With this, we have CORS enabled for all our routes. If you want to configure it by, for example, limiting the allowed origins, you can do so like this:

```
e.Use(middleware.CORSWithConfig(middleware.CORSConfig{
  AllowOrigins: []string{"https://example.com"},
  AllowMethods: []string{http.MethodGet, http.MethodPost, http.MethodPut,
                         http.MethodDelete},
}))
```

That's it – there's nothing too involved. The same happens with JWT authentication; we can use the built-in middleware to protect our routes:

```
e.Use(echojwt.JWT([]byte("my-secret")))
```

With that, we have enabled JWT authentication. Now, we only need to generate the valid JWT tokens for the users who can access the protected routes.

Do you also want metrics with Prometheus? Echo has you covered with the `echo-prometheus` middleware, which allows you to easily expose metrics for your API:

```
...
e.Use(echoprometheus.NewMiddleware("myapp"))
e.GET("/metrics", echoprometheus.NewHandler())
...
```

With these two lines, Echo will automatically gather metrics about your API, such as request counts, response times, and more, and expose them at the `/metrics` endpoint for Prometheus to scrape.

Echo makes a lot of things easy that would be harder using only the standard library. Check out the Echo documentation at `https://echo.labstack.com/` for more built-in middleware and features that you can use in your application. Things such as automatic TLS certificate management with Let's Encrypt, rate limiting, request ID generation, tracing, and recovery from panics are trivial to implement with Echo.

Summary

This chapter explored Echo, a powerful and lightweight web framework for Go. We learned how Echo can simplify many everyday tasks in building REST APIs, such as data binding and validation, which become trivial. This powerful middleware system provides a clean way to provide extra functionality across our application, and its routing and handler system allows us to write clean and expressive code.

We applied what we learned to migrate our existing shopping list API so that it uses Echo, making it cleaner and easier to read. We also leveraged some Echo middleware to provide features such as CORS and JWT with minimal effort.

As we come to the end of this book, we have learned how to build a REST API using Go from the ground up, using the standard library, and understood the concepts behind API development. We explored important concepts for building modern APIs, such as the HTTP standard, security, performance, and observability. All this was applied to our API example. There is much more to learn about these topics, but I'm sure you are leaving this book with a solid foundation so that you can keep exploring and building powerful APIs with Go.

Unlock this book's exclusive benefits now

Scan this QR code or go to packtpub. com/unlock, then search this book by name.

Note: Keep your purchase invoice ready before you start.

15

Unlock Your Book's Exclusive Benefits

Your copy of this book comes with the following exclusive benefits:

☁ Next-gen Packt Reader

✦ AI assistant (beta)

📄 DRM-free PDF/ePub downloads

Use the following guide to unlock them if you haven't already. The process takes just a few minutes and needs to be done only once.

How to unlock these benefits in three easy steps

Step 1

Have your purchase invoice for this book ready, as you'll need it in *Step 3*. If you received a physical invoice, scan it on your phone and have it ready as either a PDF, JPG, or PNG.

For more help on finding your invoice, visit https://www.packtpub.com/unlock-benefits/help.

Note: Did you buy this book directly from Packt? You don't need an invoice. After completing Step 2, you can jump straight to your exclusive content.

Step 2

Scan this QR code or go to `packtpub.com/unlock`.

On the page that opens (which will look similar to Figure X.1 if you're on desktop), search for this book by name. Make sure you select the correct edition.

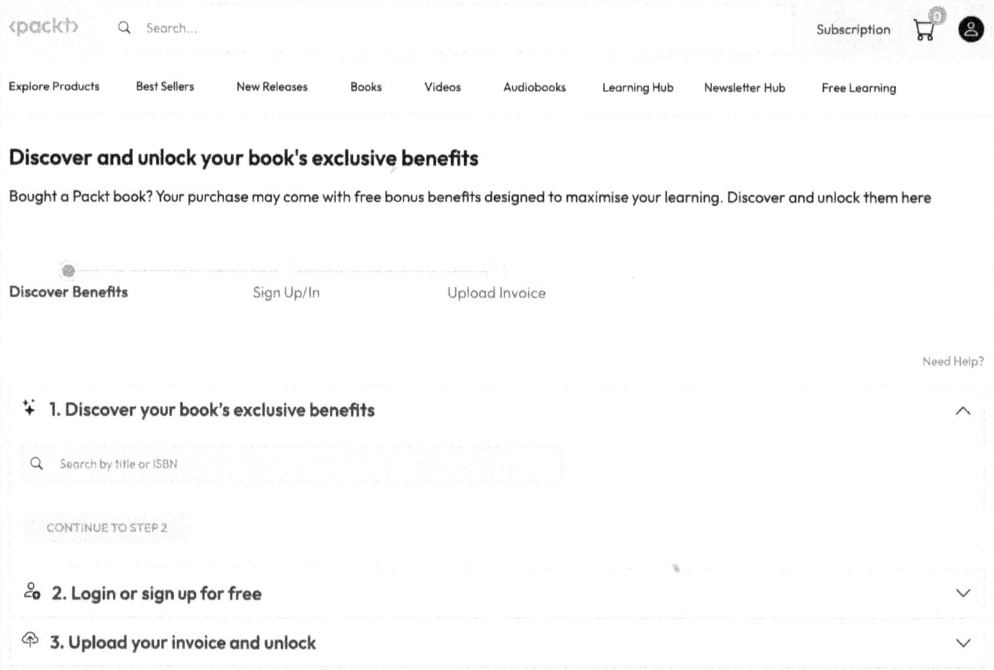

Figure 15.1: Packt unlock landing page on desktop

Step 3

Once you've selected your book, sign in to your Packt account or create a new one for free. Once you're logged in, upload your invoice. It can be in PDF, PNG, or JPG format and must be no larger than 10 MB. Follow the rest of the instructions on the screen to complete the process.

Need help?

If you get stuck and need help, visit `https://www.packtpub.com/unlock-benefits/help` for a detailed FAQ on how to find your invoices and more. The following QR code will take you to the help page directly:

Note: If you are still facing issues, reach out to `customercare@packt.com`.

‹packt›

Subscribe to our online digital library for full access to over 7,000 books and videos, as well as industry leading tools to help you plan your personal development and advance your career. For more information, please visit our website.

Why subscribe?

- Spend less time learning and more time coding with practical eBooks and Videos from over 4,000 industry professionals
- Improve your learning with Skill Plans built especially for you
- Get a free eBook or video every month
- Fully searchable for easy access to vital information
- Copy and paste, print, and bookmark content

At www.packtpub.com, you can also read a collection of free technical articles, sign up for a range of free newsletters, and receive exclusive discounts and offers on Packt books and eBooks.

Other Books You May Enjoy

If you enjoyed this book, you may be interested in these other books by Packt:

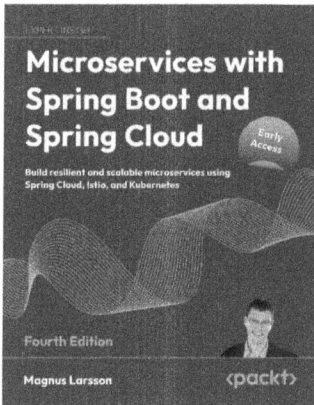

Microservices with Spring Boot and Spring Cloud, Fourth Edition

Magnus Larsson

ISBN: 978-1-80580-127-6

- Build reactive microservices using Spring Boot
- Develop resilient and scalable microservices using Spring Cloud
- Use OAuth and Spring Security to protect public APIs
- Implement Docker to bridge the gap between development, testing, and production
- Deploy and manage microservices with Kubernetes
- Apply Istio for improved security, observability, and traffic management

- Write and run automated microservice tests with JUnit, test containers, Gradle, and bash
- Use Spring AOT and GraalVM to native compile the microservices
- Use Micrometer for distributed tracing

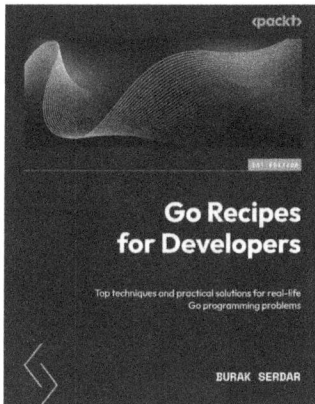

Go Recipes for Developers, First Edition

Burak Serdar

ISBN: 978-1-83546-439-7

- Understand how to structure projects
- Find out how to process text with Go tools
- Discover how to work with arrays, slices, and maps
- Implement robust error handling patterns
- Explore concurrent data processing for Go programs
- Get up to speed with how to control processes
- Integrate Go applications with databases
- Understand how to test, benchmark, and profile Go programs

Packt is searching for authors like you

If you're interested in becoming an author for Packt, please visit `authors.packtpub.com` and apply today. We have worked with thousands of developers and tech professionals, just like you, to help them share their insight with the global tech community. You can make a general application, apply for a specific hot topic that we are recruiting an author for, or submit your own idea.

Share your thoughts

Now you've finished *Modern REST API Development in Go*, we'd love to hear your thoughts! Scan the QR code below to go straight to the Amazon review page for this book and share your feedback or leave a review on the site that you purchased it from.

https://packt.link/r/1836205376

Your review is important to us and the tech community and will help us make sure we're delivering excellent quality content.

Index